The Political Economy of Rule Evasion and Policy Reform

Today's policy reforms are built upon the ashes of yesterday's policy failures. Widespread disobedience, people choosing not to abide by the letter or the spirit of the rules, is a major source of policy failure. Massive evasion of rules creates conditions conducive to policy reform. Disobedience, therefore, can be a source of improved policies, and rule breakers can unintentionally serve as public benefactors. Evasion-included policy reform is both common and important, prevalent in areas as disparate as traffic regulations and systemic change in formerly socialist countries.

The Political Economy of Rule Evasion and Policy Reform develops the logic underlying the connections between breaking the rules and making the rules. Approaching policy issues from the point of view of rule circumvention provides a perspective that illuminates a wide variety of phenomena:

- implicit tolerance of extensive illegal behavior, treadmills of reform, delays of major policy changes
- the complexity of rules
- potential for perverse outcomes from policy reforms
- corruption of enforcers
- trade-offs between a rule-based and a discretionary policy.

This ground-breaking new book is written in a clear, readable style and is replete with a wide variety of examples, including case studies on zero tolerance policies, the demise of the Soviet Union, and the ongoing transformation of firearm regulations in Britain and the US. *The Political Economy of Rule Evasion and Policy Reform* provides social scientists, legal scholars, and policy professionals with an improved understanding of public policy formation and evolution.

Jim Leitzel is Senior Lecturer in Public Policy Studies at the University of Chicago.

Routledge Frontiers of Political Policy

The Political Economy of Rule Evasion and Policy Reform

Jim Leitzel

Routledge
Taylor & Francis Group

LONDON AND NEW YORK

First published 2003
by Routledge
11 New Fetter Lane, London EC4P 4EE

Simultaneously published in the USA and Canada
by Routledge
29 West 35th Street, New York, NY 10001

Routledge is an imprint of the Taylor & Francis Group

Typeset in Goudy by
Keystroke, Jacaranda Lodge, Wolverhampton
Printed and bound in Great Britain by
MPG Books Ltd, Bodmin

British Library Cataloguing in Publication Data
A catalogue record for this book is available
from the British Library

Library of Congress Cataloging in Publication Data
Leitzel, Jim.
    The political economy of rule evasion and policy reform / Jim Leitzel.
        p. cm.
    Includes bibliographical references and index.
    1. Civil disobedience. 2. Illegality. 3. Policy science. 4. Law and economics.
    5. Public policy (Law) I. Title. II. Series.

    JC328.3 .L454 2003
    320′.6–dc21   2002028466

ISBN 0–415–28272–1

To Bob Conrad, Phil Cook, Richard Taub, and Vladimir Treml, mentors, scholars, and gentlemen all.

Contents

Acknowledgments

Time has not been the constraint. The ideas broached in the following pages have had years to age like fine wine or to rot like, er, mackerel. And many are those who have tried to nose the ideas towards a more satisfying bouquet. Yours may not have been pleasant or gratifying toil, but it will not be thankless. Thank you.

The debts that I have accumulated in preparing this manuscript have gone well beyond repayment prospects (though not repayment intentions) with respect to Michael Alexeev, Phil Cook, Clifford Gaddy, Mike Meurer, Will Pyle, Erik Weisman, and Christopher Young. These generous individuals, all mentioned repeatedly below, deserve immediate recognition for the extent of their help and my obligation.

Significant chunks of the manuscript have received the attention of Michael Alexeev and Jeff Stake, Hoosiers with hearts of gold (or is that redundant?) My gratitude to you both. Now it would not be amiss to bring up a general point, one that applies with particular force to Professors Alexeev and Stake. There are many specific ideas in the pages that follow that were drawn, with various degrees of directness, from comments or conversations with others. My memory of the source of all these ideas is not always, shall we say, infallible, and I am particularly apt to over-credit my own contribution (at least for the good ideas). The issue that has presented itself, then, is to judge when an idea merits a separate citation in the text, along the lines of, say, "I owe this point to Maynard Keynes." The problem is a familiar one, that of where to draw the line. The complication is that once any separate citations are made, it might give the appearance that ideas not so credited are somehow not drawn from Maynard or others. This would be a deceptive appearance. My compromise has been to provide only a handful of such specific citations, and to combine those with this rather wordy and yet not entirely effective apologia.

Much of this book has dribbled out in various publications and working-papers-that-will-never-be-publications, and many a good person has commented on the dribblings. My thanks to you all, with a special fillip of gratitude for those whose contributions will remain anonymous due to my oversight (as opposed to those whose anonymity is due to an understandable desire to distance themselves from the final product). Those who remain anonymous because I do not know their identities include the reviewers of the manuscript for Routledge, who made many constructive suggestions on the first few chapters.

Those who were helpful from the very early stages of this project include William Ascher, Phil Cook, David Hoaas, and Patrick Larkey. More-than-able research assistance was provided, years apart and years ago, by Janet Johnson and Nese Nasif. Sheldon Lyke read an early complete draft, and much improved the manuscript both in substance and in style. Apologies, Sheldon, for still reverting to the passive voice all too frequently. I will reform, if I ever learn what the passive voice actually is.

The genesis for this book can be traced to an article, "Breaking the Rules and Making the Rules: Evasion, Avoidance, and Policy Reform," published in *Policy Sciences* 29: 247–69, 1996. Parts of this article appear, in revised form, in Chapters 1, 2, and 4 with kind permission of Kluwer Academic Publishers. Comments on that original article were provided by Bill Ascher, Charlie Clotfelter, Phil Cook, David Hoaas, Mike Meurer, Will Pyle, Barrie Richardson, Erik Weisman, and Chris Young.

An early version of Chapter 4 was presented at the Midwest Economic Association meetings, Chicago, in April, 2000. I would like to thank Gerhard Glomm and other session participants for helpful comments.

The section on Race and Policing in Chapter 5 is a slightly revised version of my article "Race and Policing," which appeared in *Society* 38(3): 38–42, March/April 2001. I would like to thank Transaction Publishers and *Society*'s Editorial Director Irving Louis Horowitz for permission to reprint the article. Mike Alexeev, Phil Cook, Kelly Daley, Cliff Gaddy, Mike Meurer, and Erik Weisman all provided comments on early versions of the article.

The quotation that starts off the "Costs of Corruption" subsection of Chapter 6 is Copyright © 1995 *Under the Frog* by Tibor Fischer. Reprinted by permission of The New Press and Tibor Fischer.

Parts of Chapters 6 and 7 draw heavily on my article "Corruption and Organized Crime in the Russian Transition," published in *Institutional Change in Transition Economies*, Michael Cuddy and Reuben Getter, eds, Aldershot, Hampshire: Ashgate Publishers, forthcoming. Thanks to Ashgate Publishers for permission to reprint that article. Earlier versions were presented in seminars at Duke University, North Carolina State University, Indiana University, the University of Oxford, and at a conference at the National University of Ireland, Galway. I would like to thank conference and seminar participants, as well as Michael Alexeev, Clifford Gaddy, Will Pyle, Alan Resley, Erik Weisman, and Chris Young, for their attempts to educate me on corruption and the Russian transition. I would also like to thank the Galway conference organizers, Michael Cuddy and Ruvin Gekker, for arranging a fine academic program that they supplemented with unsurpassed hospitality.

Parts of Chapter 8 closely follow material that appeared in my article "Evasion and Public Policy: British and US Firearm Regulation," *Policy Studies* 19: 141–57, June 1998. Also, a couple paragraphs from that article are used in revised form in the Introduction. I would like to thank *Policy Studies* (www.tandf.co.uk) for permission to reprint. I presented an earlier version of Chapter 8 at a seminar at the University of Glasgow, and am grateful for comments from the discussant,

Professor Geoff Webb, as well as Phil Cook. Thanks to Phil more broadly for recruiting me into the world of gun control policy, and for consistently offering detailed comments on my often quirky (read: incoherent) drafts. Tom Judge and Susan Groce kindly arranged for me to present a version of this article at Sheffield, and entertained me lavishly, too.

Chapter 8 and the book more generally received their initial impetus during 1996–7, when I spent a year as an Atlantic Fellow in Public Policy at the University of Essex in Colchester, England. The Department of Economics at Essex provided an extremely congenial and intellectually stimulating environment, and the staff and students there were exceptionally welcoming to me. Those who were instrumental in making that year so enriching include Fabienne Brooks, Sarah Keeton, Byung-Yeon Kim, Sajal Lahiri, William Plowden, Elena Quercioli, and the Friday night soccer group. I think back with great fondness on the spirit and acumen within the Essex economics department and among the Atlantic Fellows.

Dr Elspeth Findlay provided amazingly painstaking and helpful comments on early and poorly printed versions of Chapters 2 and 3. I am both grateful for the comments and touched by her commitment to a task for which "tedious" is a profoundly understated description. To the extent that the later versions of those chapters make any sense at all and are readable by humans, much of the credit goes to Elspeth. I am still confused by a marginal note from Dr Findlay, one that appeared next to numerous passages in the draft manuscript: "This is Jim-speak." Elspeth, is that a commendation or a criticism?

For Chapter 3, on zero tolerance, I benefitted from the comments of Michael Alexeev, Eugene Bardach, Jonathan Caulkins, Phil Cook, Elspeth Findlay, Clifford Gaddy, Sheldon Lyke, Will Pyle, Erik Weisman, and Joselyn Zivin. Thanks to you all. A version of Chapter 3 was presented at George Mason University. I would like to thank Peter Boettke, Bridget Butkevich, and seminar participants for their constructive suggestions.

Michael Ellman read and commented on an early version of Chapter 7. A still earlier version of the first part of Chapter 7 was presented at the November, 1996 meeting of the American Association for the Advancement of Slavic Studies conference in Boston. I would like to thank participants at the roundtable, Kimberly Neuhauser, and session organizer Vladimir Treml.

Following my year in England, I had the opportunity to teach at the New Economic School in Moscow, Russia. The New Economic School (NES; www.nes.ru/english/index.htm) is a phenomenal institution that provides a two-year masters' program in economics to outstanding students from Russia and other parts of the former Soviet Union. I feel privileged to have been associated with NES, which has played a vital role in the renaissance of the economics discipline in Russia. My thanks to Barry Ickes, Gur Ofer, and Valery Makarov, both for inviting me to NES and for their years of effort in envisioning and building up this inestimable economics establishment. The students and staff at NES taught me much about the Russian transition while providing a safe and pleasant harbor from the sometimes stormy seas of transitional Moscow. Oxana Budjko greatly eased my own transition to Moscow, while preventing me from excessively shirking my duties. Stuart Shaw and Linda Ryan kept my spirits up, only in part by encouraging me to shirk my duties. Alexander Vasin, Elena Panova, and Mark Levin tutored me on tax evasion and corruption and contributed to the collegial atmosphere at NES. Leonid Polishchuk shared his deep understanding of the Russian economy and the occasional pizza, and succeeded me as Academic Coordinator at NES. Chris Young loaned me a jacket that helped me get through the Moscow winter. Others who aided me considerably in Moscow include Ludmilla Alexeeva, Eric Livny, Joel McDonald, and Vitaliy Yermakov.

Since leaving NES I have continued to stay active in Russia, most particularly through the auspices of the Economics Education and Research Consortium (EERC; www.eerc.ru), ably and admirably administered from Moscow by Eric Livny. Like the New Economic School, EERC has been in the forefront of the advance of economics in Russia. Judy Thornton, Rick Ericson, and other members of the EERC family have helped to make EERC research workshops intellectually stimulating and fun. The EERC staff, both in Washington and in Moscow, have ensured that things have run smoothly; Yulia Nikitina was particularly helpful during our magical trip to Kizhi. I would advise everyone to visit Kizhi!

Richard Taub has been supportive beyond measure in Chicago, and this has greatly contributed both to my sanity (such as it is) and to the completion of this book. Many thanks for all the help, Richard. Lee Price has helped make the public policy concentration work for students and for me. The encouragement of many other people also has been very significant for me at various times in recent years. In particular, I would like to recognize Bob Conrad, Phil Cook, Barry Ickes, Gur Ofer, Andrei Shleifer, Judy Thornton, and Vladimir Treml. In Chicago, Kelly Daley, Gauhar Turmuhambeteva (plus Alex and Elizabeth), and Joselyn Zivin have been indispensable. Sunday night LC members Sheldon Lyke and Margrethe Krontoft (Krontfort) have helped me get through many a week (with the assistance of Teresa), while Hilary Caldwell, Phoebe Rice, and Helen Thompson have tolerated, with admirable good cheer, my favorite Hyde Park and Chicago dining establishments at times other than Sunday night. Ari Adut, Betty Farrell, Heather MacIndoe, Devin Pendas, Gustav Peebles, Richard Taub, Dorothy Tsatsos, and Erik Grimmer-Solem have helped make Chicago a fun place to work. Old friends like Julius Scott (an original Sunday night LC member), Jeff and Cheryl Samuels, Chris and Eleni Scheidt, Mike and Nina Alexeev, Cliff and Kerstin Gaddy, Lydia Faulkner, Janice Hall, Carol Nahra, Nick and Teresa Malyshev, Mike and Miyuki Meurer, Barry Ickes, Jim Baer, Fallaw and Wanda Sowell, Geoff Renshaw, Sarah Caress, Randy and Leslie Beard, Chris Young, and Alan Resley have done all that old friends do, and more. My family, too, has been steady and reassuring, though Leitzels aren't good at talking about things like that (or is it just me?).

Routledge may disagree with my initial claim that time has not been a constraint. Alan Jarvis, Rob Langham, and Terry Clague have been patient and supportive. Thanks to them, and to Routledge generally; after my earlier book on Russian reform, Routledge can now be classified as a recidivist. Incidentally, the title of this book went through many iterations, and the decision pressed up against the time constraint that I claim was otherwise inoperative. And though the chosen title starts with the word "The," keep in mind that the titles of all books written by economists after 1776 implicitly begin with "An Inquiry Into."

The ideas presented in this book have been repeatedly filtered through my students at the University of Chicago, and have emerged with many of their impurities removed. Any value that experts and scholars in economics, law, and social science might find in this volume has only developed as a side effect of trying to reach students. Though this is not a textbook, or at least a standard one, in some sense students have been the primary audience during the writing of the book.

Thanks in advance to potential reviewers of this book for not referring to, or even structuring their review around, that unfortunate mackerel comment at the beginning of these Acknowledgments. The length of these Acknowledgments, incidentally, might give the impression that I don't intend to write any more books. Once again, a deceptive impression, though undoubtedly by now a happy deception for the reader. I have more books planned, oh yes I do, while recognizing the contingencies that can thwart even "best laid schemes." Should my plans come to fruition, however, those books, very interesting books at that, one day will exist. I only mention it here as an inducement to potential journal editors, colleagues, and funders, to keep in mind that in assisting me in my endeavors, your name could appear in this place in a future book! If that is not enticement enough, let me observe that particularly valuable services in the past have been met with – brace yourselves – a free copy of the final product, though slightly tainted by the autograph of the author. Even the dedication of forthcoming books is unsettled, and could be yours, oh gentle future Muse. It is not exactly the moon, but it is a promise a shade more credible – ah, since it is late, I am feeling generous, and you are a friend, I will throw in the moon, too.

Introduction

A traffic-light tale

In Bogota, Colombia, cars stopping at red lights late at night became favored targets for robbery and carjacking.[1] As a result, nocturnal drivers refused to brake for lights, preferring the possibility of a spectacular accident to that of being the victim of violent crime.

The Bogota city traffic department responded to these developments by legalizing the behavior of drivers: between 11 PM and 2 AM, red lights were eliminated, and replaced with flashing yellow signals. Note that this change was not undertaken to limit the amount of time wasted by drivers and passengers sitting at red signals when intersections were uncrowded, the more common rationale for employing flashing yellow traffic signals during off-peak hours. The fact that robbers were about indicates that these were not deserted intersections, and the switch to flashing yellow as a time-saving device, if desirable, could have taken place any time, prior to the spate of carjackings. Traffic safety, not time savings, led to the elimination of red lights in Bogota at night. The expressed hope was that the flashing yellow lights would capture the attention of drivers, and induce them to proceed more carefully through intersections – more carefully, that is, than when drivers had made up their minds that they would fail to heed red lights.

How does a weakening of the official regulatory regime – flashing yellow lights instead of standard red and green signals – lead to fewer accidents? Drivers who ignore red lights would seem unlikely to attend to flashing yellow lights. But not all drivers are accustomed to the informal ways of driving in Bogota at night. Inexperienced motorists are apt to take green lights at face value, and proceed through intersections, with potentially fatal consequences, given that other drivers are ignoring red lights. For these less savvy motorists, a flashing yellow light induces more caution than a green signal. The change to flashing yellow lights makes the driving norm (of not stopping at intersections at night) clear to everyone. Further, the policy reform identifies the precise time period during which the "no stopping" norm is in effect. The Bogota authorities were right to believe that replacing standard traffic signals with the less restraining flashing yellow lights could nevertheless increase coordination at intersections and improve traffic safety.

How far the consequences of evasion! People who evade laws against robbery induce others to evade traffic laws. To improve traffic safety, the authorities change the rules of the road and institutionalize the *de facto* situation. The response of the authorities is quite sensible, indeed it can make virtually every participant (except, perhaps, for the thieves at the crossroads) better off than they were under the old, evaded rule. But this improved policy engendered by rule evasion doesn't mean that all is for the best. Another alternative – cracking down on robbers and carjackers comes to mind – might lead to even better outcomes.[2]

We are all experts concerning some of the consequences of evasion. Private behavior continually takes account of the fact that laws are broken. We are careful where we walk at night, or avoid going out alone, knowing that others might commit crimes. We look before crossing an intersection, even when we have the legal right-of-way. We lock our doors. We run red lights if we fear carjackers. And if we perceive an increase in rule breaking by others – more carjackings, perhaps – we will amend our behavior to take the changed environment into account.

As with the "rules" that govern our private behavior, so with public policies: we choose them taking into account the propensity of humans to disobey strictures. While disobedience can be controlled, through vigilant enforcement and stern punishment awaiting malefactors, it can rarely be eliminated. Public policies reflect the inevitability of rule evasion, in Colombia and elsewhere.

The channels through which rule circumvention exerts its impact on public policies are not always as obvious as they are with private policies such as looking both ways before crossing a street. But the influence on public policies of the potential for rule evasion is omnipresent. Driving under the influence of alcohol is illegal, not because of a direct public interest in the driver's blood alcohol content – our concern is with safe driving, as opposed to the characteristics of the driver – but rather because a high blood alcohol content makes it more likely that a driver will be reckless, drive too fast, or break other driving rules. Sales of cigarettes from vending machines are regulated to control one obvious channel for evasion of rules against minors purchasing cigarettes. The government withholds taxes, in advance of the date when their payment is required, to promote compliance with tax laws.[3] Substantial resources are dedicated to attempting to reduce illegal drug use, but simultaneously needle exchange programs are sponsored publicly to help prevent HIV and hepatitis transmission among drug users. As these examples demonstrate, real world policies, public or private, differ from those regulations that would be appropriate in an alien world populated by individuals who consistently complied with rules.

Unintentional civil disobedience

"Unjust laws exist: shall we be content to obey them, or shall we endeavor to amend them, and obey them until we have succeeded, or shall we transgress them at once?"[4] The question was Thoreau's, who answered that, if the injustice of the law "is of such a nature that it requires you to be the agent of injustice to another, then, I say, break the law."[5] Open violation of a law, coupled with a willingness to bear the legal consequences, sends a strong signal to the body politic of the depth of belief that a rule is unjust and needs changing. So the notion that laws and policies respond to rule breaking is far from a novel insight. Acts of civil disobedience are undertaken precisely with the intent of changing the rules.[6]

Most disobedience, such as running red lights, could hardly be termed "civil." Rules are violated or circumvented without any intention of initiating new policies or legislation – few robbers are motivated by the desire to see theft legalized, for example. Nevertheless, widespread circumvention of a rule will likely lead to an amendment, either in the rule or in its enforcement. The likelihood of amendment remains, even if reform is neither intended nor desired by the rule breakers.

Many are the ways to get around rules. Some actions directly contravene the rules, as murder most foul; at other times, the circumvention is more subtle: "Thou shalt not kill; but need'st not strive/Officiously to keep alive."[7] "Evasion" is the term applied to direct violations of rules, while "avoidance" is reserved for actions that technically do not violate the rules, but that run counter to the spirit of the laws. Although evasion is illegal and avoidance is legal, widespread circumventions of either type tend to pave the way for policy reforms. Rule circumvention that engenders policy reform, such as ignoring red lights at night in Bogota, might be termed "unintentional" civil disobedience. That is, the disobedience is intentional but the precipitated policy changes are not intended by the rule breakers. And the induced reform might – but only might – make for better social outcomes: in a curious twist of Adam Smith's invisible hand, law breakers can improve society, even if serving the social good is the furthest thing from their minds. Unintentional civil disobedience need not be uncivil in its effects.

Evasion and change

Whether or not a specific rule violation leads to improvements in society, a policy that is widely disobeyed is, in some sense, a failure. Focusing on the lessons learned from failure is a common technique of inquiry, whether in civil engineering, medicine, or policy analysis.[8]

Policy failure occasioned by widespread rule evasion is marked by two attributes that are fundamental to reform. First, this type of failure tends to become general knowledge. It doesn't take long in a new environment to learn if red light running is widespread. Likewise, it doesn't take long to determine if corruption of government officials is widespread, even though acts of corruption are not committed as publicly as red light running. Significant rule breaking tends to receive media attention. But even without media coverage, widespread evasion often carries its own publicity, generating as common knowledge the notion that the circumvented policy has indeed failed. And among those who learn of the failure of the current policy will be the policy makers themselves. In the language of economics, the widespread evasion makes it clear to policy makers that the current rule and its enforcement regime are not "incentive compatible," i.e. many people apparently find it in their interest to violate or circumvent the rule.

The second feature of evasion-based policy failure that helps sow the ground for the succeeding policy is the more-or-less automatic creation of incentives to enact a policy reform.[9] Often, these incentives exist because a policy alternative involving a full or partial legitimation of the existing evasion will naturally suggest itself – as in the case of the Bogota traffic signals. Some incentive to change an obviously failed policy would emerge in any case, of course, even if a partial legalization is undesirable. But the fact that there are many people who are breaking the current rules, and hence are at some risk of incurring sanctions, provides a built-in constituency for liberalization – and a constituency whose existence is itself widely known. These two attributes of evasion-induced policy failure, publicity and the generation of incentives to reform, typically are shared by both intentional and unintentional civil disobedience.

Evasion, then, can spark reform. Despite the rather positive, progressive connotation surrounding the word "reform" (which survives despite the frequency of failed reforms), change need not be for the better. A reform can be worse than the *status quo*, even when evasion has caused the current policy to be widely regarded as untenable. The world is complex and interconnected, whereas rule circumvention provides but a partial guide to beneficial alterations in policy. For a reform to be successful, modification in the malfunctioning, circumvented policy might also necessitate changes in complementary rules: changes which will not be made obvious by the evasion-induced failure of the prior policy. In cases where the policy reform involves a partial liberalization, as in the Bogota traffic signal example, the remaining constraints might prove to be unsustainable. Will frightened drivers at 3 AM in Bogota, after the official time-period for flashing yellows, suddenly be willing to stop at red lights, and will novice drivers approaching a 3 AM green light rely on the law-abiding behavior of the other motorists?

Exit and policy reform

In his renowned 1970 book *Exit, Voice, and Loyalty*, economist Albert O. Hirschman examined two options – "exit" and "voice" – that are available when a customer is faced with deteriorating quality in a store or product that he or she has been patronizing. Exit involves switching to an alternative supplier. If enough customers exit, the owners of the store will face financial pressure to improve the store's performance, even if those exiting have given no thought to inducing such an improvement. Alternatively, voice consists of lobbying efforts by customers to prod the store owners into recapturing the previous standards – efforts that typically are engaged in while those doing the prodding remain as customers. Hirschman discusses those situations in which either exit, voice, or some combination are likely to succeed in restoring quality.

In the context of policy, evasion and avoidance are forms of "exit" – though the rules from which they provide exit can be either low or high quality. As with

Hirschman's exit, unintentional civil disobedience indirectly creates an incentive for policy reform, even though invoking such a reform did not motivate the disobedience.

In *Exit, Voice and Loyalty*, Hirschman highlighted the extent to which the existence of exit can incapacitate the operation of voice. Why invest in the effort needed to make voice effective in raising quality at the original firm, if you can simply exit to a now superior alternative? Further, it might be those who are most dissatisfied (or those who might be most effective at mobilizing voice) who exit, undermining the opportunity to generate an effective collective voice. Revisiting these issues in a later book, *A Propensity to Self-Subversion*, Hirschman emphasized the opposite possibility, the prospect that extensive exit could help to empower voice. An important example of this phenomenon concerns the fall of the Berlin Wall, where exit (via emigration) amplified the potency of the political demands of those citizens who remained in East Germany.[10]

Similarly, exit via rule evasion can either spur a policy reform, or retard change. One aspect of rule breaking that determines which of these two cases applies is the frequency of the evasion. Small-scale rule evasion ("exit" from the rule) often helps to solidify the rule, to pose a barrier to reform. In this case, those who find obeying the rule to be most onerous choose not to obey. As long as they can evade the rule with limited consequence for themselves or for society at large, and as long as there are not too many such evaders, there will be little impetus to alter the policy.

Widespread rule evasion, however, is likely to generate a policy reform. As noted above, widespread evasion tends to makes it clear that the existing policy is a failure, while providing incentives to alter the policy. Certainly the massive emigration from East Germany in 1989 made the failure of the existing emigration controls (and more generally of the East German regime) obvious. Simultaneously, a policy alternative – eliminate the Wall – that fairly obviously represented an improvement (for the vast majority of those affected) over the *status quo* presented itself. Such preferred alternatives tend to be available when the *status quo* involves widespread evasion. If almost everyone is evading the existing policy anyway, a legitimation (or partial legitimation) of the evasion would at least seem not to make matters worse, whether in the case of the Berlin Wall or the Bogota traffic signals.

Common knowledge that an existing policy is not working, and the availability of seemingly superior alternative policies, help to forge widespread evasion into a spur to reform. But a second dimension (beyond the extent of evasion) that influences the relationship between evasion and reform concerns the specific incentives facing policy makers. Those responsible for making or enforcing policy may not be susceptible to the usual impulses to reform, if their personal well-being is tied to the current policy. Highly placed East German officials were not enthusiastic supporters of breaching the Wall.

Corrupt incomes derived from existing policies are one avenue through which rule makers find their well-being tied to the *status quo*, at least if policy reforms will reduce the opportunities for such illicit earnings. Corruption is itself a form of rule evasion. But widespread corruption does not have the same reform-generating capacity as other types of evasion, because the rule makers (or enforcers) typically benefit from the corrupt environment. (Partly for this reason, anti-corruption campaigns often involve an increase in the legitimate earnings of officials.) Evasion involving the rule makers directly is less effective than widespread evasion of other rules at generating policy reforms – and corruption has been endemic in many countries for decades or even centuries.

Rule circumvention and policy impotence

Yet another Hirschman book, *The Rhetoric of Reaction: Perversity, Futility, Jeopardy*, examines standard arguments arrayed against "progressive" reforms. The futility argument consists of the claim that a proposed reform will be useless: the under-lying phenomenon is too deep-rooted in society to be altered by a mere change in policy. For instance, it is commonly perceived that the US attempt to prohibit sales of alcoholic beverages was futile, that people would manage to find a way around any such ban. The "perversity" argument, on the other hand, necessitates that society be mutable but marked by contrariness. According to perversity-style reasoning, a policy aimed at a specific goal eventually will result in movement away from the goal. In the case of alcohol control, it might be argued that by a "forbidden fruit" effect or by negating the previously applied taxes, Prohibition perversely resulted in more drinking, not less.

As the Prohibition example suggests, disobedience in a policy context connects "exit" with the anti-reform arguments identified by Hirschman. The typical impact of rule avoidance and evasion is to weaken a policy's desired effect. The greater the extent that a ban on cocaine, or handguns, is evaded, the less effective is the policy, at least with respect to the presumptive end of reducing the availability of the banned commodity. At times, this weakening can be so severe that a rule ultimately has no effect (Hirschman's futility), or perhaps, through a series of responses, even has the opposite effect of that intended (Hirschman's perversity). The circumstances in which enforced rules have no effect, or worse, a perverse effect, are rather limited, however – indeed, if such circumstances were common, we might term a policy "perverse" if it worked in the desired direction!

The path ahead

The first six chapters address various aspects of the general issues surrounding rules, evasion, avoidance, corruption, and policy reform. They are followed by two case studies, one concerning the Russian transition to capitalism and a second dealing with gun control policies in the US and Britain.

On the heels of Chapter 1's discussion of rules, Chapter 2 deals with illegal forms of circumvention – evasion – and the consequences of evasion for policy reform. The examination of legal forms of circumvention – avoidance – is postponed until Chapter 4, though there is substantial overlap between the implications of evasion and avoidance for reform. Chapter 3 follows up the "evasion" analysis by looking at zero tolerance policies, which attempt to eliminate evasion. The interplay between preventive, *ex ante* controls and punitive, *ex post* controls, and how that interplay is related to policy circumvention, is the subject of Chapter 5. The enforcement regime that accompanies a policy is itself a policy, and it too may be subject to circumvention. Who guards the guardians? The possibility that rule makers and enforcers might themselves be less than angelic is another factor that helps to determine whether a policy is socially desirable, or if reform is likely. Chapter 6, therefore, is devoted to corruption.

These discussions of the roles of evasion, avoidance, and corruption in making or changing policy are then applied to the two case studies. The first, the Russian transition to capitalism, identifies rule evasion as the main culprit in the collapse of the Soviet Union. The gun control case study highlights avoidance and evasion in a currently contentious policy area, the ongoing transformation of firearm regulation.

Approaching policy issues from the point of view of rule circumvention provides a perspective that illuminates a wide variety of phenomena: zero tolerance policies (and their opposite, the implicit tolerance of extensive illegal behavior), tread-mills of reform, delays of major policy changes, the complexity of rules, and the trade-offs between a rule-based and a discretionary policy. Old stories, such as Soviet collapse or the US Savings and Loan crisis, can be approached in new and, I think, elucidating ways, when rule circumvention is the focus of concentration. Policy reforms can come about for a variety of reasons, but unintentional civil disobedience is a common and important one. This book examines the interplay between rule making and rule breaking, though it stops well short of developing a comprehensive theory of unintentional civil disobedience. The goal is much more modest: to shed some light on a pervasive policy concern, the nature of rules and their transformation in a fallen world, where avoidance and evasion are expected, and sometimes condoned.

1 Rules and their circumvention

Of Man's first disobedience, and the fruit . . .

(Milton, *Paradise Lost*)

An old platitude

Rules are made to be broken. Having achieved cliché status, this piece of ancient wisdom is more enunciated than examined. But the logic underlying the adage is far from straightforward. First, because "rules are made to be broken" is itself a type of rule, a self-referential paradox presents itself: is the rule that "rules are made to be broken" made to be broken? But even leaving aside this conundrum, the saying is perplexing. Try explaining it to an eight-year-old. Why make a rule in the first place if it is to be broken? Were the great law givers of antiquity engaged in acts of futility? Should Moses, upon descending Sinai and beholding the incongruence of his laws with human behavior, have smashed those initial tablets and just left it at that?

In general, of course, the answer is "no," The existence of rules influences social outcomes, even if those rules are commonly broken. Moses' second ascent of Mount Sinai was well worth the effort, despite the regularity with which the Ten Commandments have since been violated. Rule breaking does not typically render the existence of a rule meaningless, though the contrary claim – that opportunities for disobedience will completely undermine the desired impact of a rule – is frequently made by those who oppose a proposed restriction.

While opponents of a policy might argue against it on grounds of evasion, supporters sometimes invoke the potential for evasion and avoidance to make a case for strict enforcement of the measure. Much of the attention paid to rule circumvention is perfunctory, however, whether on the part of supporters or opponents – simply one standard element in the rhetoric of public debate. And it is understandable that rule evasion tends to be somewhat undervalued. To devote primary attention to rule circumvention would be purposely to sideline the majority of activity, because it probably is the case that most people obey most rules most of the time, even in many instances when it would seem that they have little incentive to do so.[1] The influence of evasion and avoidance, however, cannot be measured solely by the extent to which these responses are actually evoked. Just as extensive circumvention does not imply that a rule is meaningless, limited circumvention does not imply that evasion is not an overarching policy issue. Policy making takes place in the shadow of avoidance and evasion, notwithstanding high levels of compliance. Few of us embezzle funds, at least on a significant scale, but accounting procedures to keep track of cash flows are useful nonetheless. Such procedures are, in actuality, a large part of the reason why so few of us embezzle, just as the lack of detail in accounting or inventory procedures explains why work-provided pens and photocopiers are not infrequently diverted to the private uses of those same employees who wouldn't think of embezzling funds more directly or on a grander scale.[2]

On rules

Rules are made to be broken, but what actually constitutes a rule? Nations have rules, corporations have rules, schools have rules, bureaucracies have rules (the infamous rigidity of which lends meaning to the term "bureaucratic"), families have rules, individuals have rules, and individuals voluntarily enter into contracts that specify still more rules. The rules that I want to explore are primarily those of governments: laws, regulations, or, more generally, public policies. One important component of the rules examined here is that they have the capacity to be enforced, at least to some extent. Other types of rules, such as rules of thumb ("don't put your thumb too close to the nail you are hammering") or guides to good living ("eat, drink, and be merry") are not the present objects of study, valuable as they may be. Indeed, most of the issues that I want to address can usefully be thought about in the rather unglamorous setting of traffic rules, as exemplified by the Bogota intersection tale.

The potentially enforceable rules have the general form "In circumstances from the set A, an action from the set B is required." Given that circumstances from A actually arise, an action from the set B is then in compliance with the rule or contract, while an action from the set "not B" is then a breaching action, or an evasion of the rule. The enforcement regime associated with a rule specifies what happens in the event that non-compliance is detected and proven, and this will generally depend on the particular breaching action chosen: murder is punished more severely than assault. Of course, many rules are written in a form that specifies not the actions to be taken, the compliance actions, but rather the breaching actions: "Thou shalt not kill." But such a formulation can be encompassed within the general form described above, since the set of compliance actions (those actions that involve no killing) is the "complement" of the set of breaching actions (all actions that involve killing), and hence the compliance actions can be ascertained given the description of breaching actions.

The distinction drawn here between a rule and its enforcement regime is not necessarily so sharp in practice. Perhaps the general form of a rule should read, "In circumstances from the set A, taking an action from the set B will result in no potential fine or other punishment, while actions from 'not B' will be punished by . . ." The rule that says that, under most (and spelled-out) circumstances, you must drive no faster than the posted speed limit, could alternatively be stated in a package with the enforcement regime, along the lines of "If you are driving a car more than 10 but less than 25 miles per hour over the speed limit you will be fined $250; if you fail to pay this fine, you will be jailed for 6 months; if you abscond to avoid jail, you will be jailed for 3 years when found . . ." And, of course, you won't really be fined $250 if you speed, but rather only if you are caught, which has some probability that is typically fairly small. (In other words, the enforcement regime itself consists of two components, the surveillance strategy by police or regulators and the sanctions imposed on those who are ascertained to be violators.[3]) Even if you are caught, the police officer might give you a warning instead of a ticket, or perhaps mercy can be purchased for some monetary consideration, either directly from the officer or later from a lawyer or a judge. And in making judgments about whether to obey a rule, perceptions of the probability of punishment for various types of non-compliance and what the extent of the punishment will be are clearly relevant. But in terms of describing a rule, the separation of the rule from its enforcement regime is both analytically convenient and generally consistent with our common, everyday understanding of rules.

The application of rules involves some obvious difficulties. The first is the determination of which rule to apply: are circumstances actually in the set A? This determination must be made both by the individual decision maker at the moment of decision, as well as by enforcement and adjudicatory authorities after the fact. (The decision maker may be more interested not in his or her personal view of the circumstances, but rather with the view that the enforcement authorities are likely to take.[4]) Once the circumstances have been adjudicated, there remains the question of whether the action chosen was actually a compliance action, i.e. in set B, or a breaching action. Again, both decision makers and enforcers have to resolve these issues, and they may well not see eye-to-eye. But imagine that they do . . .

A perfect rule

> As in other sciences, so in politics, it is impossible that all things should be precisely set down in writing; for enactments must be universal, but actions are concerned with particulars.
>
> (Aristotle[5])

Imagine everyone getting together and agreeing to a contract that will precisely specify their actions for the next year. Of course, there are many elements outside the control of these people, like the weather or natural disasters, and they cannot be sure when they write the contract what circumstances will actually come about. But assume for now that while they cannot know in advance what circumstances will arise, our contractors will at least be able to specify all of the possibilities, all the potential "states of the world" that have some possibility of occurring, at all moments during the next year. While taxing our imaginations, let's assume that the "law makers" (i.e. the contractors, the people themselves) understand each other's preferences, so they needn't fear revealing any private information during the contract negotiation, and let's also assume that the contract negotiation itself is a smooth and costless process. Further, there will be no room for later disputes as to what circumstances actually occurred and what actions were actually taken: these will be perfectly clear to all.

What would be the result of this frictionless negotiation among such far-seeing creatures? They needn't leave anything to chance, in the sense that they can perfectly specify exactly what every person should do under any and all circumstances, even if they cannot control what circumstances will occur. The contract can tell driver α that when approaching a certain intersection at a certain time on a certain day and under certain weather conditions, if there is another vehicle approaching the intersection from driver α's right, then α should stop and wait for the intersection to clear, unless the brakes have failed on the truck behind α, in which case α should honk his horn and keep going, while the other car should stop. The resulting contract, then, will be composed of a plethora of rules. For each rule in the contract, the set of circumstances A to which it applies consists of only a single circumstance or a unique "state"; further, for each state A, the action that complies with the rule in circumstance A is also perfectly speci-fied, so that for each individual and for each circumstance, the set of compliance actions B consists of a single well-specified action.[6]

The law givers, then, can specify the best actions for everyone in all possible circumstances, and subsequently go out and perform as required by the contract. There will be no room for avoidance, as in any circumstance there will be only one well-specified, compliance action. Evasion is another story, however, the rather large fly in this otherwise pleasant ointment. In the absence of enforcement, the people won't have any incentive actually to take the actions specified in the contract, to implement the plan that they themselves agreed was socially optimal. Driver α might note that if he honks his horn and doesn't slow down, the driver approaching from the right will have little choice but to stop – even if there is no truck with faulty brakes behind α. Bank employee β might notice that instead of putting a cash deposit in the drawer, he could just as easily and more gainfully put it in his pocket. Entrepreneur γ might note that there is money to be made from selling the narcotic that the social contract decided should be banned under all circumstances, where the profitable opportunity presents itself thanks to customer δ's eagerness to make a purchase in defiance of the ban. And so on.[7]

An implication of this parable is that a rule cannot be determined to be either good or bad unless the enforcement regime is also specified. In a world of far-sighted, infallible angels who would be guaranteed to obey agreements strictly, optimal policy would amount to simply signing the detailed contingent contract as envisioned above. But human beings might be tempted to disobey, as Hobbes noted in the seventeenth century, "because the bonds of words are too weak to bridle mens ambition, avarice, anger and other Passions, without the feare of some coerceive Power."[8] For humans, then, the optimal angelic contract is not available in itself, but rather, an enforcement mechanism and the resources necessary to maintain it also must be included. And it is only in rare cases that the enforcement will be sufficient to prevent all violations; some contract violators might remain undeterred even by harsh sanctions, and some violations will occur by mistake, when fallible humans, as opposed to infallible seraphs, are choosing actions. Nor can it be taken for granted that the enforcers will themselves be unerring angels, needing no supervision of their own activities. Given such impediments, perfect compliance cannot be achieved, and should not be sought. The law givers will recognize that even were it feasible to enforce so strictly and honestly that there would be no breaching of the contract, it would generally be too costly to do so. The additional resources needed to decrease rule evasion further and further would eventually become better spent in some other way, such as on more vacations, shoes, and movies.

Once the necessity for enforcement and its fallibility is taken into account, the optimal contract itself changes: the rules that would be best for angels might be extremely inappropriate for humans who make mistakes or who fall prey to the temptation to disobey strictures in the absence or imperfection of "some coercive Power." The angels might find, for example, that a prohibition on the use of heroin for non-medical purposes is the best rule. The humans might agree, but they might also decide that free needle exchange programs are likewise a good policy, to lower the social costs stemming from circumvention of the heroin ban. Angels would have no need of such a program, but mankind is fallen.

Perfect information concerning future states of the world, combined with complete information over individuals' preferences and their potential actions, is an insufficient basis for determining desirable rules: the enforcement mechanisms must be included. In many areas of social interaction, incidentally, neither the rules nor the enforcement mechanisms need be provided by the state, by the long arm (fin?) of Hobbes's Leviathan. The relevant rules, for instance, can be provided by social norms, and these may even conflict with the formal, state-provided rules.[9] With respect to enforcement, individual consciences and social sanctions can substitute for or complement explicit enforcement machinery. Informal norms and enforcement mechanisms may themselves co-evolve with the formal rules and their enforcement regimes.

The necessity of taking enforcement into account complicates the process of law making; the difficulties are further exacerbated when short-sightedness and ignorance – as well as the costs of composing ever more detailed rules – are coupled with the human penchant to disobey. Rules cannot be completely detailed, and because of the costs of trying to do so, they should not be completely detailed, even if in theory they could be. Future circumstances and compliance actions can-not be perfectly delineated, at least at reasonable cost. The set A of circumstances to which a rule applies, and the set B of compliance actions, generally have many elements. As a result, rules do not actually require the best possible action in a given circumstance. The rules will be drafted, it might be hoped, in such a way that compliance typically will result in fairly good, if not first-best, social outcomes (though there will be many different actions that constitute compliance, some more socially desirable than others). But in some cases, all of the compliance actions will be ill-advised: the socially best actions will violate the rules, as many of those frustrated with a bureaucracy will testify. Imperfect rules are made to be broken.

It might be thought that the incomplete nature of rules, which was noted by the ancient Greeks, could be avoided by a general rule along the lines of "take the socially efficient action in all circumstances."[10] But in practice, such a rule would also prove to be incomplete, in that the police and courts (or, within a firm, managers and arbitrators) would be unable to monitor and enforce such a rule at any reasonable cost. A general rule of this type simply moves the incompleteness to the *ex post* stage, after the relevant actions have been chosen, and probably makes it impossible for individuals to have any confidence that they have chosen a compliance action: whether the chosen action represents compliance with or breach of the rule will have to be determined by a court, and a fallible court at that.[11] Complete rules cannot be purchased on the cheap.

Evasion and avoidance

Evasion and avoidance are alternative ways of circumventing rules. Evasion involves choosing a breaching action, and usually trying to hide either the fact of evasion or the identity of the evader from the enforcement authorities. Avoidance, alternatively, involves choosing a compliance action, so the enforcement authorities are not a direct concern (unless there is some question as to whether the chosen action actually is of the avoidance or the evasive kind). But an avoidance action takes advantage of rule incompleteness, in that the action chosen technically constitutes compliance while presumably running counter to the goals that the legislators had in mind when they crafted the rules.

Though differing with respect to legality, evasion and avoidance are often similar with respect to the forces they bring to bear on public policy. Widespread evasion or widespread avoidance, for instance, both tend to lead to policy reforms. Indeed, public policy is in large measure about designing rules and their enforcement regimes in such a way that there will be widespread compliance, and that such compliance – even when it involves avoidance – will promote desirable outcomes.

This description of the goal of public policy contrasts with some popular notions that suggest that poor social outcomes are due to the nefarious activities of certain classes of evil people: "greedy lawyers are ruining America" is a case in point. Public policy should design the rules and their enforcement regime in such a way that even a self-interested lawyer is "led by an invisible hand to promote an end which was no part of his intention," where that end is good social outcomes.[12] This is not to say that there is no role for public spiritedness or individual conscience, on the part of lawyers or anyone else. Indeed, in worlds where there is neither public spiritedness nor individual conscience, when all individuals are like Justice Holmes's "bad man," interested only in the price exacted for his actions, then the rule making of public policy is asked to do too much.[13] Perhaps only the rule making of penitentiaries can produce anything like order given such raw material: but is this a desirable social outcome? Under any public policy regime, there will always be a multitude of avoidance actions, and therefore legal actions, that I would hope that no one would ever believe it to be in his or her best interests to choose. But given the modicum of civic virtue requisite for self-government, rules and their enforcement should be designed to make enlightened self-interest consonant with both rule compliance and the social good.[14]

Bright lines

The failure of a general rule such as "Always take the socially best action" to be a useful guide to choice indicates that rule incompleteness derives not only from the costs of drafting more detailed rules, but also from the costs of attempting to enforce what would otherwise be appropriate distinctions. While free speech is generally thought to be a good thing, we can all imagine circumstances in which prohibiting some forms of speech would lead to better social outcomes: surely falsely shouting "fire" in a crowded theater could safely be prohibited, to use Justice Holmes's famous example. Nevertheless, the First Amendment to the US Constitution says that "Congress shall make no law . . . abridging the freedom of speech." Why such an absolute prohibition? Why not allow Congress to adopt a few clearly beneficial laws restricting speech?

One reason for absolute prohibitions is that they create "bright lines" – it is pretty clear (or at least relatively clear) what "no law" means, and so the amendment is easily enforceable against Congress. But if the First Amendment made room for some exceptions, for cases of overwhelming necessity, say, or, as Justice Holmes and the Supreme Court have ruled, if there is a "clear and present danger," then the prohibition becomes much more difficult to enforce, as one person or court's view of a clear and present danger may well differ from that held by another person or court.[15]

Again, a similar issue arises in the rules that guide private behavior. A person on a diet might adopt a "no dessert" rule, even though an occasional dessert might be better than none. But any attempt at further discrimination, such as "dessert only allowed if I had a light lunch earlier in the day," greatly complicates (self-) enforcement. What constitutes a light lunch? Further, once the door is opened to exceptions, it is unclear where it should stop. What if I skipped breakfast? What if I anticipate a significant delay before my next meal? Drug abusers who seriously attempt to reduce their dependence often find that "cold turkey" is an effective strategy, though it would seem to be easier to adopt a less rigorous rule, such as reducing consumption by 50 per cent. But if you can consume 50 per cent of the drugs that you used to consume, why not 60 per cent? And maybe it isn't that easy to measure your consumption, anyway. A limit of zero makes compliance, and evasion, clear.[16]

One role played by law and enforcement is to establish bright lines when reality is much more murky. A driver who is proceeding safely but who is stopped at a check point will be arrested and face serious difficulties (in most US states) if he or she is found to have a blood alcohol content of 0.08; if the breathalyzer test reads 0.07, the driver will be allowed to continue on his or her way. For that matter, an adult who purchases alcohol in the US is within his rights, though if he purchases marijuana or heroin instead, he is committing an illegal act.

Other countries draw the boundaries differently. The Dutch, for example, have attempted to draw a bright line between "soft" drugs (marijuana and hashish) and "hard" drugs such as heroin or cocaine. Small purchases of marijuana are implicitly condoned, while enforcement efforts and harm reduction resources are concentrated against hard drugs. But no matter where the lines are drawn, the unavoidable incompleteness of rules will mean that in some circumstances, appropriate actions (i.e. those that are not socially undesirable, excepting their illegality) will fall on the "illegal" side of the line, and inappropriate actions will fall on the "legal" side. Imperfection is unavoidable, and as Justice Holmes noted: "the law does all that is needed when it does all that it can, indicates a policy, applies it to all within the lines, and seeks to bring within the lines all similarly situated so far and so fast as its means allow."[17]

Rules intended for children are particularly sensitive about adopting bright lines, because children have less ability to make responsible discriminations among circumstances. "Just say no," "Look both ways before crossing a street," and "Don't take candy from a stranger" are all rules that would admit some exceptions, but to start noting the exceptions to children could result in complete emasculation of the strictures. Better to stick with understandable and enforceable rules, unrefined though they may be.

In this, as in many things, "We are but older children, dear,/Who fret to find our bedtime near."[18] Not only do we try to create bright lines in rules designed to change our own habits, we recognize that even other adults may need to be presented with unambiguous guidelines. The ethical codes that we practice and believe in may not be the ones that we publicly espouse, in part because we fear that the distinctions that we respond to personally cannot be easily expressed, or might be misunderstood and misapplied. Potentially, such hypocrisy is optimal, and it is surely widely practiced.[19]

Enforcement difficulties, then, lead some rules to be more coarse than they otherwise would be. A second consequence of limited enforcement is that supplementary rules may be adopted to aid in enforcement of a primary rule. Consider another example from the US Bill of Rights, the Fourth Amendment prohibition against "unreasonable searches and seizures." How can this rule be enforced? Should police officers who conduct an unreasonable search be punished? Perhaps, but what if in practice the punishment is light or non-existent? Then in apprehending a suspected criminal, the police could essentially conduct a search first, and worry about the niceties of its legality later, after the criminal had been convicted. And even if the offending officer were punished, that might be of little solace to the criminal, or to those innocent victims who are also subject to illegal searches without being charged with a crime.

These thorny issues have led, in the US, to the controversial "exclusionary rule," based on a 1961 Supreme Court judgment that evidence obtained in illegal searches is not admissible in state criminal trials. (The rule had previously applied to federal law enforcers.) Supporters of the exclusionary rule argue that it improves compliance with the Fourth Amendment – though at the cost of releasing some factually guilty criminals. Simultaneously, the rule greatly complicates criminal litigation, with the admissibility of evidence often becoming a leading issue, partly because of tremendous uncertainty regarding how the rule should be applied in specific cases.[20] An unfortunately common response to the exclusionary rule, incidentally, is perjury, where police falsely testify that a suspect "dropped" a prohibited substance in the course of being apprehended, or kept a controlled substance in plain sight during a traffic stop.[21] For police, presumably, this represents one of those instances of practicing an ethical code that they would be unwilling to espouse publicly.[22]

And so enforcement complications can lead to new prohibitions that otherwise would not be in place, or to rules that are coarser or perhaps less restrictive than they otherwise would be. In the case of drug regulation, these responses have been termed "reluctant denial" and "grudging toleration."[23] A drug is reluctantly prohibited or denied to adults, for example, if its legality would make it too difficult to enforce a clearly desirable ban on its consumption by children. Alternatively, a drug might be grudgingly tolerated if enforcing its prohibition is too costly or an exercize in futility, when the extent of demand and the ease of black market circumvention is taken into account.

Computer-generated child pornography provides another "vice" example where ease of enforcement requires a certain combination of rules. Computer-generated images may involve no actual children in production; nevertheless possession of such images remains (reluctantly?) illegal in the UK, in part because of complications in enforcement. If computer-generated images were legal, police or the courts would have to go through a painstaking (and perhaps highly imperfect) analysis when any child pornography were uncovered, to ensure that it was not of the legal, computer-generated variety. The famous adage of former US Supreme Court Justice Potter Stewart concerning obscenity, "I know it when I see it," vague as it is, could not be applied to child pornography if the precise production method would first have to be ascertained before illegality could be determined.[24]

Mandates as well as bans can be driven by enforcement concerns. Violations of child labor laws might be hard to monitor, but school attendance is verifiable. Mandatory school attendance, then, can be an attractive way to promote compliance with laws that limit the working hours of children.[25]

Good and bad rules

Given that the outcomes associated with a rule depend on the enforcement regime, and that rules are necessarily incomplete, there is little that can be said in general terms about the features that good rules should possess. The dependence of the quality of laws on enforcement suggests that whether a law or policy is desirable depends on the frequency with which it is evaded. Alcohol prohibition in the US is generally deemed to have been a failure, and reconstituting Prohibition is not on the current US policy agenda, predominantly because of widespread evasion of the earlier prohibition regime. At the same time, there is little political support for repeal of the ban on heroin, in large measure because evasion of the ban, while significant, is not sufficiently widespread, at least among the politically influential. Examples abound in private settings, too. Rules that provide a ticket holder with a particular seat in a theater, for instance, with higher prices charged for better seats, work well in many instances; if evasion is widespread, however, and cannot be controlled at reasonable cost, so that low-priced ticket holders habitually and *en masse* "invade" the good seats, then a single-price system, where individuals choose whatever seat they want on a first-come first-served basis, will be preferable.[26]

Opportunities for circumvention not only help to establish whether a law is socially desirable, they can even influence the determination of the law's legality. Some US states permit casino gambling, while others are more restrictive. Can the government limit broadcast advertizing of casinos, if such advertizing reaches states with restrictive gambling laws (though the broadcasts themselves originate from states with legal casinos)? One of the tests employed in the US to determine whether a restriction on "commercial speech" meets constitutional muster is whether the restriction directly and materially promotes a substantial governmental interest. But this test depends on opportunities to avoid or evade the stricture. If circumvention is widespread and people therefore are exposed to similar commercial speech, the government interest is subverted; therefore, the restriction will not promote the government interest, and the rule is unconstitutional. On such grounds, the US Supreme Court invalidated a federal restriction on casino advertizing in 1999. Native American casinos were exempt from the challenged restriction, as were many other forms of gambling. "Promotional" ads were banned, but other types of casino advertizing were permitted. The Court therefore held that the law "and its attendant regulatory regime is so pierced by exemptions and inconsistencies that the Government cannot hope to exonerate it."[27] The issue goes well beyond this one case, and beyond commercial activity: "In the United States, at least, almost any law which a significant number of people would be tempted to disobey on moral grounds would be doubtful – if not clearly invalid – on constitutional grounds as well."[28]

Clarity would seem to be a desirable feature in a rule, as the discussion of "bright lines" suggested. With clear rules, decision makers and enforcers can tell whether or not a compliance action has been chosen. (Criminal statutes in the US are unconstitutional under the "vagueness doctrine" if they are so unclear that reasonable people cannot determine what conduct is prohibited, or if the statutes encourage arbitrary enforcement.[29]) Even here, though, it is easy to imagine circumstances in which there is virtue in murkiness: imprecision might be useful to build political support to get a rule passed; the discretion that a lack of clarity provides for enforcers might promote good outcomes;[30] or vague language can intentionally be employed "as a hedge against an uncertain future."[31] Confusing tax laws can actually increase the collection of tax revenues, and even promote social welfare.[32] Further, the process of clearly demarcating laws may itself be detrimental to the laws; it has been suggested, for instance, that in delineating the scope of the exclusionary rule, "the very specificity of the process makes it look foolish and renders it vulnerable to easy criticism."[33]

Nevertheless, the more typical case is that good rules involve clarity and bright lines. Suggestive of this tendency are bad outcomes in some areas of the law that currently lack clarity. Consider, for instance, the definition of a terrorist and the appropriate "rules" concerning terrorism. Some former terrorists have staked claims, respected by many, to being legitimate political figures. Can a terrorist be delineated from a patriot or freedom fighter, or is it simply a matter of *realpolitik*, like Adam Smith's observation "that both rebels and heretics are those unlucky persons, who, when things have come to a certain degree of violence, have the misfortune to be of the weaker party?"[34] Is there any behavior so beyond the pale that irrespective of the distribution of power, terrorists who engage in that behavior will not be permitted to evolve into statesmen? There are some obvious dimensions upon which distinctions should turn, even though the boundaries will assuredly be fuzzy. The greater the opportunity to effect change through persuasion and peaceful means, for example, the less that a resort to terror should be countenanced. Citizens enjoying full civil rights in a functional democracy, therefore, should face essentially a zero tolerance policy against acts of terror. Those who purposely target children should likewise find little solace, even when there are serious restraints on non-violent dissent, and even from those who are sympathetic with the ends in view. More generally, the deliberate targeting of noncombatants is highly problematic, and has even been offered as a definition of terrorism, if the targeting is done with utter disregard and without provocation.[35] Nevertheless, the current treatment of terrorists does not seem to draw these distinctions, either in international law or in the public mind.

All else equal, then, rules that are inexpensive to draft, comply with, and enforce – simple and clear rules – would seem to have an advantage in guiding behavior into socially desirable channels, as the "Just say no" example suggested.[36] Our personal rules of behavior similarly benefit from high fidelity, from being easy for others to comprehend and respond to.[37] But even a good rule will admit some exceptions in practice, because of the inescapable incompleteness of rules. There will always be "hard cases," perplexing situations in which it is difficult to determine what rule is appropriate, or how the existing rules should be applied, even with hindsight. Nor is it obvious if a proposed change to an existing rule will improve social outcomes.

A better rule?

In 1988, the *Journal of Economic Perspectives* solicited suggestions for a policy change that would lead to a clear improvement in US society, in the sense that some individuals would be helped, while no one would be harmed.[38] One reader responded with the following intriguing proposal: why not change the law so that cars, after stopping at a red light, could make a left turn if the intersection were clear, instead of killing time waiting for the light to change?[39] (A similar proposal could be made for traffic heading straight on). The proposer understood the reason why such a rule change would not be a good idea: people might not be all that scrupulous about ensuring that the intersection was in fact clear, or there might be too much room for different interpretations of what constitutes a sufficiently clear intersection. The "full stop" first required at a red light would, in practice, also be degraded. In short, a useful bright line – red means stop, green means go – would be dimmed. While such a rule change would be beneficial if it were always obeyed, it could be very costly given opportunities for evasion: killing time, and only time, is the preferred option.

But is that analysis sufficient? After all, the widespread adoption of "right turn on red" laws in the United States in the 1970s proved a success, or at least there is no obvious sentiment for repeal. These laws permit cars to make a right turn when the signal is red, provided that they first come to a full stop and their drivers determine that the intersection (including pedestrian traffic) is clear. In fact, however, right-on-red illustrates well the potential problems. Signs forbidding rights-on-red are often posted at crowded intersections (indeed, right-on-red remains prohibited throughout Manhattan), or at crossings with poor visibility. Cursory observation indicates, however, that these signs are frequently ignored, and that many cars at intersections at which rights-on-red are permissible do not bother first to come to the full stop required in the law. Prior to the rule change, a car approaching an intersection when the signal turned yellow was more likely to rush through the intersection (potentially running a red light) if the car was going straight on than if it was turning right, since a turning car had to slow down in any event. Now, however, a yellow light seems to be treated no differently from a green light by the drivers of many right-turning cars. Some statistical studies go beyond cursory observation, by indicating that the adoption of right-on-red laws leads to increased accidents, particularly those involving pedestrians or bicyclists.[40] The right-on-red law may be justified, but there has been some cost in dimming the previous bright line that red lights mean stop.

Likewise, the fanciful "right-through-red" proposal would involve costs as well as benefits. The magnitude of these costs and benefits depends on the precise situation. Here, it should be kept in mind that *de jure* rules often differ markedly from *de facto* rules, and many drivers at deserted intersections presumably evade the rule against running red lights. (This is speculation, not introspection.) The police and courts might – but only might – show some sympathy to drivers who are caught going through a red light at an empty crossroad after a long wait, despite the interest these authorities have in enforcing traffic laws.

Some *de jure* aspects of the right-through-red rule currently exist, too. As the gains from the adoption of right-through-red accrue through the reduction in time spent waiting at deserted intersections (assuming carjacking is not part of the equation!), the fact that there are already adaptations (both *de jure* and *de facto*) that reduce waiting time lessens the value of fully adopting the reform. Three official adaptations are rather common. First, right turns on red, as noted, are often legal. Second, the widespread use of "tripping" devices, whereby cars will not have to wait long at a deserted intersection before their traffic signal turns green, has lessened the time savings that "right-through-red" might offer. Third, some traffic signals are changed to flashing yellow or flashing red during off-peak times, providing the time savings in a way that does not offer the same potential to erode respect for red traffic signals.[41] And as cars have become more comfortable, the disutility associated with spending a few more seconds stopped "unnecessarily" at a red light has diminished.[42]

Why are rules changed?

The discussion of the proposed "right-through-red" rule was conducted under the implicit assumption that the point of public policy is to produce desirable social outcomes, and therefore that a rule will be changed when it becomes clear that an alternative to the *status quo* offers better results. Of course, there might be considerable disagreement over what constitutes a better social outcome, since almost all feasible rule changes will help some individuals and hurt others. For this reason, even under the best of circumstances, the political process which seeks to balance various interests will be contentious, and some desirable reforms will be delayed until the *status quo* deteriorates so extensively that almost everyone will find a policy change advantageous.

When there are substantial numbers of winners and losers from a policy change, the anticipated distributional consequences are a major determinant of the political saliency of the proposed reform. Many policies, such as trade protection for a minor industry, can be very beneficial for a small number of people, while imposing only a minuscule cost on each of the vast number of people who are not in the favored group. But if the group of "losers" is sufficiently large, the total social costs of the trade barriers will exceed the benefits. With such a small stake in the outcome, however, individual losers will have little incentive to organize and lobby to oppose the protective policy, while the incentive for the winners, of course, is very substantial.[43]

These standard barriers to desirable collective actions are well-known. Nevertheless, a politician cognizant of these dangers and anxious to choose only socially desirable rules might mistakenly support inefficient policies. Such a politician will still have to gauge the preferences of his or her constituents. Whose voice will be heard? It is unlikely that the inputs into lobbying will evenly reflect the totality of social interests, given the relatively strong incentive for concentrated special interests to express their opinions. The situation may be even more skewed. In addition to a limited motivation on the part of most citizens to acquire policy-relevant information, even when becoming informed is relatively easy, it simply might not be easy. Policies are complex. Diligent research and devoted thought might not provide much of a guide to the effects of a potential policy change; therefore, broad groups of people may not understand their own interests in a policy reform.

Within the political arena, the actual social benefits of a reform, and their distribution, are less important than the publicly perceived distribution of costs and benefits. The substantial expenses of acquiring better information for many citizens provide an opening for motivated individuals, potentially including legislators and regulators, to attempt to mislead the public debate, to sway policies in ways that favor their special interests.[44] As a result, socially undesirable rules that serve to enrich a few at the expense of the many can be adopted and maintained, even in polities that are responsive to broad citizen preferences.

While special interests and incomplete information complicate the determination of socially optimal policies, these could be relatively minor wrenches in the legislative machinery. Other factors may be much more damaging. For example, it may be that coming to some consensus over what constitutes a "better social outcome" is irrelevant for many real-world policy changes.[45] Policy may be driven by ideology, or by the institutional mechanics of regulatory or legislative bodies, irrespective of social welfare or efficiency.[46] Or the lobbying process might be dishonest, as when politicians essentially sell policy changes to voters or contributors in a way that maximizes the politicians' own chances for re-election, or offers corrupt earnings in other forms.

While acknowledging that these and other sources of policy reform can be influential and sometimes even determinative, I generally will focus on the net social benefits of a potential policy shift, and the distribution of the costs and benefits, when explaining policy change. Reforms, all else equal, have the best chance of being implemented when they offer substantial net benefits – i.e. more desirable social outcomes – and when there are relatively few who are harmed by the reforms.[47] The conditions that favor reform can be brought about through evasion and avoidance of the existing rules, as noted in the introduction and discussed at more length below. The role of corruption in changing the calculus of policy reform will also be addressed.

For now, though, note that there is some pressure, however dilute, against socially wasteful policies (and against inefficient private practices, too). The passage of time tends to erode the factors that lead to sub-optimal policies. Misleading claims about the social virtues of the policy become less compelling as experience accumulates.[48] Those harmed by a policy (whether or not it is socially undesirable) will seek ways to mitigate their losses, and emulate such discoveries made by others. Competitors will emerge for a share of the benefits, reducing the per capita stake that "winners" have in the continuation of the policy. The *status quo* policy has an edge, of course, in that policies that are yet to be adopted presumably are more uncertain in their effects.[49] But the outcome associated with the *status quo* policy need not itself be static, as self-interested behavior on the part of the erstwhile losers and would-be beneficiaries leads them to find novel ways either of avoiding costs, or of sharing in the bounty.[50] And while even socially desirable policies are subject to such attenuation, policy makers in responsive political regimes will be more apt to combat these avoidance responses when the original policy is socially desirable than when the policy is noticeably less than optimal.

Information and rule circumvention

Rule evasion and avoidance, which typically dampen the intended effects of a policy, often serve as the catalyst for policy reforms. Wide-scale evasion and avoidance, most particularly, regularly impel either the abandonment of a policy or a sharp increase in enforcement, just as "Man's first disobedience" led to a decidedly different policy regime in exile from Eden. As noted, civil disobedience is a form of rule evasion that its practitioners engage in precisely to set in motion forces that will change the rule, but even evasion less calculated can induce a similar response.

Whether intended, or desirable, or otherwise, rule evasion regularly dilutes the reliability of standard measures of the results of policy changes. Rule breaking (other than the civilly disobedient variety) tends to be conducted in a less than open manner, and hence is not captured fully in official statistics. Conditions prior to a rule change may therefore be misunderstood, potentially leading to the implementation of inappropriate policies. (What was the actual state of the Soviet economy in late 1991, given that a significant proportion of activity was conducted underground, outside the purview of statisticians and tax collectors?) The rule change then brings its own evasion and avoidance, perhaps equally hidden. Policy analysis is made doubly perplexing by the potential for evasion: not only is the relationship between changes in the formal rules and changes in individual behavior hard to untangle in advance, it also is complex to measure after the fact. Some policy issues remain contentious largely because the extent and effects of evasion are not well understood. Will methadone maintenance programs for heroin addicts lead to lower social costs from drug abuse? The answer, in large measure, depends on details of the methadone program, its implementation (in providing insufficient doses or, alternatively, excessive doses that are diverted to the black market), and how the illegal market in heroin will respond to the new competition. (The short-run and long-run responses could be quite different. By subsidizing methadone, heroin addiction itself might become more desirable – or less undesirable – "attracting" more addicts in the long run.) But the extent and workings of the existing illegal drug market are themselves very imperfectly known, and furthermore they will vary with enforcement efforts against heroin trafficking. Still less understood than the existing black market are the detailed responses by heroin buyers and sellers to a policy change such as enhanced availability of methadone treatment.

The informational erosion accompanying evasive activity implies that relevant empirical evidence tends to be both limited and of questionable reliability. Social scientists use a variety of methodologies in an attempt to overcome the shortage of sound data. Detailed information on some types of illegal behavior can be gathered by ethnographers, but it is bound to be drawn only from a small segment of society, and hence its more general applicability is questionable. Broader measures, such as standard national income accounts, are less likely to directly capture informal activity – though sometimes the influence of illegality or informality can be gleaned from standard statistics. The size of the underground economy, for example, has been estimated through a comparison of monetary statistics with the extent of the official economy.[51] Despite such efforts of social scientists, however, the potential for large errors in the understanding of the scope or nature of evasive activity remains. Policy experts may not be in any better position than ordinary citizens to understand the true state of affairs. Experts may even have one disadvantage, an inclination to place too much reliance on official statistics, which are likely to be the main source of information that appears "scientific," but which also tend to neglect informal or illegal activity.

A recognition of the informational shortcomings associated with evasive behavior is not a prescription for despair. Even in the most impenetrable cases, analysts can at least offer broad guidelines of the potential effects of evasive activity, and indicate the likely influence of hidden behavior on policy reforms. In many instances, rule circumvention will not play a large role in the outcome of policies. But for some policies it will be decisive, and analysts can make a contribution by indicating when and how that might be the case. Despair is more likely to occur, after the fact, when evasion and avoidance are not taken into account in formulating a policy and enforcement regime.

There is some compensation for the informational dilution that accompanies rule evasion: namely, evasive behavior in essence presents an experiment, an alternative way of arranging society. As long as it is on a small scale, it might be an experiment worth running, though it might be expected that, like the rule violations in copying DNA, most of the "mutations" will not lead to improvements – though this predisposition depends on the quality of the initial rules themselves. Nor are the experiments pure; perhaps the benefits of the alternative way of organizing society will not reveal themselves unless the alternative is legal and widely practiced. At least a common argument arrayed by proponents of social orderings that are widely thought to have proved their undesirability – including US alcohol prohibition and Soviet socialism – is that their preferred alternative was never actually tested, that it was never implemented in a sufficiently pure form. If these advocates are right, their versions of improved societies may not be achievable in the gradual manner that evasion-induced policy response offers.[52] But sometimes the gradualism of evasion works in bringing about beneficial changes: the evasive activity is quickly perceived as being desirable (or at least it is perceived that if the evasive activity were legal the social outcome would dominate that arising from the ineffectual attempt to enforce compliance), is imitated more widely, and is eventually ratified by an official change in the rules.

An example: avoidance and evasion in a price-controlled market

A long-popular demonstration in introductory microeconomics concerns how an effective price ceiling – a legal restriction on the maximum amount that sellers can charge for a good – leads to a shortage of the good, and a loss of economic efficiency. Nevertheless, when the price of an important good rises quickly, policy makers often call for, and sometimes enact, price controls, even in market economies. Perhaps policy makers never studied (or never understood) introductory microeconomics, and hence are unaware of the consequences of price ceilings, or are hoping to appeal to constituencies who themselves lack microeconomic training (or indoctrination?). Or perhaps the policy makers or their constituents view the distributional impact of a price ceiling – while the economy overall might be harmed, some individuals will benefit – as desirable in itself, and worth the cost of a loss of efficiency. (An extreme version of this possibility might suggest that it is the policy makers themselves who are the main beneficiaries of the price control, perhaps through corrupt means.) Another possibility, however, is that the introductory microeconomics analysis is not a reliable guide to the actual effects of a price ceiling. In practice, the impact of a price ceiling will hinge on a host of factors, many that depend on the nature of the good in question, and others that involve the precise mechanism by which the ceiling is enacted, how it is enforced, and the routes open to evasion and avoidance.

So, consider a new government regulation that establishes a price ceiling for a good, at a level somewhat below the going market price. What will be the impact of the new regulation?

Employing the standard supply–demand framework for a competitive market, the price ceiling, if effectively enforced, will result in a diminution of the quantity sold, and the nominal price will be lowered to the controlled level. Because the control results in excess demand, there remains the issue of which consumers actually receive the good. For many commodities such as gasoline, first-come first-served becomes the allocation rule, leading to queuing. For other goods, alternative rationing methods are more likely. With rent-controlled apartments, for example, existing tenants are generally given the option to continue in their occupancy, and vacancies might be filled through waiting lists. The distribution of ration coupons, with or without permissible resale, is another possibility.

Consider the case with queuing. In the standard analysis, the full price of the good, including the value of time spent waiting in line, will actually be higher than the pre-control price, on average. Thus, to the extent that the intended effect of price controls is to make goods cheaper for the average consumer, the policy will likely have a perverse impact, if queue-rationing develops.[53] There generally will be distributional consequences, too – actual consumers are not average consumers. Some buyers will pay a lower effective price for the good, while others will pay more.

The price control, however, might be evaded or avoided. Evasion basically amounts to illicit, black-market transactions, at prices higher than those allowed by law. Generally such sales are more difficult to arrange than legal sales, because they must be conducted away from the purview of enforcement agents. And there are some simple ways to raise barriers to evasion. For example, the law can make only the seller involved in the black-market transaction guilty of a crime: in other words, it can be illegal to sell the good at a price above the controlled level, but not illegal to buy the good at that price. In such circumstances, sellers will be wary of buyers whom they do not already trust, because of the increased possibility that the buyer will later testify against the seller.[54] Buyers who do not have a credible threat to go to the enforcement authorities, perhaps because they are involved in illegal activity of their own (they could be illegal immigrants, for instance), will then have an "advantage" in evading the constraint. In any case, price ceilings often stimulate a fair amount of evasion, as was evidenced in both Britain and the US during World War II.[55] Legal minimum prices (price floors) also can be evaded: it has been estimated that as many as one-third of the employees for whom the US minimum wage is binding are paid less than the minimum wage, and in some developing countries noncompliance with minimum wage laws is the rule rather than the exception.[56]

Avoidance of a price ceiling can come in various guises, often connected with changing the nature of the good either to put it outside the jurisdiction of the controls, or to lower the quality (and hence the production costs) of the good to bring it more in conformance with the controlled price. For example, a tie-in sale might be used, whereby the controlled good is sold (or given away "free") with the purchase of another, non-price-controlled good. One example comes from transitional Russia, which imposed a minimum price on imports to protect the domestic vodka industry: a price floor, as opposed to a price ceiling. To elude the controls, some shopkeepers adopted "buy one, get one free" promotions for foreign-produced vodka.[57] A similar dodge involves marketing a nominally altered product as though it represents a vastly different good, one outside of existing price controls. If such a nominal change were both costless and effective at circumventing the price control, then the control would be meaningless. There are still more methods of avoiding a price control, of course. Auxiliary services that were previously included in the purchase of the good without separate charge, such as assistance provided by an informed and responsive sales staff, might be reduced. Consider some of the dimensions of a gasoline purchase that sellers could alter when faced with price controls: octane, hours of service, acceptance of credit, and even the cleanliness of restrooms could be adjusted in response to price regulation.[58] Not all routes to avoid the control need be minor, either: a substantial change in the character of the good might actually be induced, or the quantity supplied might be significantly reduced.

After witnessing the various forms of evasion and avoidance that arise in response to price controls, policy makers might be tempted to amend the rules or the enforcement regime to combat some of the most prevalent rule-circumvention methods. Perhaps minimum quantity constraints would be added for sellers, or restrictions placed on tie-in sales. Of course, amended rules will induce their own avoidance and evasion responses; there then can be further policy responses, etc. The economist Steven Cheung has described this process with respect to Hong Kong rent controls of the 1920s.[59] At first, landlords could legally raise the rents when new tenants entered an apartment. As a result, some landlords under- or over-repaired their tenements in an effort to get existing tenants to move. Fines were then introduced to discourage this behavior (in effect, changing a legal avoidance response into an illegal evasion). When landlords began to reconstruct apartment dwellings instead (because new or reconstructed buildings were exempt from the rent controls), another amendment to the law mandated government permission before an existing tenement could be reconstructed.

Evasion and avoidance put a much different light on the standard conclusion that price controls lead to efficiency losses. Many trades that a perfectly enforced control would prevent from occurring – the potential source of efficiency losses from price regulation – actually do take place if the control is evaded. More importantly, the incentive to evade or avoid the control tends to be greatest precisely when the efficiency costs are high, when there is a large private gain from noncompliance.[60] Opportunities for evasion basically imply that bad policies generally are not quite as bad as they look – though in some cases the evasion, even of bad laws, may produce side effects that would reverse this conclusion. Further, the incentive to evade often exists for good policies, too. If a price control is enacted because some third party (i.e. someone other than the buyer and seller) is harmed by high-priced sales, then evasion can lead directly to efficiency losses of its own. But at least those deals that tend to go forward in evasion of the ban are those that offer a relatively large surplus to the transacting parties themselves, so they also tend to be (all else equal) the most socially desirable or the least socially undesirable of the potential circumventions.

Finally, there is also the possibility of avoidance, not of the price control itself, but of the costs of queuing. A market for waiting in line might develop, whereby time-pressed professionals hire retirees or teenagers to purchase the price-controlled good on their behalf. Consumers might begin to "hoard" the good, increasing their quantity purchased per trip, in order to avoid the waiting costs of subsequent trips, or to engage in re-sale, possibly at above-control prices. For these reasons, price ceilings are often teamed with restrictions on the quantity that can be purchased at one time. One familiar example is the time limits that are often imposed for low-priced street parking: some jurisdictions, for instance, do not allow parking for more than an hour, even if the requisite coins are continually fed to the meter. Queue jumping also might develop, in the form of dealing on connections with sellers, or by other means of establishing priority, including coercion. Public parking spaces in crowded downtown areas are frequently "privatized" by large men ("parking jockeys") who charge market-clearing rates, ostensibly to "watch" parked vehicles. For limited-seating government hearings, firms hire college students and others with relatively low values of time to wait in line for high-priced lawyers and lobbyists who want to attend the hearings, and government insiders, who have access to buildings prior to normal working hours, have been known to jump the queue.[61]

Like the Bogota traffic tale, the example of a price ceiling highlights several features of evasion and avoidance that will be examined in more detail throughout this book. First, evasion can be beneficial for all involved, as might be the case for some black-market trade, particularly if the rule being evaded is ill-advised; such a conclusion, however, need not apply if the illegality of the evasive transaction in itself is harmful, perhaps by undermining respect for the law. Second, there are often many different ways to avoid or evade regulations, even if some effort is made at enforcement, and supplementary rules (e.g. maximum purchase limitations) might be necessary to control the most direct kinds of circumvention. Third, extensive evasion and avoidance could completely undermine the intended effect of a policy. Fourth, evasion and avoidance of existing regulations can be the spur towards further regulations or altered enforcement, in a cycle of response and counter-response. And finally, the potential for avoidance and evasion complicates the cost–benefit calculus of possible policy changes, rendering first-cut analyzes such as the introductory microeconomics approach to price ceilings highly suspect, if not clearly insufficient. Rule breaking matters.

2 Evasion

> . . . a world of perfect enforcement could be an intolerable place.
> (Economist Frank A. Cowell[1])

People evade rules, both major and minor. Recorded violent crimes in the US numbered some 1.4 million in the year 2000, and more than 15,500 Americans were murdered.[2] Mundane rules are broken with even greater abandon. Most cars on US highways exceed the speed limit, and individuals who scrupulously obey the limit are not infrequently resented by the high velocity majority.[3] Another crime that ubiquity has rendered almost respectable is tax evasion; it is estimated that some 17 per cent of US household tax liabilities are not reported and voluntarily paid on time.[4] Journalists strive to uncover reliable information on evasive activity, though it is often hard to come by, particularly when there are no obvious victims motivated to report the violation. Most instances of trade in illicit commodities or corruption of government officials never come to light, presumably. Nevertheless, a large percentage of news reporting relates to various forms of rule breaking, despite the fact that people generally try to avoid publicity of their illegal behavior. Few of us would be found wholly innocent of rule breaking if scrutinized intensely: witness the frequency with which nomination to a high-ranking government position is rapidly followed by the revelation of some past questionable or illegal behavior, perhaps in the area of taxes, immigration, or drugs, though the most blatant offenders are screened out prior to nomination.

Tolerating evasion

Why do organizations (a government or firm) permit evasion of their laws or policies? One reason is that enforcement is costly. Monitoring compliance, identifying and apprehending malefactors, and imposing punishment all require resources, so organizations typically will not attempt to enforce complete compliance. There are some very obvious costs of enforcement – courts and prisons, for instance – while other costs are quite subtle: monitoring employees more closely against theft can engender distrust, and decrease their work effort.[5] Almost any specific type of evasion could be reduced significantly if enough resources were poured into enforcement. But there are other things we value, so resources have alternative uses that eventually become more pressing than diminished evasion. At some point additional reductions in evasion surely become increasingly costly for an organization to achieve, in part because of the extended efforts of rule violators to avoid detection as enforcement mounts.

Enforcement may not be absolute but it is generally not completely absent, either. The level of "expected" punishment for a rule violation is the probability of punishment (that is, the probability of getting caught) multiplied by the size of the punishment. You can step up enforcement by increasing either or both elements of expected punishment, through higher probabilities that a rule violator will be caught or augmented punishments for those rule violators who are apprehended. Instituting a regime of higher probabilities of apprehension, perhaps the more typical meaning of tighter enforcement, requires enhanced and more costly policing. Higher penalties, alternatively – particularly if they consist of increased fines – may not involve socially costly outlays. Fines are not a "net" social cost, because the enforcer or the government receives the money paid by the violator. To achieve a given level of deterrence against rule evasion – or a given expected punishment – it might be cheapest to combine low probabilities of being apprehended (keeping policing costs low) with high fines imposed on those evaders who are caught.[6]

Nevertheless, reducing evasion by increasing the size (as opposed to the probability) of punishment for rule breakers is no panacea. Higher penalties themselves can indirectly involve substantial expenses, especially if the penalties do not take the form of fines. Few people want to pay higher taxes in order to build prisons for jaywalkers, even less so if the taxpayers enjoy the odd jaywalk themselves on occasion. In many instances the possibility of more severe punishment is either precluded (e.g. an employer can fire a rule-breaking employee but in general do little else, and poor people are limited in the extent to which they can pay a fine), or restricted by the necessity to provide marginal disincentives for more serious offenses: if the death penalty is applied to jaywalkers, jaywalkers might resort to extreme violence to try to elude capture.[7] In the US, the Eighth Amendment (precluding "excessive fines" and "cruel and unusual punishments") restricts the extent to which the state could employ a low probability/high severity approach to crime control.

Other factors that serve to limit the use of low probability/high punishment regimes are risk aversion, the potential for judicial error, and notions of fairness. Is it right to punish someone severely for a minor transgression when many other people behaving similarly are unpunished?[8] Even when the transgression, within its context, is not so minor – plagiarism by college students, for instance – if there is enough of a gray area with respect to what constitutes a violation, or if the evidence for the violation falls short of a smoking gun, harsh penalties are unlikely to be exacted.[9]

For minor offenses that can be monitored relatively cheaply, the system of fines that is chosen creates an (expected) "price" of evasion, perhaps sufficient to cover the social costs arising from the evasion. People who still choose to evade the rule and pay the expected price, then, presumably find the trade-off acceptable: in their view, perhaps, the penalty is more like a tax than a fine. If the expected fine does indeed reimburse the social costs of the evasive activity, the government will have little interest in increasing compliance. Payments of fines for conducting illegal activity can become as standardized as tax payments for legitimate, regulated business. In some US towns during Prohibition, bootleggers paid regular fines that mimicked the saloon licensing fees that had prevailed prior to the Volstead Act.[10] Unofficial fines, such as regular bribes to police officers for ignoring or protecting illegal activity, also share many of the features of an official fee or tax. Contracts between private parties often incorporate (implicitly or explicitly) a similar "price" for evasion of the contract terms. The legal regime governing most contracts in the US, for instance, commits a contracting party either to perform to the terms of the contract, or to breach and to pay damages, with little or no preference by the courts as to which alternative is chosen.[11]

Evasion might even form part of the intention of a policy. Making an activity illegal, coupled with some meaningful enforcement of the prohibition, drives the activity underground, probably at a reduced level. The creation of a black market might be seen as quite desirable, at least relative to the situation with unregulated, legal sales. One might even suspect that most prohibited, "victimless" activities aim at exactly such an outcome, given that the attempted suppression of the underground transactions is often quite limited. Bans on prostitution, for instance, generally are not enforced with complete commitment. Rather, the seeming aim of the enforcement is to restrict prostitution to certain neighborhoods, and to types of prostitution (involving consenting adults, for instance) that entail lower social costs.[12] John Stuart Mill made the point with respect to bans on gambling:

> (it may be said) . . . public gambling houses should not be permitted. It is true that the prohibition is never effectual, and that whatever amount of tyrannical power may be given to the police, gambling houses can always be maintained under other pretences; but they may be compelled to conduct their operations with a certain degree of secrecy and mystery, so that nobody knows anything about them but those who seek them; and more than this society ought not to aim at.[13]

Subsidizing compliance

For someone deciding whether to comply with a rule, presumably it is the differential between the payoffs anticipated from compliance versus breach that guides behavior. (If everyone is punished, innocent and guilty alike, the enforcement regime provides no deterrence against evasion whatsoever.) An alternative to punishing or taxing undesired evasion, then, is to subsidize compliance. Being fired is often the most severe feasible punishment that can be imposed on corrupt officials or shirking employees. One way to limit corruption or shirking, therefore, is to pay premium, above-market wages to officials and employees. In essence, these premium wages are legal bribes that employees will have to forgo if they misbehave, thereby lowering the appeal of misbehavior. Such "legal bribes" occur in other regulatory settings, too. Consider the licensing of economic activity. If the number of licenses is kept artificially low, holders of licenses can earn excess profits. The threat of losing a valuable license, then, helps to enforce other legal controls, such as liquor regulations or taxi rules. Nor need it be the case that providing such legal bribes for compliance is particularly costly for the government. If the license holders have to pay for the license in advance, the excess profits associated with owning a license can largely be transferred to the government, via a high initial price for the license.

Toleration of some evasion in one area can itself be used as a subsidy to promote compliance in other areas where evasion is deemed more costly – a strategy used both by parents and regulatory agencies.[14] But direct subsidies to compliance can lead to a form of blackmail. Recipients of the subsidy might threaten to withhold additional compliance or better behavior (either in similar or unrelated fields) unless a further subsidy is provided – a situation all-too-familiar to many parents.

As with punishing breach, subsidizing compliance has severe limits in practice. It may not be possible to finely tune a system of subsidies to provide greater rewards for "higher" levels of compliance (even in the absence of blackmail). Subsidies can be expensive, too. The provision of a subsidy will itself prompt more people to engage in the subsidized activity, raising the expense. For these reasons, direct subsidies to compliance are not as common in public policies as are penalties for non-compliance.

In short, the costs involved either in punishing evasion or in subsidizing compliance can be so large, or the benefits so small that, on these grounds alone, for many rules it is desirable to tolerate a significant amount of evasion – a comforting thought, given the levels of evasion actually observed.

In praise of evasion

> Disobedience, in the eyes of any one who has read history, is man's original virtue. It is through disobedience that progress has been made, through disobedience and through rebellion.
>
> (Oscar Wilde[15])

There are further reasons for the toleration of evasion; indeed, were enforcement perfect and costless, significant levels of rule evasion should still be tolerated. Some rules are misguided, perhaps because the costs of the compliance that the rules mandate are too high or the benefits questionable. Frequent evasion of such rules might be welcomed: smuggling, for example, reduces the burden of ill-conceived trade restrictions. An understanding that people should be free to evade laws that they believe to be misguided, however, would not make for desirable public policy, to say the least. While evasion sometimes is beneficial, it usually is harmful. Disobedience may be, according to Wilde, man's original virtue, but it is also man's original sin.

Still, breaking bad rules can be a good thing. Even generally "good" rules (those for which compliance generally results in desirable social outcomes) can benefit from a degree of evasion, because rules are perforce incomplete, as noted in Chapter 1. Some technical violations may not violate the spirit of the laws. Regulations, even good ones, tend to be quite coarse and unresponsive to detailed individual preferences or circumstances, in part due to the high cost of drafting detailed rules. Costless policing and good rules, then, are insufficient to exclude the toleration (or even encouragement) of some evasion. This is true of both private and public rules. The importance of rule evasion (and avoidance) in promoting the goals of private firms, for instance, is highlighted by the use of "work to the rules" as a strategy taken by employees to impose costs on management during labor disputes. And again, the legal regime governing private contracts, which to some extent has evolved to promote economically efficient outcomes, recognizes that some breach of contract is socially desirable.[16] (Indeed, any breaching action that a contracting party chooses, while fully compensating the breached-against party, would seem to be socially preferable to the alternative of compliance with the contractual terms.[17])

Occasional avoidance or evasion offers an opportunity for flexible responses in various circumstances, employing better information than that contained in a coarse rule. Consider rules within a firm or the civil service that limit the monetary compensation of employees. To motivate and keep valued employees – when the source of their value is behavior that cannot easily be described in an employment contract, or verified by third parties after the fact – informal rewards that avoid the standard compensation limits will be beneficial, and such devices are widely used.[18] An employee who undertakes herculean efforts to deal with an urgent issue at work might be compensated with tacit permission to take some additional time off, even if such "comp time" is not part of the formal labor agreement. The discretion that becomes available in tolerating rule evasion can, of course, be employed for good or ill. The selective intervention might be used to reward favorites, as opposed to those who are performing well, and might rightly be viewed by those not favored as unfair.[19]

Letting people evade rules is potentially itself a rule violation, and the punishments attached to such violations might similarly benefit from some avoidance or evasion. Rules for punishment, as with other rules, are not as nuanced as would be desirable for their firm application to real-world situations. For example, official penalties for many rule violations are not dependent on the personal characteristics or circumstances of the violator. (Mandatory sentencing laws adopted in recent decades provide one limit to the extent to which judges can tailor punishments based on individual characteristics.) While such rules appear to be even-handed, their rigorous implementation could lead to dissimilar consequences among individuals. A respected high-ranking official often has much more to lose from charges of gross misconduct (whether the charges are true or false) than a lower-ranking official, both in lost earnings and perhaps in the increased visibility of the charges and official punishment.[20] Furthermore, an organization might itself be harmed significantly by public revelation of high-level misconduct. (Perhaps a more sympathetic instance is the additional distress that a sizable fine presumably will bring upon a poor person as opposed to a rich person.)

Praise for evasion can easily be taken too far.[21] While some evasion can be beneficial, there also are costs associated with evasion, as the previous discussion of informally rewarding employees makes clear. Indeed, in situations where policies tend to be "good," compliance with rules generally is desirable. Evasion, then, often comes with high social costs, such as those imposed by violent crime. There are further costs of evasion that are less direct. In many instances, for example, the purpose of rules is to foster coordination of the activity of diverse individuals – traffic rules are a paradigmatic example. If significant evasion takes place, it is likely that coordination among drivers will be impaired. Individuals will stop when the light is green, as an old joke has it, in anticipation of the other guy running the red light. (Though in this circumstance, coordination might be almost as well served by complete evasion on the part of all drivers – continuing when the light is red, and stopping when the light is green – as it is by complete compliance.) Another important cost of a regime of widespread evasion, noted in Chapter 1, is that standard measures of economic or social activity are rendered less reliable if there is a good deal of hidden (or at least unmeasured) evasion. Poor information can lead to inappropriate policies, and the actual effects of policy interventions can be misconstrued.[22]

Cascades of disobedience

Evasion of rules has a tendency to snowball. In other words, rule evasion is marked by "positive feedback," wherein evasion begets evasion, with potentially explosive consequences. Some evasion that would be "efficient" or beneficial in itself might be undesirable when this effect is taken into account.

The sources of positive feedback in evasive activity are numerous. If it is widely believed – rightly or wrongly – that crime has increased, formerly law-abiding individuals might be more likely to engage in criminal activity, since police resources are perceived as being spread more thinly. The perception of a crime wave could itself cause a crime wave.[23] Likewise, the perception that a social norm of compliance has changed could have a similar outcome, even if enforcement remains constant: the belief that red light running by other drivers is widespread might make a driver more likely to run a red light herself, possibly because of the increased likelihood that the car behind her intends to run the light. Increased availability of the information that makes evasion possible is a third potential source of positive feedback in rule breaking. If my close friend starts to acquire illicit drugs, my own access to a reliable drug supply might be considerably improved.

Some forms of crime almost naturally bring forth further crime. For example, the relatively well organized portion of the illegal drug trade generally is accompanied by the additional crime of corruption of the would-be enforcers, and a single act of violence often provokes a second in retaliation. Even at the level of an individual, disobedience can multiply. Once the threshold has been crossed, once steeped in evasion, as Macbeth was steeped in blood, "Returning were as tedious as go o'er." In economic terminology, the marginal cost of additional evasion apparently is lower for an individual, the more extensive the evasion he has already engaged in – prompting divines like Thomas à Kempis to warn that "He who shunneth not small faults falleth little by little into greater."[24] One cost of prohibiting recreational drug use is that users who are not deterred by the prohibition might become more willing to break other laws, too.[25]

The incentives that lead to cascades of disobedience can be generated through regulation. Many states in the US, for example, require automobile drivers to purchase minimal levels of automobile insurance. This insurance must include coverage in the event of an accident with an uninsured driver.[26] The cost of the insurance coverage, then, will depend on the frequency of accidents with un-insured drivers who lack the means to directly reimburse the damages for which they are legally liable. If for some reason a locality has a high frequency of such accidents, automobile insurance will be expensive in that locality. But the high cost of insurance will then induce more local drivers to evade the requirement to purchase insurance, so they become uninsured drivers, too: further increasing the probability of having an accident with an uninsured driver, raising the costs of insurance again, and so on. (Incidentally, most states require proof of insurance before a driver's license is issued or renewed, to help enforce the insurance requirement.)

The snowballing of evasion could involve forms of evasion that are virtually unrelated to the original offense. Rule violations could spill over into other areas by inducing a general disrespect for rules, as noted in the drug use example. In the extreme, a "slippery slope" of evasion engendered by changes in perceived social norms could lead to the total breakdown of law and order. A broken window left unrepaired eventually will result in a building with no unbroken windows, and perhaps in a neighborhood that is unsavory in many other respects – the unfixed window serves as a signal to potential violators that the owners or managers of the building do not really have a strong interest in maintaining their property.[27] Evasion can cascade even in the very short run; indeed, the tendency for evasion to propagate lies at the heart of riots and mass insurrection. A riot can be "sparked" by some focal event that creates the expectation that many others will join in riotous behavior, and hence offers a degree of immunity to first movers. The spark can be some public news announcement, such as the verdict in a trial or the assassination of a highly visible individual, an announced price increase for food or gasoline, or a fiery speech. Later entrants in the riot may not even be aware of the precipitating event; it suffices that they can see that others are rioting.[28]

Those engaging in civil disobedience, as opposed to riots, also can promote their cause by taking advantage of the possibility of overwhelming enforcement authorities with violations. In the mid-1990s, a new bridge to Skye in Scotland opened. The toll was extremely high, however, and hundreds of people refused to pay.[29] The issue has lingered for years, but the protestors have won on many counts, including a large reduction in tolls for frequent users of the bridge. People who favor decriminalization or legalization of marijuana occasionally organize smoke-ins, where hundreds of people gather in public and openly smoke marijuana, generally with little or no response by the enforcement authorities. In Stockport, England, an illegal Amsterdam-style coffee shop selling marijuana was opened in September, 2001, but then raided three times by the police over the next few months. As a result, in early 2002, nearly 100 people descended on a Stockport police station in open possession of marijuana, insisting on being arrested. At first the police obliged, but then they gave up – arrests and prosecutions are quite demanding of police time and resources – in a move that could signal the *de facto* legalization of possession of small amounts of marijuana in Stockport and possibly beyond.[30]

Evasion and policy reform

Faced with a perceived increase in evasion of its policies, a government or firm has available a variety of potential responses. Two common responses are to do nothing (i.e. tolerate the evasion), or to increase or redirect enforcement. Often "doing nothing," the absence of real action, is accompanied by verbiage about getting tough (like my repeated threats to students that I will not accept late homework assignments). Given the potential for positive feedback in evasion, an optimal countermeasure to the perception of increased (though still minor) rule evasion might well involve strong but more-or-less toothless rhetoric. If the rhetoric can make some people less likely to believe that their future evasion would be tolerated, then this form of "doing nothing" could have very beneficial effects. Like all threats, get-tough oratory, if sufficiently credible, need not be matched with future action. Nevertheless, occasional crackdowns might still be required to purchase belief, to prevent the rhetoric from being completely and rightly dismissed.

Rather than doing nothing or increasing enforcement, policy makers can respond to increased evasion by changing the rule that is being evaded. Rule modifications impelled by evasion can be relatively minor, such as codifying some allowable exceptions, perhaps in combination with heightened penalties or enforcement aimed at the remaining violations. Alternatively, evasion can prompt significant policy change, including the elimination of the rule. The introduction of a new policy regime in response to evasion is much more likely, however, when the rule evasion is on a very large scale. First, let's examine the less sizable policy adaptations that evasion can engender.

Marginal policy changes

If doing nothing or changing the enforcement regime does not sufficiently reduce the social costs associated with a small increase in evasion, then a potentially valuable alternative might entail a minor alteration of the policy. (Unlike evasion, avoidance of a policy does not lend itself to stricter or differently targeted enforcement. The option of amending the rules, therefore, plays a more significant role when the circumvention is legal, and it is examined in more detail in Chapter 4.) The two main (and nearly opposite) alternatives can be characterized as (1) closing loopholes, and (2) delineating exceptions.[31] Loopholes will be narrowed if the evasion is believed to be socially detrimental, and if the evasion can be made more cumbersome by a small extension of the policy. In the price control case discussed earlier, for example, the prohibition of tied sales would close a loophole. Note that the term "loophole" is often used to characterize a part of a rule that allows legitimate avoidance (as opposed to evasion) of the rule's purpose. The usage here is meant to encompass not only the avoidance sense, but also to include characteristics of the policy that provide a ready channel for evasion. For example, the unregulated sale of cigarettes through vending machines can be thought of as a loophole permitting relatively easy evasion of rules forbidding sales to minors.

If some evasion is indeed sensible, then perhaps the policy could be modified to indicate the acceptable deviations. Going through a red light in Britain was once an offense, without exception. This situation placed drivers of fire engines in a bit of a quandary, because sometimes the public good depended on their not waiting for a green light, and some chief officers of fire departments demanded that their drivers ignore the law. An exception was finally carved out for fire engines and other emergency vehicles, first in the common law (but not until 1971!) and later by an Act of Parliament.[32] One problem with a general policy of delineating exceptions is that the level of complexity required could make the drafting of the policy prohibitively costly, or not worth the effort given the virtue of simplicity in rendering rules understandable. Again, rules are necessarily coarse relative to the intricacies of the various circumstances that can arise. Allowable exceptions might be easier to identify when they arise than to define precisely in advance; then the exceptions can become legitimated, like red light running by emergency vehicles, as common law evolves. Note, however, that the complexity of potential circumstances can render it infeasible even to validate and to codify existing forms of tolerable or encouraged evasion, much less to anticipate further permissible "evasions" down the road.

Reluctance to making minor policy changes

There are some situations, however, where complexity surely doesn't prevent the codification of the *de facto* regime: a rule making the formal speed limit 60 miles per hour is no more complex than a rule of 55 miles per hour. A 60 mph speed limit, rigorously enforced, would seem to nearly be equivalent to a 55 mph speed limit, if the lower limit is coupled with an enforcement regime that won't ticket drivers unless they are going more than 5 mph above the limit. If the *de jure* speed limit is 55 mph but the *de facto* limit is 60 mph, why not amend the official limit to 60 mph, and then enforce it rigorously? In that way, the written law matches the actual law, and compliance with the law coincides with the behavior that you wish to encourage.

In the case of exceeding speed limits and many other violations, measurement inaccuracy provides a technical reason for not changing the rule to reflect reality. A sizeable cushion is needed between the measured speed and the legal limit before the probability that a driver was speeding (or the willingness of a judge to take the violation seriously) meets court norms. Judges might not be very impressed if police officers testify in court that a ticketed speeder was clocked doing 57 miles per hour in a 55 miles per hour zone.

A less conspicuous reason that rules are not changed to reflect the *de facto* situation, despite the obvious acceptability of the existing evasion to the relevant authorities, is based on a concern with reputation. As long as the nominal rule remains in place, it is easier to increase enforcement at a later date without violating any "vested" interests. Making an informal exception to a rule, even if the exception is visible and expected, tends to reduce the reputational forces brought to bear on future actions. An employer who informally rewards an employee for extraordinary diligence is less committed (than she would be if the compensation were formal) to provide similar rewards in the future – both to the employee in question or to other employees in similar circumstances. A perfectly enforced rule represents a strong commitment on the part of the rule maker. Imperfect enforcement loosens the commitment and provides discretion, but generally less discretion than if there were no rule at all. As noted earlier, however, the discretion made available through the toleration of some evasion can be abused, potentially by the harassment of disfavored groups.

Furthermore, the continual toleration of widespread evasion can itself take on the character of a commitment. Sudden police enforcement of routinely violated laws – such as when Antonio has Claudio arrested for fornication in Shakespeare's *Measure for Measure*, after more than a decade of non-enforcement – would likely be met either by prosecutorial reluctance to bring charges or by refusals of juries to return convictions. While almost everyone might prefer a low-evasion setting to a high-evasion one, once the high-evasion setting is established, there might be little sentiment for increased enforcement. When everyone is evading taxes, an increased risk of being punished for tax evasion for each individual might seem to outweigh the public advantages of a return to widespread tax compliance. And the practical barriers to actually increasing enforcement are significant, too: "Where would one find a jury pool that did not contain a majority of tax evaders?"[33]

Even with widespread evasion and without reputational concerns, policy makers might be reluctant to change the law to reflect actual practice, as a way of making a moral statement (or as a way to avoid seeming to make the opposite statement). For example, the 1986 Meese Commission that examined pornography policy in the US argued against explicit decriminalization of some forms of pornography, though it recognized that there would continue to be little or no enforcement of the existing rules: "there are vast real and symbolic differences between not doing what has not been done before and undoing what is currently in place. To undo makes a statement much stronger than that made by not doing."[34] A similar argument is put forth by law professor Randall Kennedy, with respect to his proposal that there be a fairly broad prohibition against the police use of race as a signal of potential criminality – a prohibition that might be frequently evaded: "Even when rightful rules are underenforced, they are still worth fighting for because they set the standards for legitimacy, standards which, like magnets, exert a pull that affects the order of things."[35]

When evasion takes place at more modest levels, as opposed to being wide-spread, the toleration of evasion can serve as a substitute for an explicit policy reform that would further delineate among various contingencies. One advantage of such an approach is that it can be reversed relatively easily, if necessary, simply by increasing enforcement, without precluding the option to formally change the rule at a later date.[36] In the case of marijuana regulation, drug policy expert Mark Kleiman has suggested that "a policy of continued prohibition plus salutary neglect has a great deal to be said for it, compared with either formal legalization or a vigorously enforced prohibition."[37] If explicit policy changes involve some expense, policy makers might be unwilling to incur these costs for relatively minor changes to the rules, particularly if the substitute of altering enforcement is available.[38] And because enforcement can be changed less publicly than the law or regulation itself, the same amount of political support need not be garnered for an enforcement change than for a statutory change.[39]

The reluctance to alter rules to recognize the *de facto* situation is bolstered by the concern that the altered rule might prove unstable, that it could lead to greatly increased evasion. Tolerating a small amount of evasion of a rule might involve vastly different outcomes from what would occur if the existing evasions (and only the existing evasions) were legalized. Officially ratifying the existing evasion could create new opportunities for rule evasion, i.e. opportunities that are unattractive or unavailable under the existing rule. For this reason, policies often take the form of general prohibitions, when certain unobjectionable exceptions could easily be adopted. There is a wealth of experience of situations in which legalizing some exceptions has provided a ready channel for evasion in other instances when such evasion is socially costly; in other words, sometimes policy provisions that would be beneficial in themselves create loopholes for undesired activity. In transitional China, foreign investment was singled out for favorable regulatory treatment. One result was that domestic investment became disguised as foreign investment, to take advantage of the advantageous regulations. According to one estimate, the statistics on foreign direct investment in China in the early 1990s were inflated by a factor of six through the informal arbitrage – most of the recorded foreign investment was really disguised domestic investment.[40]

Examples abound of how codified exceptions can informally serve to undermine the remaining controls. Adopting convertibility of a currency for current account transactions (foreign trade in goods and services) often provides a route for some capital account (investment) convertibility as well. Free photocopying or free long-distance telephone calls for work-related purposes gives employees the opportunity to use these services for personal purposes, too; e-mail and internet access provide similar opportunities for activity unrelated to employer require-ments. The legal and free-price collective-farm markets in the Soviet Union greatly eased the evasion of state-sector price controls for food products, while in the US many underage consumers can purchase cigarettes and alcoholic beverages with little difficulty, thanks in part to the large legal market for adult consumption of these goods.[41] By enacting a general (no free long distance, no legal alcohol sales) as opposed to a selective prohibition, such loopholes are avoided, while the enforcement regime can grant more toleration to evasion in the less costly circumstances.[42]

Major policy reform

Pervasive evasion of existing policies can lead to policy changes akin to closing loopholes or delineating exceptions, but of greater magnitude. The closing of loop-holes, at the extreme, results in the implementation of a much stricter regime, while the delineation of exceptions can become a wholesale liberalization.

Population flows out of East Germany provide telling evidence of the difference between small-scale and wide-scale "evasion," as well as between the two types of policy reforms, a much stricter regime and a liberalization. In the late 1950s, migration from East Germany was enormous, with an average of some 200,000 East German citizens leaving annually. As a response to this wide-scale emigra-tion, the Berlin Wall was constructed. Between 1962 (after the Berlin Wall was built) and 1988, annual emigration from East Germany was greatly reduced, ranging between 11,000 and 43,000 people.[43] This moderate level of migration probably helped sustain the East German regime, as it included many who were quite dissatisfied with the internal political situation, and some vocal and promi-nent critics of the system. In 1989, Hungary removed barriers on its Austrian border, so East Germans travelling to Hungary could then easily migrate west. Largely as a result of this chink in the iron curtain, over 340,000 East Germans migrated in 1989; the regime (which soon was taken over by the West) ceased to control emigration, and reluctantly (in fact, more-or-less accidentally) allowed the Wall to be breached.[44] Wide-scale evasion, therefore, can promote significant policy shifts, whether for good or ill; it can raise or destroy imposing walls.

One needn't look at system-level transformations in socialist regimes to find evasion-induced policy changes. Consider two less prominent proposed reforms, recently brought to the table by evasion of existing constraints. The first case concerns the Church of England, which since the seventeenth century has not allowed second weddings in church for divorced individuals.[45] Nevertheless, approximately one-third of Anglican priests remarry divorced individuals in defiance of the ban; some 10 percent of Anglican marriages already involve divorced people. Not surprisingly, then, Anglican bishops have proposed a partial relaxation of the ban. (The proposed liberalization is only "partial" in that some conditions, such as leaving a spouse precisely for the purpose of marrying someone else, or being twice-divorced, might still disqualify a divorced person from being remarried in the Church.)

The second potential reform could not be further removed from serial marriages, except for the shared motive force of rule circumvention, and the resulting partial legalization. This case concerns abandoned babies in the United States.[46] Following a spate of abandoned baby incidents in the Houston area, the state of Texas passed a law (implemented September 1, 1999) that shields parents from prosecution if they abandon their infant by bringing it to an emergency medical technician. Other states, including California and West Virginia, are considering similar legislation, and informal programs for protecting parents who safely give up their children have arisen elsewhere. Some Anglican priests who married divorced individuals in defiance of the ban might have viewed their marriage services as acts of civil disobedience; those parents who abandoned infants harbored no such illusions. Both priests and parents, however, are motivating policy change, even if they were not themselves motivated by the desire to amend policy.

The political economy of evasion and reform

Why should wide-scale evasion lead to significant reform, while small-scale evasion often serves as a substitute for an explicit amendment that would delineate the rule more finely? Much of the difference can be traced to the two factors identified in Chapter 1 as being key determinants of policy reform: the net social benefits of a policy shift, and the distribution of the benefits. Massive reforms have the best chance of being implemented when they offer significant net social benefits, and when there are relatively few who are harmed by the reforms. When evasion of existing rules is quite extensive, these two conditions are likely to be met.

How does widespread circumvention render policy reform congruent with social gains? Consider, for instance, monetary reforms in a high inflation setting. The high inflation acts as a tax on holding domestic currency. People will try to rearrange their affairs to avoid this tax. One possible form of inflation tax avoidance is to keep savings in the form of foreign, not domestic, currency. (The government might try to limit this route of avoidance with currency and capital controls, but these controls themselves can be evaded.) Monetary reforms aimed at ending inflation often are undertaken only after significant flight from the domestic currency – avoidance of the national monetary system, an implicit reform – already has occurred. The implicit reform brought about by circumvention of the domestic currency not only shields citizens from the inflation tax, but it also reduces the gains to the government from further inflating the currency. The constituency for inflation is thus undermined by the circumvention, and a monetary reform that will produce a disinflationary regime grows in popularity. Thanks to the preceding implicit reform, the distributional impacts of the explicit monetary reform are small, while the social gains can be significant in providing a stable local currency.

A second example of how widespread evasion or avoidance sows the seeds for reform can be found in transitional socialist countries. Starting from a regime of fixed prices for goods in state-owned shops, post-socialist societies that embraced capitalism had to move to a regime of free, market-determined prices. But liberalizing prices can make many people worse off, even if the economy as a whole benefits from the reform.[47] In countries such as Russia and Poland, a spontaneous price reform muted the distributional effects of formal price liberalization. Increasing informal diversion of goods from the state shops to parallel, free markets meant that the fixed prices became less and less relevant for consumers in these countries. This diversion of goods from the state sector provided a *de facto* reform, so the distributional impact of official price liberalization was dampened.[48]

Significant official reforms, therefore, are generally not as radical as they appear, because they typically follow a long period of spontaneous, unofficial reforms. New requirements on a regulated industry tend to be preceded by growing pressures from the regulators and the public for the firms in the industry to address some concern, prior to the statutory requirement. Bans against drugs or alcohol tend to follow a long period of increased social intolerance and intensified regulation. Many US states, for example, had banned alcohol sales, and *per capita* alcohol consumption was declining, prior to the imposition of national Prohibition. Land reforms in Latin American countries have frequently followed waves of land "evasions" and squatting.[49] Deregulations are likewise preceded by informal slackening of rules. For instance, many states had stopped enforcing Prohibition prior to its repeal, and state-level abortion regulations in the US were becoming significantly more liberal before the Supreme Court ruling in *Roe* v. *Wade* found broad abortion prohibitions to be unconstitutional in January, 1973.[50] There is a profusion of examples of official deregulations following informal ones. "History suggests that for the U.S. financial-services industry, before an exclusionary statute [for instance, a prohibition on multi-state banking] comes to be formally rescinded, most of the effects targeted by the recission will have already been tolerated by the enforcement system for years."[51] This tendency for official reforms to follow, rather than to lead, major social changes, lies at the heart of a common "reinterpretation" of a significant historical event, in which a seemingly major policy adjustment is argued to have had little real impact, as exemplified by de Tocqueville's argument that many changes associated with the French Revolution had already taken place under the *ancien régime*.[52]

The fact that formal policies respond to informal evasion complicates the determination of the effects of policy. If a drug is legalized because it has become increasingly popular, then we must be careful about attributing higher usage to legalization. Legal scholar Franklin Zimring makes the same point in the opposite direction, for the case when a drug is rendered illegal:

> if regimes of prohibition are usually initiated and maintained only under conditions of low social usage, it is highly misleading to compare the two strategies [prohibition versus regulation] in terms of the use rates associated with them. In other words, a large part of the difference in usage that we find associated with prohibited drugs is the condition that made the prohibition possible rather than the result of legal status. Crediting the criminal law for

the low usage levels of prohibited substances is a bit like congratulating children for the fine job they did raising their parents.[53]

The East German emigration example suggests that the tendency for widespread evasion to lead to better policies, as opposed to simply different ones, is greater in systems where the policy process is responsive to individual preferences. Under any circumstances, the political power of those who gain from the reform relative to those who lose will affect the probability of reform, and government responsiveness can be undermined if large corrupt incomes accrue to officials in the absence of reform. But given a fairly responsive political system, wide-scale evasion can be a force that promotes the efficiency of policies. If "good" rules (such as those against violent crimes) are frequently evaded, the social costs inherent in such crimes will tend to make the policy response one of stricter enforcement. Socially inefficient restrictions that are widely evaded, however, will likely be liberalized, through either explicit legalization or, implicitly, through reduced (perhaps to zero) enforcement.

One of the reasons why widespread evasion favors major reform, while small-scale evasion often promotes the stability of the existing policy regime, concerns the incentives of those who are doing the evading. Take, for instance, smuggling, the evasion of trade restrictions. If there are only a few smugglers, then those engaged in the smuggling might find it to be quite lucrative. The limited competition gives the smugglers some monopoly power, which they can exercize in the form of higher prices for the smuggled good. Such smugglers might well prefer that the trade restrictions continue, to reduce the supply of the smuggled goods and keep prices and profits high.[54] Once smuggling is widespread, however, the smuggled goods will carry much less of a premium; many of those involved in the trade will be amateurs, operating on a small scale for personal use. With few profits to be made from smuggling, but still some risk of arrest, the (now large) smuggling community would typically favor liberalization.

Of course, policy makers could simply ignore even wide-scale evasion, and not alter either the evaded rule or its enforcement regime. It is probable, however, that widespread evasion of a rule, to the extent that it is visible, would bring the rule to the attention of policy makers.[55] In Hirschman's terminology, the "exit" from the rule via evasion promotes the "voice" calling for change. There are thus two components to the process by which wide-scale evasion contributes to better policies (including enforcement regimes), as noted in the Introduction. First, widely evaded policies will be disproportionally represented among those policies that come under consideration for review. Second, the response of policy makers (to the extent that the government is attentive to the welfare of its citizens) is likely to favor socially desirable changes in the evaded rule: either stricter enforcement of good rules, or a change or liberalization of bad policies.

Further, even if policy makers make a mistake, choosing to enforce more strictly a bad rule that is being widely evaded, for example, this very response may produce the incontrovertible evidence that the rule is indeed bad. Some historians have traced the end of alcohol Prohibition in the US to the passage of the Jones Act in 1929, which increased penalties for first-time offenders who violated the Volstead Act.[56] The draconian penalties applied to small-scale operators – five years in jail and a $10,000 fine – to enforce a policy that was widely evaded and increasingly unpopular helped to mobilize opposition to Prohibition. The Soviet Union effectively dissolved with the putsch of August, 1991, in which an attempt to re-introduce some elements of the old controls collapsed within a few days. And those engaging in civil disobedience often attempt to encourage or provoke enforcement of a rule against their behavior to bring attention to the undesirability of the rule: "The leaders of the civil rights movement exposed the evils of segregation by inciting enforcement of its laws – and seeing to it that the results appeared on prime-time television."[57]

This efficiency dynamic is an underappreciated element of disobedience, a further argument in praise of evasion. In practice, however, evasion may be tolerated (and evaders respected) in part because of an implicit recognition of the benefits of disobedience. It has been argued that courts tend to tolerate "diligent evasion" of regulation, for instance, when the evasion consists of the creation of new markets on the borders of old ones – even when the purpose of the new markets is precisely to escape the existing regulation.[58] A novel evasion is an innovation, and in many circumstances innovation is welcome. One weighty instance is the "household contract responsibility system" in China, probably the key element in initiating the tremendously successful economic reforms of the post-Mao era. This reform, which essentially freed Chinese peasants from the straitjacket of collective agriculture, was outlawed by the central government in 1979. Widespread evasion of the ban, and the enormously beneficial results in terms of massive increases in agricultural productivity, later led to official endorsement of the previously banned system.[59]

In common law legal systems, judicial decisions are a source of new rules. The actions of judges, then, like the actions of legislators, provide a channel through which widespread evasion can lead to legal reforms. Customary behavior can form the basis for new rules, even trumping the existing formal rules with which the customary behavior conflicts. If evasion of the explicit rules is so widespread that it becomes expected and customary, it may then achieve legal status through court opinions that validate the evasion.[60] Property law rules surrounding "adverse possession," for instance, endorse longstanding evasion: failure to assert ownership rights against a trespasser eventually results in the legal title shifting to the (former) trespasser.[61] The "community standards" approach to the regulation of obscenity in the US implies that once a given standard is sufficiently evaded, there is a new standard, and obscenity that was formerly illegal to distribute becomes transformed into legal, First Amendment-protected speech.

Other factors can reduce or overwhelm the tendency for evasion to lead to improved policies. A sudden perception of widespread evasion may create an atmosphere where policy makers believe that they must act quickly, almost regardless of the consequences.[62] A hasty reform, like a hasty marriage, can lead to a leisurely repentance. And societies are changing continually, of course, causing the mix of desirable policies and enforcement regimes to change over time, too.

The "efficiency dynamic" of evasion is less able to exert itself if the rules that need revising are so rigorously enforced that there is very little evasion. Evasion of a rule generates information about the value of alternative social orderings, and one argument for less than perfect enforcement of rules in some arenas is to keep open this channel of information.[63] Thus the constitutional guarantees in the US against "excessive fines" and "cruel and unusual punishments" not only constrain tyrannical government behavior, but they also promote policy experimentation, by (somewhat) limiting the penalties that can be applied to those who undertake such experiments in violation of the existing law. (Adam Smith praised standing armies in part for offering security to the sovereign, who can then "safely pardon or neglect" non-compliant behavior, even "the most licentious remonstrances." Standing armies, then, can be "favourable to liberty."[64]) Two decades prior to the collapse of socialist regimes in Eastern Europe, Hirschman noted the long-term instability of organizations that unduly restrict dissent: "exit and voice being illegal and severely penalized, they will be engaged in only when deterioration has reached so advanced a stage that recovery is no longer either possible or desirable. Moreover, at this stage, voice and exit will be undertaken with such strength that their effect will be destructive rather than reformist."[65]

Perhaps the major factor that can prevent wide-scale evasion from leading to better policies within responsive political systems, however, lies precisely in the notion that policies come as part of a "mix." Evasion tends to select relatively bad rules for change, but for the changed rule to be effective or even to represent a minor improvement, other rules or their enforcement regimes might also have to be changed. Evasion provides the information and the incentive to alter a bad rule, but it is only partially informative, and "a little learning is a dang'rous thing." Policy analysts cannot simply sit back and let evasion do their work for them, like landscapers who first let trails develop before they decide where to place sidewalks. Rather, policy makers must be proactive, because wide-scale evasion might be a very costly way to acquire information, and because evasion might point out only a subset of the policies that require amendment to achieve improved social outcomes.

Prohibition, taxation, and evasion

Prohibitions are rarely complete. Addicts manage to find heroin, and inexperienced users of illicit drugs manage to become addicts. Prisoners consume banned substances and acquire prohibited weapons. Underage consumers smoke and drink. The world's oldest profession finds new recruits and customers.

Legal prohibition raises the costs of engaging in some activity or consuming some commodity. But it seems that bans don't ban; rather, a prohibition shares many features with a tax. For some people, the "tax" will be sufficient to drive them out of the illicit market (on either the supply or the demand side) for the activity; others, however, will continue to operate on the market, all the while looking for ways to reduce the cost that the "tax" of prohibition imposes on them. The more extensive the evasion of the prohibition, the more likely it is that replacing the prohibition with an actual, statutory tax will be an advantageous policy reform, as I demonstrate below.

The form in which the tax of a prohibition is exacted is very different from that of a statutory tax. Instead of simply paying a premium to the state for the opportunity to buy or sell a commodity, a prohibition requires market participants to behave covertly and to take other steps to secure their activity. Underage drinkers might need to obtain fake identification, and drug users might have to cultivate a reliable source of supply. The protections of contract and tort law, as well as of the police, are no longer available (at least on the same terms) for those who violate a prohibition. Uncertainty in the quality of goods, then, tends to increase in a prohibited market, and dispute settlement procedures take on an informal, frequently violent character. Prostitutes often have (or fear that they have) little legal recourse against rape, assault, or robbery, for instance, and buyers on illegal markets also are differentially exposed to violent crime or fraud.

When a statutory tax is paid, the state receives the revenue. Though the tax influences the incentives of individuals to engage in the activity, the payment of the tax is itself a transfer: someone pays the tax, and someone else (the government) receives the revenue.[66] Not so with the costs of evading a prohibition. The "costs" of behaving stealthily, or of having to cultivate a trusting relationship, or of being exposed to theft, are paid by illicit market participants, but these costs are not received as government revenues.[67] Some of the costs imposed on illicit market participants, such as the threat of imprisonment, are not only not received as revenues by the government, but imposing the costs itself requires large government expenditures. The organization of illicit markets, perhaps by mafia-like structures, can reduce the costs of engaging in an illicit activity, while simultaneously converting the remaining costs of operating on the market into something more akin to a tax: buyers and sellers pay a premium, collected by the mob, which serves as the informal substitute for the government. Some of the informal tax revenue might then be funneled to corrupt elements of the state, in the form of regular payments to the police, for instance.[68]

Replacing a prohibition with a tax

Consider, then, the choice between a policy of prohibiting an activity and a policy of keeping the activity legal, but taxing it. If the prohibition were sufficient to dissuade everyone from taking part in the activity, then the costs of evading the prohibition would not arise. The only cost borne by would-be participants is that of not taking part in an activity that they view as desirable – though the prohibition presumably exists because society does not share their view. But what if the prohibition is imperfect? Then some people are engaging in the activity despite the prohibition, and they are bearing the kind of costs discussed above. In theory, it would be possible to replace the prohibition with a statutory tax that would be of sufficient magnitude to bring about the same amount of the controlled activity as takes place under prohibition.[69] Replacing a prohibition with such a tax, then, would not change the amount of the drug actually consumed, or the amount of alcohol beverages imbibed by nineteen-year-olds. But the cumbersome and wasteful "tax" associated with secrecy and the other adverse characteristics of illicit markets would be avoided, and replaced with a formal tax that simply transferred purchasing power to the government. Society as a whole would be better off, roughly by the amount of tax revenue collected. In most cases, it is probably less expensive to collect a tax than to police a prohibition, too.

The main obstacle to replacing a prohibition with an appropriately chosen tax is that the tax might itself be evaded.[70] Such tax evasion becomes more likely the higher the requisite tax. But the appropriate size of the tax depends on the amount of evasion of the ban. If almost no one violates the prohibition, then a huge tax might be necessary to achieve the same low level of consumption; a tax of such a magnitude would then make tax evasion a relatively attractive prospect. But while it may not be feasible to replace a near-perfect prohibition with a tax, there is little potential gain from doing so, anyway. With extremely limited consumption, almost no one is paying the cumbersome prohibition tax in the first place, so the benefit of replacing the cumbersome tax with a more efficient (though potentially evadable) legal tax is inconsequential.[71]

If consumption is significant despite the prohibition, however, the case for taxation is stronger. First, the tax will not have to be all that high in order to achieve the same level of consumption, so evasion of the tax will be less of an issue. Second, the fact that there is significant consumption in the face of the ban indicates that many people are paying the cumbersome tax, so replacing it with an efficient tax offers large social gains.

What about well-organized illicit markets that arise following a prohibition? The fact that they are well organized suggests that the cumbersome tax has already, to some extent, been informally replaced with a more efficient one. For that reason, the more organized the market – or more broadly, the better the form of the evasion of the ban – the less are the social benefits of replacing the prohibition with a statutory tax. From a political economy standpoint, however, well-organized illicit markets may be more, not less, ripe for legalization and taxation. The fact that such illicit markets are well organized renders more palpable the alternative of a legal, but taxed regime, even though the social gains from legalization may not be as great as they would be in less organized markets. The public may rightly be led to wonder why the mafia should collect the "tax" revenues in an illicit market, rather than having the receipts accrue to the legitimate government, which could formally tax a legalized but regulated industry.

While the amount of consumption of an illicit commodity might remain unchanged under a tax system, the individuals who choose to engage in the activity typically will differ between the two regulatory alternatives. The prohibition will tend to screen out potential consumers who are law-abiding, or who have the most to lose if they are identified as law breakers. The tax will tend to screen out the poor, those with a low ability (or low willingness) to pay for the commodity. For these reasons, replacing prohibitions on drugs with taxes might involve a shift from inner-city to suburban or middle-class and upper-class use, even if the tax is high enough that total consumption stays the same. A regulatory regime that does not involve complete prohibition, however, might also provide opportunities to target enforcement resources at specific users or uses that are most harmful, in a way that is much more difficult with prohibition. For example, suppliers in illicit markets often have little compunction against selling to children (or even employing them in the business), while in a regulated industry children might be more effectively screened out. In the case of some currently illegal drugs, a regulatory regime that involved legalization might be able to promote a substitution to less harmful forms of the drug.

This discussion by no means exhausts the issues involved in comparing prohibition with taxation. One important omission is that making a commodity or service legally available to adults eventually might undermine the interest – by the police, say, or by society more generally – in enforcing forcefully the continuing prohibition against consumption by children. Similarly, leading drug policy analysts Robert MacCoun and Peter Reuter suggest that under contemporary conditions in the US, it would generally not be possible to legalize a currently illicit drug without simultaneously paving the way for "commercialization" of the drug, including many forms of advertizing.[72]

A second topic neglected here is whether legalization coupled with taxation sends an inappropriate message about the consumption of the good or service, though perhaps the law should be primarily concerned with what is legal and what is illegal, while other forces in society are better suited to inculcate values concerning right and wrong. (And the visibility of significant evasion of a ban also might send a worrisome message about the legitimacy of the law more generally.) The main point of this section, however, is to demonstrate how evasion influences (and should influence) the choice of regulatory regime applied to a problematic activity or commodity: the more widely evaded a prohibition, everything else equal, the more desirable is the alternative policy of legalizing and taxing the controlled activity or commodity.

Small-scale evasion and major policy shifts

I have argued that small-scale evasion tends to produce responses of "doing nothing," nearly empty rhetoric, increased enforcement, or perhaps minor policy changes; alternatively, wide-scale evasion often prompts a major reform. But if there is sufficient positive feedback in evasion, a society faced with a small increase in rule circumvention could soon end up with widespread evasion. In such circumstances, there is little distinction between small-scale and large-scale evasion, other than the passage of time – and perhaps not very much time. For this reason, an increase in evasion, even at a low level, sometimes provokes major policy change. When positive feedback is believed to be a substantial threat, there will be little perceived distinction between small-scale and wide-scale evasion, and they can then generate similar policy responses.

One example, discussed in more detail in Chapter 8, concerns British firearms policy. Following a massacre of sixteen people in the town of Hungerford in 1987, Britain tightened its firearms restrictions by banning new classes of rifles and shotguns. A more significant tightening, this time banning first high-caliber and then virtually all handguns, occurred following the massacre of sixteen primary school children and their teacher in Dunblane, Scotland, in March 1996. In overall terms, firearm crime in Britain is quite small, certainly in comparison with the US, and the vast majority of the gun crime that does take place in Britain apparently does not involve legally owned weapons – though both the Dunblane and Hungerford massacres were perpetrated by legal gun owners.[73] Many members of the legal shooting community in Britain viewed the significantly increased restrictions following these two tragedies to be the result of ill-considered, panic legislation. But given the positive feedback dynamics that characterize arms races, the tragedies may well have been seen as placing Britain on a slippery slope to greatly increased levels of gun crime. Supporters of the stricter legislation often pointed to gun crime in the US as the type of situation that they were hoping to avoid in Britain through the increased controls. In other words, the rather limited (though of course very costly) evasion of laws against gun crime in Britain was also seen as potentially bringing on much increased evasion, and it led to significant change in British firearms policy.[74]

In some circumstances, in terms of social welfare, there might be little to choose between low and high evasion situations. In the case of firearms, once illegal firearm carrying spreads so far that otherwise law-abiding citizens are carrying guns (and perhaps, in recognition of the perceived need to do so, the laws governing the carrying of firearms are liberalized), it is conceivable that actual gun violence may not be much or any greater than in a situation with only small-scale evasion of gun laws, when potential victims choose to be unarmed. Or, in the case of economic controls, perhaps tight controls that by and large are obeyed work reasonably well, while widespread evasion (which could impel liberalization) would also make for satisfactory economic outcomes. Nevertheless, in both of these cases, the transition phase between the low and high evasion "equilibria" could be very costly, marked by criminal or economic "chaos." For this reason, there might be large benefits in avoiding a transition to a high-evasion situation, even if the endpoint of the transition is not itself undesirable – imagine a gradual transition from no red light running to complete evasion of the stop on green, go on red variety![75]

Delayed reform

Many governments appear to delay necessary policy reforms – for that matter, firms and people do, too: I really should get more exercize. Government budget deficits, for example, might be kept at unsustainably high levels. To cover their excess expenses, the governments eventually turn to printing currency. The result is hyperinflation and economic crisis. Finally, the country is forced to adopt a severe stabilization package. The sequence is foreseeable. It would seem that there are major advantages to stabilizing prior to the hyperinflation. Why do governments wait?

One possibility is that governments have extremely short time horizons, perhaps because they believe that there is a good chance that they will not be in power very long, whether through electoral or social upheaval. Under such circumstances, they may view it as serving their interests to shift necessary but painful action onto the next government or administration. But in most countries, there is either a modicum of political staying power, or political parties and their concern with their reputations lengthen the effective time horizon of the current government. Hyperinflations, then, are more likely the cause than the result of political instability (or perhaps both the hyperinflation and the instability are caused by some third factor, one that impels a continuing government budget deficit, for instance).

Various explanations for the delay of desirable reforms have been offered.[76] One possibility is that people are uncertain about whether they will personally benefit from the reform. Even if everyone understands that a policy change is beneficial in overall terms, uncertainty about the reform's effect on individuals can impart a *status quo* bias, a reluctance to reform.[77] (The *status quo* can be buttressed even without uncertainty over the individual outcomes, of course, if the pro-reform majority is not as motivated, well-organized, or politically powerful as the "entrenched" elite.[78]) A second possibility is that there may be a struggle among competing groups to shift the costs of the reform onto others, and reform could be delayed until this struggle is resolved.[79] Under such circumstances, an economic crisis that forces reform can be advantageous, by accelerating the adoption of the necessary policy.[80] Hirschman's "exit–voice" framework offers a complementary explanation. If those most disgruntled by the current policies choose to "exit" – as opposed to adding their "voice" to the calls for reform – then a crisis is averted and an unsatisfactory *status quo* can be maintained.[81] Or perhaps the widespread dissatisfaction is never revealed, as people choose to hide or misrepresent their private preferences in public, and the political force for reform remains latent.[82]

The political economy of evasion and reform, as developed above, offers another approach to delayed policy changes. Consider again the example of an unsustainable government budget deficit that eventually results in hyperinflation. As the policy continues, and as inflation mounts, more and more people will find it in their interest to "evade" the domestic currency, by shifting their wealth into foreign currency (usually dollars), foreign financial assets, or real assets such as art, carpets, or furniture.[83] (This flight from the domestic currency produces some positive feedback, as the rush to unload the inflating money itself generates further inflation. While an individual can reduce her own stock of the currency, a simultaneous attempt by everyone to do so will not reduce society's stock of currency at all. Instead, prices will rise.) Other responses might include a lessened willingness to accept the domestic money in payment, decreased work effort if wages are paid in the domestic currency, or an increase in barter deals. As argued earlier, these evasive responses essentially introduce an informal monetary reform:

the country informally, and in a decentralized fashion, adopts dollars or some other stable foreign currency as the medium of exchange and store of value. When this behavior becomes widespread, which will happen when the domestic inflation rate gets high enough, there are not many people left to be directly harmed by an official monetary reform.[84] If I am only transacting in dollars, why do I care what is happening to the local currency? Simultaneously, those who do not have access to dollarization or other costly methods of shielding themselves from the inflation eventually find the current system intolerable, because of the huge inflation tax that they must bear. Crises generally spark reform not because one side capitulates and accepts the costs of reform, but rather because the informal reform that occurs prior to the official reform reduces, sometimes dramatically, the number of people who could be harmed by official reform: the "political cost–benefit ratio" of policy reform improves as the informal reform proceeds.[85] Governments can delay official reform, but *de facto* reform through evasion and avoidance continues just the same, eventually paving the way for the official policy change.

Rules v. discretion

Many policy controversies fall under the general rubric of "rules v. discretion."[86] While the dichotomy is rarely so absolute, the tension between these alternative approaches is rather common, arising in such disparate areas as criminal sentencing and the conduct of monetary policy. Should a situation be governed by a fixed rule, which cannot possibly be sufficiently detailed and far-sighted to induce optimal behavior in all contingencies, or should it rather be handled via the discretion of decision makers? Discretion allows decisions to respond more closely to actual conditions, though in the hands of a fallible or corrupt decision maker, a greater reliance on judgment may not be such a good idea.

One disadvantage of discretion, it would seem, is that it gives those affected by decisions an incentive to lobby for favorable treatment. A fixed rule that is implemented automatically, like a machine, eliminates this incentive for politicking. Machines are notoriously difficult to persuade, being immune to the blandishments of reason, love, or money. But the comparison between fixed rules and discretion with respect to lobbying is not clear-cut. First, a fixed rule does not eliminate lobbying, and may not even decrease it. Rather, the lobbying is front-loaded, occurring primarily when the rule is itself being developed, or perhaps in ongoing attempts to change the rule.[87] Second, because rules are incomplete, there will still be some discretion available – and hence a continued rationale for lobbying – even to a decision maker who views himself or herself as being completely bound to the strictures of a rule. Third, despite its less-than-sterling reputation, lobbying is not altogether without social merit. (Think what trouble lobbyists could cause if they were forced into other pursuits!) Policy makers are not perfectly informed about the effects of various rules, and about how individuals perceive themselves as being affected by the rules. Lobbying is one method of transmitting this information (and, occasionally, disinformation) from the ruled to the rulers.

A second potential cost of discretion, relative to a fixed rule, is that the option to choose can expose the decision maker to difficult dilemmas concerning the trade-off between short-term and long-term interests. Life is full of situations where the expeditious policy, that which offers the best outcome in the short run, invites disaster – or at least sub-optimality – in the long run: yes, thank you, I will have another doughnut. A decision maker endowed with discretion, then, may fall prey to the seduction of expediency; a fixed rule, alternatively, can presumably implement the long-run optimal policy, without calling on limited reserves of resistance to temptation.

The trade-offs are stark in the case of hostage taking.[88] A nation could adopt a "no negotiation with hostage takers" stance, as unpleasant as it may be to comply with once hostages are taken. Alternatively, a nation could choose to negotiate with hostage takers on a case-by-case basis, but this strategy may increase the number of hostage incidents in the long run.

In many "fixed rule v. discretion" situations, evasion of the rule (or, relatedly, the possibility of varying the enforcement of the rule) lessens the distinctions between the alternatives. The US negotiated what came close to being an "arms for hostages" deal with Iran, despite claims that such considerations were ruled out, and even the Israeli government has engaged in a massively unequal trade of prisoners, in *de facto* contravention of its official "no negotiation with terrorists" stance. And so it is with many policy rules. Consider the machinations that the US government has gone through to circumvent the "fixed rule" of deficit reduction targets, or other budgetary limitations. Expenditures can be ruled to be off-budget, thus yielding compliance with the letter though not the spirit of the law, or budget baselines can be altered through various accounting devices.[89] Rules can make it a little easier to resist temptation, but they cannot remove temptation. When those who are governed by the rules also have the power to enforce or amend or avoid the rules, resistance cannot be purchased cheaply.

Within the economics discipline, the most famous of "rules v. discretion" debates concerns the conduct of monetary policy.[90] Nobel-prize-winning econo-mist Milton Friedman suggested that the economy would be better governed by a rule in which a given measure of the money supply is allowed to grow at some fixed rate (the "x percent" rule) year-in and year-out, as opposed to a situation wherein the money supply could be altered based on the continuous discretion of the monetary authorities. The chief reasoning behind Friedman's suggestion is to sidestep the conflict between short-term expediency and long-run optimality. A monetary authority endowed with discretion might succumb to the short-term benefits of increasing money growth – which are generally viewed as being an expansion in output and employment – at the cost of producing inflation in the longer term, accompanied by no increase, or even a decline, in output and employment.

Friedman's x-percent rule, however, as with rules more generally, could be undermined by "evasion" and "avoidance." There are many different measures of the money supply. Once a rule governs growth in one of the measures, private actors could introduce or increase the use of various near-monies. The pre-existing relationship between growth of the controlled monetary aggregate and the overall economy will be altered by this substitution to different forms of money.[91] So, the x-percent growth rate in the controlled aggregate that seemed appropriate before the induced adaptations may turn out to be counterproductive. Further, even without monetary substitution, a fixed rule could be undermined by the coarseness of the levers that are available to the monetary authorities. Attempts to keep a monetary aggregate growing at a fixed rate could fail – the monetary authorities cannot control the growth rate of a monetary aggregate precisely – providing a second route by which a fixed monetary growth rule could become either inappropriate or meaningless over time. Of course, a more detailed monetary rule covering a plethora of monetary aggregates could be developed and rigorously enforced, though opportunities to evade and avoid the strictures would undoubtedly remain. And rigorous enforcement of a rule that would sometimes, and perhaps often, be inappropriate would itself be a questionable practice. In this case, as in others, the caution of George Stigler, another Nobel-prize-winning Chicago economist, should be taken into account: "Variation in enforcement provides desirable flexibility in public policy."[92] But with variable enforcement, the distinction between rules and discretion dissipates.

3 Zero tolerance

No more evasion.

(Shakespeare, *Measure for Measure*)

Disillusion with the efficacy of traditional regulatory structures in recent decades has resulted, in many jurisdictions, in the introduction of "zero tolerance" policies. The purported goal of such policies is essentially to eliminate evasion, by stepping up enforcement while severely restricting or eliminating the discretion available to rule enforcers. Zero (or near-zero) discretion is an inherent part of most zero tolerance policies.

Now widespread, zero tolerance policies continue to be adopted by schools, municipalities, and private businesses that hope to make headway against some longstanding problem such as alcohol or drug abuse. Simultaneously, existing zero tolerance policies are criticized, even ridiculed, when they lead to severe punishment for behavior that technically is forbidden, but that judged on the merits might not deserve a reprimand.[1] Zero tolerance might be accompanied by zero discretion, but such policies have not been accompanied by zero controversy.

Evasion can prompt reform, and the initial adoption of zero tolerance policies often occurs as a response to a perceived increase in rule breaking. But zero tolerance policies themselves are susceptible to being altered through two different types of evasion: continued occurrences of the targeted, prohibited activity in significant numbers, even in the face of the zero tolerance policy, and evasion of the "zero discretion" feature of such policies on the part of enforcers. In many circumstances, however, zero tolerance is an inappropriate enforcement regime, as I demonstrate below. In these cases, the evasions that lead to the demise of zero tolerance are forms of unintentional civil disobedience, rule circumventions that generate improved policies.

Characterizing zero tolerance

No widely accepted, precise definition of "zero tolerance" exists, but there are some common features to the types of policies that are adopted under this rubric. A tightening of enforcement against rule violations is the chief characteristic of a newly adopted zero tolerance policy. Zero tolerance connotes that minor infractions (which might otherwise be overlooked) will be punished.[2] The sorts of behavior that constitute an infraction might be widened under a zero tolerance regime, too. Anti-drug policies in schools, for instance, might newly include over-the-counter medicines such as aspirin when a zero tolerance policy is introduced.

Some zero tolerance policies might go no further than a willingness to prosecute minor offenses. The punishment itself might be minimal. Errors in calculating US federal income taxes are adjusted and additional payments and interest collected by the Internal Revenue Service, even if the mistake only amounts to a few dollars. A zero tolerance policy against speeding might involve issuing tickets to those going even one mile per hour above the limit, but the fine might be small. For offenses that previously had been ignored, the introduction of a trifling penalty can bring a substantial decrease in violations. Many people who would jaywalk when there is no penalty will be dissuaded from jaywalking by the possibility of a nominal fine.

Frequently, however, a zero tolerance policy suggests not only that violators will be prosecuted, but also that few distinctions will be made in terms of punishment between a minor infraction (say, a short pushing match between students in a hall where no one is injured) and a more severe infraction of the same type (an all-out fight between two students that leaves both of them hospitalized). Minor violations are punished under typical zero tolerance policies, and are punished relatively harshly.

As noted above, zero tolerance implies diminished (or zero) discretion on the part of enforcers. Any violation within the targeted class that comes to light, no matter how minor, is supposed to be punished under a zero tolerance regime. The cop on the beat or the principal in the office isn't supposed to informally excuse or lightly punish those violations that are deemed to be less important: these enforcers are supposed to enforce, not to "deem."[3] Often the implementation of zero tolerance is accompanied by a visible expansion in the number of enforcers, too: not only will infractions that come to light be punished, but more light is generated. All else equal, a larger proportion of those infractions that do occur will be observed and punished under zero tolerance, whether the infractions are minor or significant, and for small violations the magnitude of the punishment will be raised.

As noted in Chapter 1, rules have two components: the rule itself, i.e. what behaviors constitute compliance and breach under what circumstances, and the enforcement regime. The enforcement regime can itself be divided into two components: the monitoring or policing strategy and the punishments inflicted upon violators.[4] Zero tolerance policies frequently involve heightened strictness in all three components of rules: more behaviors are declared to be violations, the probability that a violation will be detected is increased, and the sanctions imposed on violators are raised. Further, the discretion available to both the police and judges (or, those who detect violations and those who determine punishments) is scaled back, potentially to zero.

The adoption of a zero tolerance policy is meant to signal a changed stance, a new toughness towards a type of infraction.[5] For this reason, the enforcement regime against serious violent crimes is generally not described as one of zero tolerance, despite the willingness to prosecute all such violations. Unlike standard zero tolerance policies, the enforcement regime against major crimes such as homicide and armed robbery allows for meaningful distinctions in the gravity of the violation to influence the punishment inflicted upon the offender. More importantly, the fact that serious violent crimes have long been subject to tough enforcement is precisely why they are not described as being governed by zero tolerance.

Benefits of zero tolerance

Why would authorities adopt enforcement regimes that limit the discretion of enforcers and call for punishments that are arguably disproportionate to offenses? The main reason is the hope that a zero tolerance enforcement strategy will deter potential offenses that would not be deterred by a standard discretionary enforcement strategy. Enforcement, though, is expensive. Devoting substantial resources to policing minor infractions (including those that might otherwise have been ignored) looks like a fairly undesirable long-run strategy, requiring significant expenditures for inconsequential gains. The hope is that by upgrading enforcement in the short run, habits of compliance will be induced that will outlast the stringent policing.[6] Threats to punish are cheap if they work in deterring the targeted activity, because then the punishment itself does not have to be implemented.[7] So zero tolerance policies needn't involve large expenditures in the long run, if they succeed in providing credible deterrence. But the more often that the threatened punishment actually has to be implemented (i.e. the greater the number of violations that occur and come to light despite the threatened punishment), the more expensive and ultimately less viable a zero tolerance policy will be.

The attractiveness of a zero tolerance policy is augmented if it is believed that a single minor infraction will lead to further and more severe infractions in the future. A zero tolerance policy that prevents the initial infraction will then also deter those violations that otherwise would have been induced. Rule breaking, as was noted in Chapter 2, frequently is marked by "positive feedback," wherein evasion begets evasion, with potentially explosive consequences. For instance, if it is widely believed – rightly or wrongly – that crime has increased, formerly law-abiding individuals might be more likely to engage in criminal activity. Police resources will be perceived as being spread more thinly, if the number of enforcers stays the same while the number of violations increases.[8] The perceived probability of being apprehended following a crime therefore falls, perhaps enticing more individuals into crime. Even in circumstances where the potential for violations to cascade is not clear-cut, the *failure* to punish a given infraction does nothing to deter future infractions of the same type.

Positive feedback in rule breaking provides one explanation for why enforcement authorities employ periodic crackdowns or zero tolerance campaigns against minor offenses; it is not so much that the additional enforcement (either increased probabilities of detection or stiffer penalties for violators, or both) is worth the effort in itself, but it may deter a later cascade of evasion. Situations in which positive feedback is a particularly salient concern tend to be countered with zero tolerance-type policies. Effective (though imperfect) tools to prevent riots include strong and visible reprisals against the early movers to discourage the others, and limiting assemblies of individuals to such small size in relation to the forces of law and order that such reprisals are expected to be effective.

The possibility of positive feedback in evasion tends to be more pronounced when the legitimacy of the enforcement powers is questionable; then, every visible act of evasion calls that legitimacy further into question. Partly for this reason, informal enforcement authorities are particularly likely to adopt forms of zero tolerance policies. Mafia members, "men of respect," are renowned for forceful responses to any evasion of their strictures, any besmirching of their reputation, however slight. In American inner cities, where formal enforcement bodies are often discredited, and in part replaced by the informal authority of gangs or drug dealers, a small, even unintentional act of "disrespect" can – sometimes, virtually of necessity – bring forth what would in other circumstances constitute an irrationally excessive counterattack. Similar processes are at work in the area of international relations, where again there is no recourse to an overarching formal authority. During the Peloponnesian War, the small island of Melios rashly attempted not to support Athens actively, but rather to remain officially neutral, though it had Spartan sympathies. The Athenian response was first to issue the warning: "Your hostility cannot so much hurt us as your friendship [i.e. amiable neutrality] will be an argument to our subjects of our weakness, and your enmity of our power"; when the Melians refused to fall into line, Athens besieged the island state, demonstrating in the cruel post-surrender massacre the validity of another observation made by the Athenians at the pre-invasion conference: "The strong do what they can and the weak suffer what they must."[9]

The "marketing" of a zero tolerance policy is essential for its success. The benefits of the policy depend on the extent to which the heightened threat of punishment for minor offenses actually curtails those offences (and hence also curtails the further offenses that might have cascaded from the existence of the original offenses). The social payoff is in deterrence, not in punishment; indeed, punishment is socially costly. To limit the extent to which the punishment has to be applied, the authorities attempt to signal that a new regime is in place. The greater the belief among potential malefactors that the crackdown will indeed be implemented – that the authorities have both the capability and the intention to enforce stringently – the more successful the zero tolerance campaign will be. The fanfare that typically accompanies the introduction of a zero tolerance policy in itself helps make the crackdown credible. By putting their reputation on the line, enforcers will have little choice but to follow through on the threatened punishments.

Decreased violations are not the only benefit associated with credible zero tolerance policies. Theoretical models of the slippery slope of rule evasion highlight the possibility of two distinct outcomes, one with low levels of evasion and a second with high levels of evasion.[10] The positive feedback that can characterize evasion tends to make the low evasion outcome unstable: if for some reason, rule breaking increases somewhat above a longstanding low level, it could snowball until the high evasion outcome is established instead. In practice, of course, it is hard to know the precise location of the "tipping point" between the two outcomes.[11] This uncertainty suggests an additional benefit to credible zero tolerance policies: while the exact tipping point at which high levels of evasion become the norm is unknown, zero or near-zero evasion is almost certainly below it. Alternatively, if the setting already involves high levels of evasion, a temporary policy of greatly increased enforcement might be needed to re-establish a low evasion environment.

Another ancillary benefit of zero tolerance could reside in the very lack of discretion that such a policy implies. Decisions can be costly to make, and enforcement authorities might welcome the imposition of a fixed rule that (at least officially) eliminates their discretion. (Increased litigiousness in the US has raised the perceived costs of exercising judgment, helping to spur policies such as zero tolerance that restrict discretion.[12]) The elimination of discretion also will bring with it a reduction in lobbying for preferential treatment by affected parties.[13] Zero tolerance makes enforcement automatic, and hence, in theory, beyond the reach of persuasion. Relatedly, simplicity tends to be a virtue in rules, and maintaining a publicized regime of zero tolerance makes the rules quite transparent. And if the behavior that is targeted is precisely defined and of near-constant social undesirability, consistent punishments might be more just than the varying punishments that discretion might engender.

Drawbacks to zero tolerance

> I think life too complex a thing to be settled by these hard and fast rules.
> (Oscar Wilde, *Lady Windermere's Fan*)

Reluctance to carry out the threatened punishment, however, calls into question the credibility of zero tolerance policies, which impose harsh penalties for relatively minor violations. When a good student is suspended from school for an insignificant or perhaps even involuntary infraction, voices are sure to be raised that this suspension is unjustified and not sensible. The fact that harsh punishments for inconsequential or understandable infractions are widely regarded as senseless, then, also suggests that, formally or informally, the enforcement authorities themselves will use some discretion, and not implement the zero tolerance policy to the letter. The class valedictorian who is seen taking a sip of a friend's beer after the school dance (in violation of the zero tolerance policy against student alcohol consumption, and perhaps not knowing that the cup contained an alcoholic beverage) is more likely to be informally reprieved than is the troublesome student who is seen gulping from a pint of whisky and is noticeably drunk at the same dance. But once it is recognized that there is unwillingness to live by the letter of the zero tolerance policy, the policy is undermined. The troublesome student can rightly say that both he and the valedictorian broke the rule, and the policy calls for suspension alike. So if the offenses at which the zero tolerance policy is aimed nevertheless occur with sufficient frequency, especially in their minor form, then the zero tolerance policy will be formally or informally abandoned.

Enforcement authorities can find zero tolerance policies to be a sort of trap. For such policies to be effective, they must be believable. To make the policies believable, authorities put their reputation on the line, by making public commitments to the heightened punishments. When faced with an inconsequential or inadvertent violation, then, enforcers can either destroy that credibility by forgoing the punishment, or face ridicule for showing what in the absence of the policy would be a foolish lack of judgment.

Credibility of a zero tolerance policy can be undermined not only by reluctance to carry out the policy to the letter, but also by an inability to do so. Specifically, some violators may avoid apprehension and punishment, irrespective of the enforcement regime. The unfairness will be magnified with a zero tolerance policy, however, because those minor violators who happen to get caught receive severe penalties, while other (and potentially more serious) violators go unpunished. The fact that others are not apprehended is generally not a strong argument for failing to punish those who do get caught – try explaining to a traffic court judge that other drivers were going even faster but they weren't apprehended – but the more disproportionate the punishment to the offense, the stronger the argument becomes. And it may be that the serious or repeat offenders are the ones who are least likely to be punished, as they might have heightened incentives and resources to avoid detection.

Perceived unfairness in punishment is not only bad in itself, it also can undermine deterrence. Just as enforcers might look for informal means to avoid fully implementing zero tolerance policies, members of the public might diminish cooperation with the authorities if they view the system as unfair. But public cooperation is necessary for enforcers to learn about infractions, and to identify, apprehend, and successfully prosecute malefactors. As a result of public antipathy towards the harsh punishments of a zero tolerance regime, then, the probability that an offender will be punished is reduced, potentially even below the level that would prevail in the absence of zero tolerance.[14] There may also be dynamic considerations: the perception of unfair treatment in the past makes individuals less willing to obey laws in the future.[15]

Even credible zero tolerance policies involve costs beyond those of prosecuting offenders. First, recall Chapter 2's praise of evasion: not all violations are socially undesirable. It might be best for a driver in an emergency to exceed the speed limit. If a zero tolerance policy will punish speeders severely without regard to the circumstances, then some beneficial violations might be deterred. Second, well-intentioned people could inadvertently violate a strict zero tolerance policy, by absentmindedly bringing a nail clipper to school, for instance, in violation of a zero tolerance policy against weapons at school. To avoid the harsh punishments attached to such technical violations, people will have to be extremely vigilant regarding rather minute aspects of their behavior. The problem is particularly acute if the proscribed activity is not well defined – it might be very hard for a student to ensure that he or she does not engage in any "disrespectful" behavior, for instance. Vindictive "framing" of foes is also eased and must be guarded against in a zero tolerance regime. Your rival for class president could quite effortlessly slip an aspirin into your locker and have you suspended. Living in a zero tolerance world can be stressful, even for the law-abiding.

The disproportionate punishments for relative minor infractions that tend to mark zero tolerance campaigns carry some heavy costs in other forms, too. The advisable punishment for an offense is limited by the need to provide some disincentive against undertaking more serious offenses. (As noted earlier, this is referred to as the need to provide "marginal deterrence.") If students who engage in any fight will be suspended for a year, irrespective of the severity of the fight, then participants in a minor shoving contest have reduced incentives to avoid escalation to an all-out fight. Further, labeling and treating insignificant breaches of rules as criminal will result in the criminalization of almost all of us. The stigma associated with being labeled a criminal will surely erode.[16] Simultaneously, the deterrence value of the zero tolerance policy will be undermined as the number of technical, unintentional violations grows. If both good behavior and bad behavior receive the same punishment, the enforcement regime provides no reason to avoid bad behavior.

Enhanced penalties lead to other changes that can diminish the desirability of zero tolerance policies. Violators will go to more pains to avoid detection – pains which might be viewed as a benefit to the rest of society, which isn't so keen on rule evasion, but are costly to the violators. Once apprehended, violators will respond to higher penalties by investing more resources in conducting their defense. And the need for additional resources isn't limited to the defense side of the legal confrontation. Administrative penalties such as small fines can be assessed and adjudicated at small cost. Mistaken prosecutions are not too damaging if the penalties imposed on those judged guilty are minimal, so intricate protections against mistakes are unnecessary. Higher penalties, however, increase the damage associated with errors: miscarriages of justice become more serious when punishments involve long prison terms or worse. Criminal prosecutions, therefore, must comply with rather elaborate and costly procedural safeguards – though even with these precautions, the criminal justice system is often extremely fallible.[17]

Recall that one of the potential benefits of zero tolerance is that incentives of violators to lobby enforcers for favorable treatment are reduced if the enforcers possess little discretion. Discretion, however, cannot be eliminated simply by the adoption of a policy. There are always higher levels to which appeals can be made, and even sovereign governments can change a rule after the fact. In practice, some zero tolerance policies appear to have resulted in increased lobbying, as the harsh punishments imposed on violators create firestorms of protest.[18] In Decatur, Illinois, following a fight at a high school football game in the fall of 1999, six students were expelled for two years, as the result of a newly adopted zero tolerance policy against violence.[19] Prior to the policy, a ten-day suspension would have been the typical punishment for a fistfight. National and international attention was brought to Decatur, including the involvement of Reverend Jesse Jackson and the governor of Illinois. And though the Decatur Board of Education was rather steadfast in its commitment to the original term of expulsions, in the end discretion was indeed available. The Illinois governor issued an executive order that allowed the expelled students to enroll in an alternative education program, and eventually the expulsions were scaled back, too.

So discretion and lobbying are not eliminated by zero tolerance. Nor is it automatic that the adoption of a zero tolerance policy leads to increased transparency in the rules. A zero tolerance policy against weapons at school still has to determine what qualifies as a weapon: fists do not qualify, presumably, but what about keychain-size Swiss army knives or a small pair of scissors? Sometimes zero tolerance policies are adopted against behaviors that are even more difficult to define than "weapon," such as "sexual harassment" or "defying authority." In delineating the scope of zero tolerance policies, discretion will still be required, and rules can remain murky at the margins. While zero tolerance "horror stories" generally concern rules that are overinclusive, as with nail clippers being considered as weapons, sometimes they can be underinclusive, too. Bringing a threatening metal-spiked ball into a New York City high school did not result in a suspension for the offending student, because such devices were not specifically included in the laundry list of proscribed weapons.[20] Once again, the exaggerated penalties for nail clipper "violations" make the unfairness all the more glaring.

Finally, the fact that in practice zero tolerance policies do not and generally cannot eliminate discretion implies that there is a chance that the residual discretion will be used to discriminate on racial or other grounds.[21] The potential misuse of discretion is shared by virtually all enforcement strategies, of course. The additional element that zero tolerance brings is an enhanced possibility to harass targeted groups on the basis of common, minor violations, given that such violations would be lightly punished or not addressed at all under other enforcement regimes. A zero tolerance policy potentially offers a plausible "justification" for harassment that might be more difficult or impossible to justify under a less severe enforcement regime. If the proscribed behavior is one that is hard to define precisely – such as "defying authority" in a classroom – then abuse of discretion is magnified by the harsh penalties that accompany zero tolerance.[22]

Let me summarize, both here and in Table 3.1. Enforcement and punishment are costly, so a policy that involves substantial enforcement and frequent punishment can be very costly. The adoption of such a policy tends to be a short-run measure. The hope is that the heightened punishments deter violations, so that in the long run, fewer resources are needed for both enforcement and for punishment. The sustainability of the relatively severe penalties associated with

Table 3.1 Some potential consequences of zero tolerance

Positive features	Negative features
Increases deterrence, reducing the number of rule violations.	Applies harsh and costly punishments to minor or inconsequential violations.
Lessens the impact of positive feedback in generating more violations.	Forces discretion in enforcement to become hidden.
Provokes a lasting shift from a high violation setting to a low violation equilibrium.	Deters some beneficial violations.
	Reduces the disincentive for violators to engage in more serious violations.
Makes the *de facto* rules clear, and equivalent to the *de jure* rules.	Increases the per-violation costs of prosecuting and defending cases.
Makes the job of enforcers clear.	Provides increased "rationale" to harass or frame targeted groups, and increases the penalties unfairly imposed.
Reduces the incentive to lobby for favorable treatment.	
	Lowers the stigma associated with penalties such as suspension from school or imprisonment.
	Causes well-intentioned people to devote considerable attention to avoiding technical violations.
	Raises the stakes associated with "errors" of under- as well as over-inclusiveness.

zero tolerance policies, then, depends on the extent to which the threatened punishment actually deters the proscribed behavior.

Credibility of the policy is the key to deterrence, but credibility itself can be undermined by two types of rule evasion. First, the targeted activity itself might continue at high levels, perhaps through inadvertent violations or perhaps because the probabilities of apprehension and punishment remain low, despite the zero tolerance policy. In this case, punishment and enforcement expenditures stay at a high level, too. The policy will then be called into question, as people recognize that they are paying high enforcement costs but receiving little benefit in the form of deterrence. Second, the "zero discretion for enforcers" feature of zero tolerance might itself not be credible, if the significant penalties associated with minor or inadvertent violations are widely perceived as being senseless and unfair. But it is very hard to achieve true zero discretion, in part because precisely following the tightened rules sometimes involves taking overly harsh actions against well-intentioned individuals. The zero discretion component of zero tolerance policies presents a near-universal bar to their credibility, an inherent contradiction that in many circumstances unintentionally demonstrates the wisdom of traditional, discretionary enforcement.

But what if the credibility of a zero tolerance policy somehow is maintained? The heightened punishments associated with violations of credible zero tolerance policies tend to enhance deterrence and lead to fewer rule violations. It remains uncertain, however, whether the enhanced deterrence serves the overall social good: increased penalties for rule violations typically involve higher average social costs for those violations that do take place.

Harm reduction

Zero tolerance can deter much evasive behavior, but that which endures is often accompanied by significant social harms, including police, court, and prison expenditures, as well as the efforts undertaken by rule breakers to avoid apprehension and conviction. Minimizing evasive behavior, therefore, need not minimize the social costs of evasion.[23] A more general approach to regulating evasion is termed "harm reduction" or "harm minimization," an enforcement strategy aimed at reducing the social cost of that evasive activity that does take place, as opposed to the amount of the evasion itself. The fact that the average social costs of violations tend to go up with increased enforcement of the zero tolerance type implies that a universal policy of zero tolerance does not minimize harms. Cases mentioned earlier, such as the elimination of red lights at night in Bogota and the legalization of safe methods of infant abandonment in the US, both can be viewed as responses to evasion with the view not of reducing the overall amount of rule circumvention, but of limiting the harm caused by the evasive activity.

A popular harm reduction strategy in policing goes by the label "order maintenance" or "broken windows." Recall that much of the interest in zero tolerance is driven by concern with positive feedback, the idea that crime can easily snowball. The "broken windows" approach shares zero tolerance's concern with positive feedback in crime. Indeed, the label derives from the notion recounted earlier, that a broken window in a building, if left unrepaired, will soon result in a building with all of its windows broken, and perhaps a neighborhood that deteriorates in other dimensions, too.[24]

Order maintenance differs from zero tolerance, however, in two respects.[25] First, order maintenance policing does not reduce or eliminate discretion. Rather, it encourages the police to use their discretion to try to resolve threats to public order without resorting to arrest.[26] Second, and relatedly, a "disproportionate" response to minor violations is not a necessary feature of a broken windows approach.

Order maintenance policing acknowledges that there will be continual threats to public order, but that most of them will be minor. That is, deterrence will be far from perfect, irrespective of the enforcement regime, but many violations are inconsequential. These are precisely the conditions that recommend against a zero tolerance approach, and instead recommend a strategy aimed at lowering the overall costs associated with offenses. Order maintenance provides such a form of harm reduction, but one that recognizes that due to positive feedback, the ramifications of some seemingly small offenses can be significant. The discretion of the officer is employed to determine which minor offenses merit an arrest – due to the social costs that would accompany a failure to arrest – and which can be dealt with less formally, or even ignored.

Police discretion can be used, and traditionally has been used, to provide a sort of targeted zero tolerance within an overall harm reduction (order maintenance) framework. In certain areas of a city, for instance, disorderly behavior is policed aggressively. In other parts of town ("skid row"), the same behavior is dealt with much more leniently. This targeted zero tolerance, or informal zoning, recognizes that small violations will occur, but as long as the social costs are low (which might mean simply that the behavior is not visible when or where it is most undesirable), the violations largely go unpunished.[27] When or where the perceived social costs are high, however, the behavior is not tolerated.

The geographical targeting of zero tolerance frequently is applied within restricted settings, such as schools, airports, or subway stations. Given an appropriate monitoring technology for the proscribed offense, it is feasible in restricted areas to detect and punish nearly all violators. If the targeted behavior is one that can be almost eliminated by such an approach – for instance, if inadvertent offenses are not a major difficulty – then much of the downside of a zero tolerance policy is avoided. An influential instance of zero tolerance in a closed setting has been the successful campaign against fare beating and graffiti in the New York City subway.[28] The US military's drive against illicit drug use by soldiers is another example where zero tolerance in a closed setting has done much to reduce the proscribed behavior. In this instance, drug testing provided the monitoring that was necessary to insure that most violators were apprehended.

The geographically targeted zero tolerance approach to harm minimization can be generalized to "temporally" targeted enforcement as well. Periodic crackdowns of the zero tolerance type can prevent forces of positive feedback in rule evasion from getting out of hand, even if in the long term zero tolerance is neither desirable nor sustainable. Limited duration events, such as soccer tournaments, might be good candidates for zero tolerance policing, especially considering the propensity for the main proscribed activity – fan violence – to display positive feedback.[29] Targeting can go beyond the geographical and temporal dimensions, too. Police officers (or school principals) might target zero tolerance on an individual basis. Kids who are generally law-abiding might be treated with leniency when they do transgress a rule. For unruly kids (repeat offenders who might be more susceptible to cascades in their own rule-breaking behavior, or whose example might provide guidance to those less inclined to violate rules), a zero tolerance approach might be adopted.

Drug policy provided the genesis for the terms "zero tolerance" and "harm reduction." Harm reduction in drug policy is driven by two considerations.[30] First, for most addicts and in most treatment programs, total abstinence is not achieved, and for many popular illicit drugs, significant evasion of the ban is quite evident. Second, the majority of users of illicit drugs use their drugs in a controlled way, without the need for treatment. (To this might be added the notion that for many people, the major drug-related concern is not drug use *per se*, but drug or drug-law related violent crime.[31]) Again, these considerations are precisely those that render zero tolerance regimes less attractive: deterrence is not particularly effective, but much of the evasion is insignificant, involving little social cost. Together, these observations imply that a zero tolerance policy (except, potentially, in relatively closed settings, or where widespread drug testing provides the requisite evidence to make the punishment threat credible) will result in a plethora of costly punishments for rather minor drug offenses. The harm reduction approach, alternatively, would propose that little enforcement effort be aimed at non-problematic users, and that problem users receive treatments (and perhaps free or subsidized needles) that lower the harm related to their drug use.

More generally, the trade-offs that are presented by zero tolerance policies tend to be particularly acute with respect to "victimless" crimes among adults, such as drug trafficking or prostitution. While these activities may be unsavory, unhealthy, or worse, they are consensual, and (at least in some of the manifestations of these endeavors) no individual is directly victimized. Zero tolerance-type crackdowns on consensual crimes, then, fill courts and jails with people who have not done anything coercive or violent: indeed, the participants in the crime presumably view their activities as personally beneficial and perhaps not a matter of public concern. If the consensual crimes continue at significant levels even in the face of the zero tolerance policies, then the credibility that tends to make zero tolerance work more effectively is undermined. Simultaneously, if the harm to others is negligible, the enforcement regime will have to relaxed, at least in a society with a government that is responsive to the preferences of its citizens: the costs of zero tolerance in such instances are very high and the benefits may not even be discernible. For this reason, a harm reduction approach involving geographically targeted zero tolerance, or informal zoning, has long been a standard strategy for regulating consensual crimes among adults.

4 Avoidance, futility, and reform

The balloon effect

> ... make the doors upon a woman's wit, and it will out at the casement; shut that, and 'twill out at the key-hole; stop that, 'twill fly with the smoke out the chimney
>
> (Shakespeare, *As You Like It*)

A government regulation on one dimension of a problem frequently induces avoidance responses involving other dimensions: an apt metaphor is that of squeezing a balloon, where any air pushed out of one area moves to another region, without any fundamental change in the balloon. Such "balloon effects" are pervasive, though often hard to predict in advance.[1] Requirements that safety caps be placed on aspirin bottles led to no change in the trend of aspirin poisonings – almost half that did occur were from bottles that were left open – while resulting in more poisonings from other medicines, probably because consumers "were lulled into a less-safety-conscious mode of behavior by the existence of safety caps."[2] Balloon effects also can arise through illegal, evasive behavior. For example, stricter controls on legal immigration may result in more illegal immigration, and stricter gun control laws might increase illegal acquisitions of guns.

Futility and perversity

A surprisingly frequent claim is that avoidance or evasive behavior will *completely* undermine a policy change – no air escapes from the balloon. Nearly as frequent is the argument that a policy change will worsen the condition that the policy is aimed to ameliorate. These types of policy analyzes can be termed the "futility" and "perversity" arguments, respectively, following Albert O. Hirschman, whose 1991 book *The Rhetoric of Reaction* was subtitled "Perversity, Futility, Jeopardy."

The economics literature contains many results that can be interpreted as claims of futility. The notion that individuals form their expectations about future government policy in a rational way has led to the "policy ineffectiveness" proposition, wherein any attempt by the monetary authorities (the central bank) to increase output by expanding the money supply will be offset completely by the changed expectations and behavior of individuals.[3] A second futility-type result is the well-known "Coase Theorem," one statement of which is that in the absence of transaction costs, resource allocation is independent of the initial distribution of property rights. In terms of futility, this result might be recast as saying that a change in legal entitlements will not influence what quantity of goods (and "bads," such as pollution) will be produced, as long as there are no impediments to the exchange of those entitlements.[4] A third example concerns generational redistribution schemes, such as Social Security, which can be informally undone by changes in transfers among family members.[5] One of the first "theorems" in economics, Thomas Malthus's claim that population expansion would wipe away any temporary advances above subsistence made by society, is stark in its portrayal of a world of futility, and helps explain how economics became known as the "dismal science."

"Perversity" results in the economics discipline are also quite common: the demonstration of how a minimum wage can raise unemployment and thereby hurt low-wage workers taken as a whole is a familiar example. Many perversity results rely on various forms of secondary responses or feedbacks emanating from a policy, such as when attempts to improve a nation's security through increased defense spending end up reducing security, because adversaries view the defense buildup as threatening to their own security.[6]

Consider the following examples, which some authors have put forth as cases where policies have resulted in either no change, or in a change precisely opposite to that intended:

Automobile safety

Perhaps the paradigmatic presentation of the futility argument is economist Sam Peltzman's analysis of safety regulations and traffic fatalities, in which he concluded "that safety regulation has had no effect on the highway death toll."[7] Peltzman's empirical evidence suggested that drivers responded to regulation-induced improvements in the safety of automobiles by driving more intensely – thereby partly avoiding the safety-enhancing features of the regulations – and lower driver deaths were offset by increased pedestrian deaths.

Criminal justice

Higher penalties for convicted criminals may have no impact on the frequency of crime commission, in part because police may enforce less intensely.[8] Another source of futility from increased official penalties is the potential for offsetting behavior by prosecutors, judges, and juries, as well as the greater care that will be exercised by criminals.[9] Heightened police enforcement also may have limited effect on crime, if private crime prevention spending falls in response. It is conceivable that because of substitutability between private and public enforcement, there is "a *natural* rate of crime driven by supply and demand that may be difficult to influence by public programs for combating crime."[10]

Drug prohibition

It frequently is argued that drug prohibition is futile, as long as there exists a sizable demand for drugs, and a ready supply of young males who have very limited prospects in legitimate activities. It is possible, via the "forbidden fruit" effect, that prohibition itself glamorizes drugs and increases demand. Further, the necessity to illegally distribute drugs hinders quality control, leading to user deaths from overdoses, while dealer deaths are high because of the inaccessibility of the standard formal channels of protection and contract enforcement. For these and other reasons, US drug policy in general has been attacked as being perverse: "Drug abuse is a serious problem, both for individual citizens and society at large, but the 'war on drugs' has made matters worse, not better."[11]

Performance appraisal systems

A "performance appraisal system" is a formal, quantitative or qualitative reckoning of the relative or absolute achievements of employees, in the manner of grades for students. Compensation or promotion possibilities may then be tied to the performance assessments. Large firms and government agencies often employ such systems in an effort to provide improved incentives for employee achievement. Managers may attempt to avoid these systems through grade inflation, or through rotation of the best evaluations among the employees. One analysis concluded that more than 100 years of experience with performance appraisal systems had failed to uncover a single success story, and furthermore that such systems often produced outcomes opposite to their intended effects of improved productivity or morale – for example, appraisal systems are disliked by most employees and supervisors, and frequently are viewed as unfair.[12]

Earmarking tax revenues

To help build a constituency for a state lottery, for instance, legislators might precommit the revenues raised by the lottery to some existing program, such as education. Total state spending on education, however, might not be increased despite this "earmarking" of lottery funds, as other state appropriations to education can be reduced: there is some evidence that programs designated for earmarked lottery funds end up with smaller budgets than they otherwise would have obtained.[13]

Anti-futility

Futility in one dimension of a policy change need not imply that a reform is useless. If criminals respond to gun control by resorting to the home manufacture of firearms, the number of guns in criminal hands may be unchanged. Nevertheless, the home-produced weapons likely will be substantially less lethal than the commercially produced alternative – at least less lethal for the intended victims of firearm violence. Stiffer penalties for crime commission may be offset by plea-bargaining, but the costs of the judicial system simultaneously might be reduced. Further, what appears to be futility or perversity in a policy change might actually reflect confusion over the true intention behind the new policy. Price ceilings, as previously noted, in many circumstances increase the average costs of acquiring goods – a seemingly perverse outcome. At the same time, however, price controls can redistribute income among heterogeneous consumers, and the redistribution, not lowering the average costs of obtaining goods, may in fact be the desired effect.

Claims of futility and perversity for proposed policy changes often are quite riveting, as a logical chain of reasoning leads to an unexpected result. Nevertheless, real-world policy changes would seem unlikely to be marked by futility or perversity, in part because policy makers can anticipate some of the more apparent possibilities for evasion and avoidance.[14] Squeezing the balloon displaces some air, but in general also pushes some air out, or at least the deformations matter. Automobile fatality rates have fallen as roads and cars are made more safe, and people get to their destinations more quickly, despite offsetting driver behavior.[15] Some US states have earmarked lottery revenues for programs that otherwise would receive no state funding, and many lottery revenues in the UK are directed to various "good causes," with the distributions shielded from government control.

Let me outline the logic that seems to underlie standard futility or neutrality results. People care about the outcomes of some economic process; in other words, people have a certain "demand" for various outcomes. The outcomes themselves depend on many factors, including the behavior of a given individual, the behavior of other individuals, and public policy. Consider starting from some initial situation – a situation brought about by the combination of the factors noted above, including the decisions of individuals that reflect their "demand." Now, change one of the factors, say, public policy, or the behavior of just one individual. The other individuals can now adjust their own actions in ways that will bring about the same outcome as before, and may well do so, given their revealed demand for the original outcome, if it is not costly to them to alter their behavior. The more costly adjustment is, the less the extent to which they will offset the initial change.

How does this process work in specific instances? In the monetary economics "policy ineffectiveness" result, outcomes depend on the policy choices of the central bank as well as the behavior of individuals, which itself is based on expectations about the policy choices of the central bank. If the monetary authorities change their policies, individuals will change their expectations and therefore their behavior accordingly, and bring about the same level of economic activity as before the policy shift. In the Peltzman automobile safety regulation example, individuals have a certain demand for safety. Outcomes are determined by the inherent safety of cars and the behavior of drivers. Change the inherent safety of cars, and individuals will adjust their driving to achieve outcomes similar to those that were achieved before the change in car design. In one version of neutrality in criminal justice, crime outcomes are determined by the anti-crime efforts of both the public sector and of private citizens. Increase public anti-crime efforts, and private anti-crime exertions will adjust downwards, again bringing about outcomes similar to those that occurred before the change in public sector crime control policy.

A complementary lens through which many futility results can be viewed centers on opportunities for arbitrage. Assume that there are many ways of achieving a certain goal, some legal, say, and some illegal. People choose among these various routes to their intended end. If one route were clearly preferable, people would choose that route, until "congestion" or the response of officials made it no longer desirable: the analogy with traffic jams is straightforward. That is, people will sort themselves so that at the margin, all routes (among those that are actually used by anyone) are equally desirable. (If this were not the case, then, for example, some drivers would leave the highway for the local routes, reducing congestion on the highway and increasing local traffic. This process will continue until there is no perceived advantage to switching routes.) After this initial "equilibrium" is established, imagine a policy change that effectively raises the costs of one of the routes. Some individuals will then shift to other routes, but, at the margin, these routes were no less desirable, anyway. Substitution among routes is essentially "free" at the margin, and the policy change is rendered ineffective. Real-life attempts to reduce traffic congestion illustrate this point: increased road capacity generally has little or no effect on peak-hour congestion, as more drivers are induced to take the enlarged routes.[16]

The arbitrage logic also indicates why the futility result is more extreme than the actual results of most policy changes. First, in situations with poor information, as often characterizes illegal (and hence hidden) transactions, the initial indifference at the margin among routes cannot be taken for granted: individuals with good knowledge of local roads, for instance, might be able to profitably circumvent a traffic jam or other barriers. But more importantly, even if all routes are equally valuable (or, equivalently, equally costly) at the margin before the policy change, marginal costs typically are rising. For the first person to change his behavior as a result of the policy change, perhaps the substitution is essentially free. But as more and more individuals find their original route has gotten more costly because of a policy change, they are then likely to find that other routes have also become more costly.[17]

Increased costs at the margin are particularly clear if routes that were not profitable at all before the policy change suddenly come into use after the change. Virtually no one currently makes his or her own automobile at home, but if sales of cars were made illegal and the prohibition were enforced rigorously, some home production might be induced – but it would be much more costly than the current alternative of legal market sales. Of course, the longer-run consequences of a policy change cannot easily be predicted. Many forms of production profit from learning-by-doing. Home production of automobiles might become easier over time, and in theory, eventually technological progress induced by home production could make it cheaper than the current system with legal market sales. But such long-run, speculative effects are by no means assured, and so they generally cannot be determinative in the choice of policies: the more likely result is that a new legal barrier raising the cost of one route to a desired end will result in higher costs on all routes.

The effects of policy over time

The extent to which policy changes are rendered ineffectual by avoidance and evasion depends on the time frame. Finding the best way to adapt to rule changes can be time-consuming, whether the adaptation is consistent with the spirit of the rules or represents avoidance or evasion.[18] All else equal, then, it can be expected that policy changes that put new constraints on the choices of individuals will have their greatest impact (in the desired direction) soon after they are implemented. As time passes, individuals will develop avoidance and evasion strategies, and the intended impact will diminish. Simultaneously, the side effects associated with a policy reform will tend to increase over time, as evasion and avoidance increase. This dynamic pattern has been found to apply in a wide variety of circumstances. Motorcycle-helmet-wearing laws have their greatest impact on motorcycle mortality in the short run; in the longer term, the mortality reductions dissipate, as motorcyclists adjust their driving behavior.[19] A similar time profile was associated with the prohibition of alcohol in the US. The immediate impact of Prohibition was a 70 percent fall in alcohol consumption; within a few years, however, consumption had reached 70 percent of pre-Prohibition levels.[20] (Unintended outcomes associated with Prohibition tended to increase over time, too, including the growth of organized crime and a substitution to more potent forms of alcoholic beverages and to marijuana usage.[21]) Even experienced criminals seem to require time to adjust "optimally" to a policy change. It has been suggested that learning by criminals explains why in the short term, increased police expenditures seem to decrease crime, while in the long run, there is a positive relationship between the level of crime and police expenditures.[22]

Contributing to the delay in finding ways around rules is inertia: individuals' choices may be governed by social norms or habits of behavior that are slow to change, even in the face of new incentives that are opposed to the norms. Many people comply with taxes that they could easily evade, for instance, or fail to apply for social benefits to which they are legally entitled. Social norms may display inertia, but they do not display permanence, and they will be threatened by significant economic incentives to deviate from the norm. Enhanced levels of deviance can cascade quickly throughout a population, as people perceive that others are profitably deviating. The increased deviance, then, can undermine the existing norm and perhaps establish a new norm antithetical to the original one.[23]

This claim that policy changes will have their greatest impact at their inception assumes that the enforcement agencies are well poised to enforce the new rule from the beginning. If, alternatively, effective enforcement also requires some time to develop, then evasion could be higher in the initial stages of a policy reform than later. Would-be evaders often have strong incentives to discover profitable routes of evasion, and these routes are hard for either policy makers or enforcement agents to anticipate. Perhaps the standard situation is where avoiders and evaders respond most quickly to reform, and then enforcement officials or policy makers learn how best to deploy their resources or amend their rules; there is then further response and counter-response, etc. (One version of this process is termed the "Regulatory Dialectic," in which the costs imposed by a regulation represent the thesis, the avoidance responses represent the antithesis, and the resulting rule change is the synthesis.[24]) For this reason, simply indicating potential undesirable side effects of a policy change that are associated with avoidance and evasion is far from sufficient evidence that the reform should not be tried. There may well be unanticipated changes in the enforcement or policy regimes down the road that will make the reform continually effective, while limiting adverse side effects.[25]

The discussion so far has been based on the underlying notion that the enforcement authorities remain committed to the policy change. Alternatively, enforcers eventually may lose interest in enforcing diligently, perhaps in collusion with rule evaders, particularly for "victimless" crimes: potential evaders might discover that the easiest method of circumvention involves corrupting those charged with enforcement.[26] In the regulatory domain, the "capture" theory of regulation suggests that over time, the overseers of an industry will begin to identify with the interests of the industry that they are charged with controlling.

The treadmill of reform

> We must change everything – in order that nothing change.
> (Tomasi di Lampedusa, *The Leopard*[27])

Prior to radical economic reform in the former Soviet Union, planners implemented a continual series of more minor adjustments, aimed at "perfecting" the planning mechanism. Despite these ongoing policy changes, documented in a well-known article by Gertrude Schroeder, "The Soviet Economy on a Treadmill of 'Reforms'," the problems that the reforms were aimed to solve – low quality output, sub-optimal assortment, poor incentives to cut costs, etc. – continued unabated.

This process is replicated in policy environments in the West. Problems are identified and reforms are enacted; a few years later, the same or similar problems are re-identified and further reforms are enacted, and the process continues. One example is the "treadmill" of commissions comprised of distinguished worthies aimed at improving weapons system procurement.[28] Welfare, public education, criminal justice, police corruption, public housing, and performance appraisal systems are other areas that perhaps can be characterized as being on reform treadmills. Within bureaucracies responding to problems, treadmills are a standard outcome: it is often the case that the "only weapon that can be used by the people who must make decisions is a greater elaboration of the rules and further centralization."[29]

Avoidance behavior frequently is the driving mechanism behind reform treadmills, as discussed in the previous section. A policy is implemented, but the intended effect is diluted by offsetting responses. Stricter enforcement is not an option (as it would be with evasion), since the avoidance is perfectly legitimate. The next step might well be to identify the form of avoidance that is muting the impact of the original policy, and to adopt a policy that essentially closes the loophole. Then there is a whole new opportunity for avoidance (as well as evasion), of course, and so on. As with offsetting behavior, the side-effects of reform also are likely to reveal themselves over time, and additional policies might be adopted to counter them.

As the Soviet planning case indicates, even authoritarian regimes have to cope with evasion and avoidance. Nor is this a particularly new phenomenon. Suetonius tells us that Augustus Caesar

> revised existing laws and enacted some new ones, for example, on extravagance, on adultery and chastity, on bribery, and on the encouragement of marriage among the various classes of citizens. Having made somewhat more stringent changes in the last of these than in the others, he was unable to carry it out because of an open revolt against its provisions, until he had abolished or mitigated a part of the penalties, besides increasing the rewards and allowing a three years' exemption from the obligation to marry after the death of a husband or wife. When the Knights even then persistently called for its repeal at a public show, he sent for the children of Germanicus and exhibited them, some in his own lap and some in their father's, intimating by his gestures and expression that they should not refuse to follow that young man's example. And on finding that the spirit of the law was being evaded by betrothal with immature girls and by frequent changes of wives, he shortened the duration of betrothals and set a limit on divorce.[30]

Treadmills of reform generally are portrayed as evidence of the futility of reform. Nevertheless, if behavior is changing over time, and new information is becoming available, a seeming treadmill could represent an optimal dynamic policy – though it would be hard to justify that claim with respect to Caesar's marital reforms. Given that, all else equal, the desired impact of a reform will tend to diminish over time, an ongoing treadmill of reforms may be required to achieve near-constant results. As the avoidance and evasion responses to a policy become more noticeable, i.e. as policy makers learn, new rules can be enacted to limit (or to condone, or to channel in another direction) the existing rule circumvention.[31] And while problems such as police corruption do seem to display a cyclical pattern, the precise form of such problems changes over time, sometimes in ways that suggest that the most socially costly forms of the problem have been curtailed.

Still, treadmills are not always optimal, even if you just want to stay in place. One cost of the frequent rule changes that characterize treadmills of reform is that they make it difficult for individuals to plan their behavior, by increasing the uncertainty over the future policy environment. The stability of a policy regime tends to be a good in and of itself, and it might be worth forgoing some otherwise desirable rule changes for the sake of creating expectations of rule stability.[32]

Rule complexity

Treadmills of reform also can result in a morass of rules and regulations, as amendments are added to deal with new forms of avoidance and evasion. Many commentators suggest that US governmental regulatory complexity has gone too far, and that detailed regulations not only produce higher administrative costs, but also create socially sub-optimal incentives: better outcomes could be achieved, in this view, at lower cost.[33] The formerly socialist states provide evidence that beyond a certain point, increased state control over the economy *de jure* leads to less control *de facto*, as more activity is conducted underground – a sort of generalization of the Laffer curve, which indicates that excessively high tax rates, by reducing taxable activity through avoidance and evasion, can result in less government revenue than would be collected with lower rates.[34] Treadmills of reform ultimately can lead to their own perverse consequences.

Why should sufficiently complex rules lead to less control over behavior? First, complex rules are costly to learn, so many individuals, including the rule enforcers, will be unwilling or unable to invest the resources necessary to learn the rules.[35] Second, excessive rule-making can make it very difficult (i.e. costly) for even well-intentioned actors to be completely law-abiding, assuming that they understand the applicable rules. The resulting widespread non-compliance in turn fosters discretion among enforcement agents, and corruption: with everyone guilty, authorities can selectively prosecute whomever they choose. And the fact that everyone is guilty reduces the incentives for people of good will to attempt to separate themselves, in terms of their virtuous actions, from scoundrels: since everyone is breaking a multitude of rules, it will be very hard for outside observers to determine who is a scoundrel and who is not. The result will be an increased supply of scoundrels, as the return to virtue falls.

Complexity in rules can arise from having a multitude of rules, of course, but it can also be fostered by poor quality rules that fail to create bright lines. The information that can be included in rules to distinguish cases varies in its precision. Simple rules tend to rely on relatively precise measures, such as sex or age or the occurrence of some fairly well-defined event. More complex rules often are based on much less precise criteria. Consider, for example, the rule that permits firing an employee only for "just cause."[36] Unlike the "at will" doctrine, in which an employee could be dismissed at any time, for any or for no cause, implementation of the "just cause" rule requires much more information than whether or not dismissal occurred. Even someone who knows the rules may be unable to predict accurately whether a given employee dismissal is likely to be judged allowable or not – the line created by the just-cause rule is relatively murky, so there are many hard cases.

The two routes to complexity just discussed, either through a plethora of rules or through vague rules, are actually two sides of the same coin. When there is a multitude of rules, it is hard to know which rule applies, whether the chosen action represented compliance given the actual state of the world, because so much depends on details of the action and the "state." Similar situations arise from vague rules that do not create bright lines. In the extreme case of a completely vague rule, all cases are hard cases and compliance cannot be ascertained beforehand, but only by an after-the-fact judicial decision. In essence, every case is unique, and *ex post*, each case is judged by its own rule. Vague rules can be just another version of a profusion of rules.

So, more complex rules can be less effective than simpler rules at channeling behavior into socially beneficial avenues. But the creation of easily understandable bright lines is not the only criterion for a simple and effective rule. Another element that must be taken into account is ease in enforcement. If cigarettes are sold through vending machines, and such machines are pervasive, a rule forbidding minors from purchasing cigarettes, while perhaps simple, is unlikely to be effective; further, in making it effective, the simplicity is lost, as a host of police officers, probably undercover, would be needed to stake out vending machines. And so a simpler and more effective route would be to have such a child-purchase ban, mildly enforced, combined with a ban on vending-machine sales of cigarettes in areas where children have free access. (Whether this combination of bans is sound social policy is another matter.) A sales (or value-added) tax based on when goods are paid for (a "cash-basis" tax) appears to be simple, but to be effective it requires sophisticated enforcement: not only does the fact that a sale has occurred have to be known to the tax collection authorities, but so does the date of payment (and in practice there frequently are low-cost methods of avoiding the revelation of the date of payment). An alternative tax, which becomes effective at the time the goods are sold, irrespective of when they are paid for (an "accrual basis" tax), requires less information to enforce, and in practice, then, is simpler.[37]

Finally, it was suggested in the previous section that some stability in rules is itself desirable, and it may make sense to forgo what might otherwise be policy improvements for the sake of stability. Aristotle made the trade-off explicit: "For the habit of lightly changing the laws is an evil, and, when the advantage is small, some errors both of lawgivers and rulers had better be left . . . For the law has no power to command obedience except that of habit, which can only be given by time, so that a readiness to change from old to new laws enfeebles the power of the law."[38] Starting from a situation of excessive rule complexity, however, this consideration presents a potential trade-off between simplicity and stability. Alexis de Tocqueville noted just such a trade-off in some of the legal changes undertaken prior to the French Revolution: "It is easy then to see how large a part is played by habit in the functioning of political institutions and how much more easily a nation can cope with complicated, well-nigh unintelligible laws to which it is accustomed than with a simpler legal system that is new."[39] In other words, rule stability is itself one component of rule simplicity.

Treadmills, radical reform, and collapse

One "solution" to reform treadmills, as recent experience in Russia and Eastern Europe indicates, lies in a massive reform. A radical change in the policy environment can result in rapid changes in behavior. Consider the example of public education in the US. Real and perceived shortcomings with public schools (that is, state schools) have been met with a host of reforms over the years, as well as a fair amount of "avoidance" via private schools, and more recently by a rise in home schooling. (Such avoidance can cascade, as the disappearance of those students whose parents are most concerned about the quality of education can result in less pressure on the original school to maintain or improve its performance. Quality at the original school could therefore decline, causing still more parents to choose non-public alternatives for their children, and so on.[40]) Minor adjustments to incentive schemes within public schools, such as national testing or an increase in merit pay for teachers, are unlikely to have much of an impact – which is not to say that they are not worth doing in some instances, nor that the accumulation of minor rule changes over many years cannot have significant consequences. A large change in environment, such as an increase in consumer choice by a voucher scheme that extends to private and for-profit schools (or, alternatively, a substantial centralization of education authority), does hold the potential for significantly different (though not necessarily better) outcomes in the short term. Recall the political economy of evasion and reform: large-scale policy transitions tend to occur when they offer significant net social benefits, and when there are relatively few who are harmed by the reforms. These conditions are likely to exist when the *status quo* is widely recognized to have degraded to such a point that there is little downside risk, or when evasion or avoidance of the existing regulations has become so widespread that the reform largely ratifies the *de facto* situation.

Avoidance and reform: the US Savings & Loan crisis

From the mid-1930s, when a federal regulatory structure and deposit insurance system was established, until the late 1970s, the Savings & Loan (S&L) business in the United States was by-and-large stable, even staid. Each federally chartered S&L had its deposits insured by the Federal Savings & Loan Insurance Corporation (FSLIC), and state-chartered S&Ls could voluntarily join the FSLIC program; the maximum insured deposit amount rose in steps from $5,000 to $40,000 between 1934 and 1979. S&Ls (or *thrifts*) contributed to the insurance fund, but there was a subsidy component: the premia were not based on insurance principles, and they did not vary based on the riskiness of an S&L's asset portfolio.[41] The risk was modest, however: the regulatory structure constrained thrifts to invest primarily in home mortgages – their *raison d'être* – within a small geographic radius of their location. S&Ls tended to be rather small, largely because of legal restrictions on branch banking, and they could not be established by a lone entrepreneur: thrifts were required to have at least 400 stockholders, and no single stockholder could have more than a 25 percent ownership stake.

Beyond the provision of deposit insurance and geographic constraints, the regulatory structure offered a further protection to S&Ls, in the form of buffers against competitive forces. Not only were new entrants into the thrift ranks closely supervized (complementing the controls on new branches of existing institutions), commercial banks, which were the chief rivals of S&Ls for depositors, were not allowed to engage in price competition: checking (or current) accounts could not pay interest, and the interest rates on savings accounts at commercial banks were also controlled. For decades, this regulatory cocoon for S&Ls worked well. The assets of S&Ls increased steadily after World War II, and S&L failures were small, comprising approximately 0.1 percent of S&L assets per year. At the same time, millions of American families received relatively low-cost, thirty-year mortgages to finance their purchases of homes.

> The postwar period was clearly the heyday of the thrift industry. Business was good; profits were healthy. One observer of the thrift industry described it as the world of '3–6–3': Thrifts could take in money at 3 percent interest on deposits; they could lend it out at 6 percent interest on mortgage loans; and thrift executives could be on the golf course by 3:00 in the afternoon.[42]

This idyllic world began to crumble in the 1960s, however, and in the 1980s the widespread collapse of S&Ls led to losses measured in excess of $100 billion. What caused the S&L industry to go from seeming regulatory success to unprecedented financial fiasco within the course of twenty years? The primary agent was rule avoidance, and the regulatory changes engendered thereby.

A preliminary bout was played out in the 1960s, as market interest rates began to rise.[43] Higher market interest rates threatened the profitability of thrifts, because most of their assets (long-term mortgages) were tied up in investments earning only 6 percent annual interest, while their costs (interest rates paid to depositors) were rising. To help relieve this pressure, as well as to limit a shift in deposits from the interest-controlled commercial banks to the market-interest-paying thrifts, in 1966 legislative ceilings were placed on the amount of interest that thrifts could offer their depositors; savings accounts at commercial banks had been subject to such ceilings since 1933. (The S&Ls were permitted to offer a slight interest premium over that allowed commercial banks, to offset the relatively restricted services that thrifts could provide.) As with other forms of price controls, the rate ceilings pushed competition into other dimensions. Commercial banks and S&Ls began to offer prizes to individuals who opened new accounts – prompting an additional regulation on the monetary value of such prizes – and service quality received increased attention.

Commercial banks and thrifts are part of a larger financial services industry, however, so it was possible for their depositors to avoid the interest ceilings through non-bank, non-thrift investments. To limit customer switching to one relatively close substitute, the minimum denomination of US Treasury bills was raised in 1970 from $1,000 to $10,000, placing T-bills beyond the means of the majority of thrift depositors. Additional regulations on commercial banks were adopted to try to forestall the departure of their large depositors to non-bank alternatives.

The hope that interest rate ceilings and a few complementary measures would be sufficient to restore the golden age of S&Ls, however, was undermined by one very specific non-bank alternative: in 1972, initially in Massachusetts, financial institutions that were not as constrained as commercial banks and S&Ls with respect to pricing or the nature of their accounts introduced money market mutual funds. These funds paid interest and allowed limited "check" writing, making them attractive relative to both traditional checking and savings accounts. Money market mutual funds, and the closely related NOW (negotiated order of withdrawal) accounts, were innovations that avoided the price controls placed on banks and S&Ls. As they were attractive to savers (who saw the real value of their deposits in commercial banks and thrifts substantially eroded during the high inflation of the late 1970s), such accounts spread, with the indulgence of the regulatory authorities of various states. These new financial instruments, however, were not consistent with the continued well-being of commercial banks and thrifts under the prevailing regulatory regime, particularly in times of high market interest rates. And in 1979, annual market interest rates rose to above 10 percent, levels at which, except for a few months, they remained through mid-1982. Such high interest rates rendered the S&L industry as a whole insolvent: thrifts lost deposits to financial instruments that paid market rates – the rapid growth of money market mutual funds did not begin until the high interest years of the late 1970s – while the thrifts themselves were typically earning only 6 percent on their outstanding mortgages.[44]

The competitors who were undermining S&Ls in the 1970s and early 1980s were less regulated financial institutions. Technological change augmented competitive forces by making credit-worthiness information widely available, thereby lessening the informational monopoly that S&Ls possessed on the prospects of their local borrowers. Simultaneously, the political popularity of government regulation was in decline across a wide array of industries, beginning in the mid-1970s and continuing through the Reagan administrations. And so it was not surprising that the eventual policy response for the thrift industry was primarily one of deregulation.

And it was a very substantial deregulation. Federal legislation passed in 1980 phased out interest rate ceilings, authorized interest payments on demand deposits (NOW accounts), and extensively liberalized the types and geographic location of S&L investments. Also in 1980, controls were lifted on the acceptance by thrifts of "brokered" deposits. This decontrol greatly increased the ability of financial brokers to aggregate the funds of many small individual savers, parcel them into $100,000 bundles (the federal legislation in 1980 had raised the maximum insured deposit from $40,000 to $100,000), and then to place them at any (FSLIC insured) S&L in the country that offered the best return. Prior to the rule change, brokered accounts could amount to no more than 5 percent of an S&L's deposits;

the extent of brokered accounts skyrocketed following the liberalization. The deregulation was accelerated by additional federal legislation in 1982, and it was specifically stipulated that S&Ls were to be allowed a deposit instrument that would be competitive with money market mutual funds. Also in 1982, the barriers to entry into the Savings and Loan industry were drastically reduced. The rules requiring 400 owners and the 25 percent ownership ceiling were eliminated, allowing a single individual to start up an S&L.

Coupled with the market-oriented deregulation of S&Ls was, as noted, an increase in the size of federally insured deposits. The inconsistency among three factors – increased competition to attract depositors, little oversight over the riskiness of assets, and the provision of deposit insurance at premium rates that did not vary with the riskiness of the lender's asset portfolio – led to much of the ensuing debacle. The fact that state-chartered thrifts had access to FSLIC insurance was also important, as those states that were most liberal (or perhaps reckless) in their thrift requirements were able to attract deposits from out-of-state residents through brokered deposits, creating a competition among states to deregulate, which was further fueled by the possibility that state-chartered thrifts in relatively strictly regulated states could avoid the regulations by re-chartering as federal S&Ls.

Avoidance by depositors and non-depository institutions of the price restrictions on S&Ls through money market accounts (which were uninsured, but generally of very high quality) eventually required that the price controls on S&Ls be dispensed with. But the countenance of price competition by S&Ls was incompatible with insured deposits (with non-actuarially based premia) and little oversight over the riskiness of the asset portfolio.[45] Had price competition been introduced without simultaneously expanding the investment opportunities for S&Ls, and while providing appropriate monitoring to ensure that S&L investment of their insured deposits was prudent, then there need not have been a crisis. (Likewise, a crisis could have been averted if the insurance was eliminated.) But the recognition that S&Ls were losing an unavoidable price competition with non-depository institutions became entangled in a broader wave of deregulation.

While with hindsight the dangerous inconsistencies in S&L regulation are easily perceived, few contemporaneous observers warned of the perverse incentives that were being generated. Perhaps one reason that the peril was not obvious at the time was the notion that even with the new regulations, S&L owners and managers presumably would still want to protect their jobs and equity holdings. While FSLIC insurance implies that depositors need not much care about the assets in which their S&Ls invest, S&L owners should still care. With some of their own funds at stake, the owners shouldn't want to see their thrifts fail.

The normal prudence of owners was undermined in the S&L case, however, by a panoply of factors. The standard limited liability of corporations implied that losses in excess of an owner's equity would be borne by others. This limitation on liability was enhanced by the liberalized rules, which meant that individuals could become owners with little of their own cash at risk. A complementary ingredient was that the widespread insolvency of S&Ls by 1980 implied that the owners had in essence already lost their stake. As long as their S&L was operating, however, owners could gamble with the FSLIC's money: they could attract deposits by offering high interest rates, and then invest the funds in very risky but potentially very lucrative assets. If they were lucky and the ventures paid off handsomely, all was well; otherwise, the FSLIC would have to recompense the depositors. Finally, running an S&L deep into bankruptcy could be directly rewarding: you could live extremely well – even disgustingly well – as the owner of a thrift that was headed towards failure, and you'd generally be fine after failure, too.[46] Stories of thrift looting, essentially for the private consumption of owners, management, and their friends and relatives, were highly publicized during the 1980s, along with the unseemly political influence that some S&L owners used to try to keep regulators at bay. The attention paid by the media to this seeming corruption may have created a perception that it was fraudulent rule evasion that drove the S&L crisis. While no doubt fraud did play a role in the failure of some thrifts, the inappropriate regulatory response to the avoidance of the prior rules and regulations was the chief culprit.

The US thrifts crisis demonstrates how avoidance can promote reform, but not necessarily in a manner that leads to a social improvement. Policies are always part of an interconnected system, and avoidance behavior can create the conditions that favor changing some of the policies. In the case of the S&Ls, liberalization of the interest rate ceilings, which depositors were avoiding by going elsewhere, could itself hardly be avoided. But the resulting system need not be stable, and enormous costs might be imposed before the sources of the instability are recognized and eliminated – an outcome shared by the US thrift deregulation and by the *perestroika* reforms in the Soviet Union.

5 Preventive and punitive controls

> ... when taking a journey, he armes himselfe, and seeks to go well accompanied; when going to sleep, he locks his dores; when even in his house he locks his chests; and this when he knowes there bee Lawes, and publike Officers, armed, to revenge all injuries shall bee done him ...
>
> (Hobbes, *Leviathan*[1])

Many regulatory situations involve a choice between intervening before the activity that involves some social harm takes place – an *ex ante* control – versus dealing, *ex post*, with the consequences of the activity. Often, a combination of *ex ante* and *ex post* approaches (or, employing the terminology of John Stuart Mill, preventive and punitory approaches) is adopted. Speed bumps are placed on some roads, though apprehended speeders will also be fined (in addition to the potential damage to their vehicles). Safety features are mandated for certain consumer products, at the same time that manufacturers may be liable for injuries caused by products that satisfied the mandates. Private behavior frequently involves *ex ante* measures, as Hobbes pointed out, despite the availability of *ex post* public enforcement.

The relative ease of avoidance and evasion plays a major role in the determination of the desirable mix between *ex ante* and *ex post* controls. In many instances, if *ex post* enforcement were inexpensive and pervasive, *ex ante* controls would be unnecessary: anti-social behavior could be effectively deterred through the credible threat of punishment. Locking your doors would be superfluous if all potential trespassers were dissuaded by the prospect of going to jail. But as *ex post* controls become less effective – some robbers may not be apprehended, or some people might be incapable or unwilling to make the expected behavioral adjustments to a credible punishment threat – supplementing after-the-fact punishment with *ex ante* regulation becomes more desirable. This may be particularly true if *ex post* punishment is skirted through legal avoidance behavior, even though the social harm remains.

"Command and control" regulatory approaches to such problems as environmental protection are commonly attacked by economists, often for good reason, for being much more costly than alternative approaches that (presumably) can achieve similar reductions in pollution.[2] For example, it might be very expensive to install emissions-reducing equipment in smokestacks. A tax on emissions might result in similar environmental improvements at much lower cost, as the owners of the factory will be motivated by the tax to find the cheapest methods of lowering pollution. But if the emissions tax can be circumvented while the emissions themselves continue, "command and control" solutions might be necessary to achieve the desired reduction in pollution.

Or they might not be necessary: evadable or avoidable emissions taxes might still be workable – as is often the case, the potential for evasion need not imply regulatory futility. Just as complete evasion of traffic signals – everyone stops on red and goes on green – works almost as well as complete compliance, a universal ability to conceal, say, 50 percent of pollution emissions is no worse for the regulatory authorities than zero evasion. The requisite emission tax can simply be doubled, in recognition of the 50 percent evasion, with the same result in terms of fees and overall emissions.[3]

In any case, the general economic approach to such regulatory questions invokes the notion of a production process, in which combinations of inputs can be transformed into outputs, some of which are desirable (refrigerators, say), and others of which are undesirable (smoke). In other words, inputs are means to various ends. An *ex ante* regulatory strategy, from such a perspective, involves control over the inputs. The notion that regulation is more efficient if it is more closely tied to the object of direct public concern, the undesirable output, lies at the heart of many economists' predisposition towards *ex post* regulatory strategies: regulate the ends, and there would seem to be little reason for public concern about the means. Nevertheless, both *ex ante* and *ex post* approaches are imperfect. Output regulations, for example, may reduce but cannot eliminate the problem that what is being regulated is not the precise object of concern. A rule regulating an output will not perfectly control the actual "end" in view.[4] Consider, for example, one of the well-known problems with central planning in the Soviet Union. Planners would sometimes specify production quotas in terms of weight. For instance, a nail factory might be instructed to produce ten tons of nails per year – an output regulation. The factory could most easily meet its plan by producing large, heavy nails, and so it would, while avoiding the production of small nails. This tendency for output measures based on weight to result in oversized production, at the expense of optimal assortment, was dubbed the "big nail" problem.[5] In the Savings and Loan example in the previous chapter, accounting conventions that did not provide good measures of the actual value of firms contributed to the ability of owners to profit while driving their thrifts into bankruptcy.[6] In other words, output controls in practice rely on measures that are not perfectly correlated with what the public is concerned with, though presumably the correlation is high, and almost by definition higher than the correlation between the means (i.e. inputs) and the end of interest.

Futility and *ex ante* controls

The economists' predisposition towards output controls, therefore, is not unfounded. *Ex ante* controls are based on factors – inputs, or means – that present a relatively imperfect correlation with what is actually of concern, the ends. If the correlation were perfect, then the choice between an input and an output control would be of no more consequence than the choice of whether a fee to use a park is collected at the time people enter or at the time they leave the park – though even this straightforward regulation in practice may have to take into account opportunities for avoidance and evasion. At most restaurants, diners receive their food before they pay, but in drive-through settings, where customer evasion is easier, the fee generally is collected first.

Typically, inputs will be less than perfectly correlated with the end that is of interest, and more importantly, the relationship between inputs and outputs generally will not be stable when a new policy based on that relationship is introduced. This breakdown in the prior connection between inputs and outputs, in the face of an input regulation, often is driven by avoidance: a new tax placed on an activity for the purpose of raising revenue tends to reduce the frequency of the activity, and hence the revenue raised is less than if this usual "avoidance" response did not take place. In the extreme, a control placed on one input will tend to provoke substitution to an uncontrolled alternative input, with little or no change in the undesired output. There is more than one way to skin a cat, and regulating or prohibiting one skinning method, or one input into skinning, as gruesome as the thought is, may not reduce the number of skinned cats.

The "policy ineffectiveness" proposition, noted earlier, is one example of how the relationship between inputs (the money supply) and outputs (GDP) will change when policy makers attempt to take advantage of it, just as the prior relationship between the number of windows in a dwelling and the wealth of the household changed with the introduction of an infamously misguided tax on windows. A general statement of this proclivity is known as Goodhart's Law: "any observed statistical regularity will tend to collapse once pressure is placed upon it for control purposes."[7] Nevertheless, the forces leading to such a collapse could take a good while to coalesce; otherwise, almost all input controls (and many output controls, too) would be doomed to rapid futility. Further, a tendency is not a certainty, and despite avoidance and evasion, wealthier people tend to pay more in taxes than do significantly poorer people, notwithstanding their incentives to substitute away from those components of wealth that are taxed most highly.

The collapse in a relationship between inputs and outputs need not always be due to conscious avoidance or evasion efforts, or to changed expectations. Technology progresses over time, new ways of doing things emerge, and so an input regulation will tend, for this reason, too, to become less well-targeted as a control over output with the passage of time. Many archaic laws that are left on statute books, such as restrictions on goats in a city center, seem silly now because the harm that they regulated (pollution in a congested area) has changed form considerably over time. Whether because of avoidance and evasion, or because of technological change, *ex ante* regulations, like *ex post* controls, are far from perfect; indeed, there is often a strong case for employing both types of controls simultaneously. In any case, avoidance and evasion are fundamental determinants of the desirable design and combination of input and output regulations.

Means, ends, and liberty

Inputs can be means to desirable ends, as well as to undesirable ends. Poisonous or hazardous chemicals, for example, often have important industrial uses, but also can be used for murder. Knives and guns have legitimate uses, but are sometimes employed in criminal violence. Nothing is either good or bad, but its application makes it so.

The multiple uses of inputs present a dilemma for policy makers who wish to complement *ex post* controls (laws against murder, say) with *ex ante* controls (such as restrictions on the distribution of poisons). While it may be desirable that misuse of the input be restricted, it is hard to do this without simultaneously creating some barriers to the legitimate uses. Law-abiding citizens might resent "being treated like a criminal" when they attempt to procure, for innocent ends, an input that is regulated as a means of reducing some socially undesirable end. If onerous enough, such regulation smacks of punishment of the innocent, without trial, and with no defense admitted. The constraint on liberty will seem all the more galling if it is believed that those with bad intentions will be motivated and able to evade the regulations anyway, so that in practice it is only the law-abiding who are harmed. Further, what *ex ante* regulation could not be justified on the grounds that it reduces the potential for mischief? As J. S. Mill wrote: "The preventive function of government . . . is far more liable to be abused, to the prejudice of liberty, than the punitory function; for there is hardly any part of the legitimate freedom of action of a human being which would not admit of being represented, and fairly too, as increasing the facilities for some form or other of delinquency."[8]

The trade-off between restrictions on beneficial uses and the erection of barriers to undesirable uses is one that simply must be faced, and despite the warranted concerns with preventive controls, there is no reason to believe that *laissez-faire* on inputs combined with *ex post* controls on illegitimate use will be optimal. After warning of the dangers of too great a reliance on preventive controls, that stalwart defender of personal liberty, John Stuart Mill, recognized the desirability of some input regulations, within the context of the sale of poisons:

> Precautions of a similar nature [to those formalities observed in entering a legally binding private contract] might be enforced in the sale of articles adapted to be instruments of crime. The seller, for example, might be required to enter in a register the exact time of the transaction, the name and address of the buyer, the precise quality and quantity sold; to ask the purpose for which it was wanted, and record the answer he received. When there was no medical prescription, the presence of some third person might be required to

bring home the fact to the purchaser, in case there should afterwards be reason to believe that the article had been applied to criminal purposes. Such regulations would in general be no material impediment to obtaining the article, but a very considerable one to making an improper use of it without detection.[9]

Race and policing

A reliance on noisy, *ex ante* indicators as opposed to actual harmful acts is common in both public and private affairs. One important and controversial example concerns the role of race in policing, an issue that has been particularly acute in the US in recent years, due in part to some highly publicized cases of extreme police maltreatment or abuse of minorities: for example, in February 1999, unarmed African immigrant Amadou Diallo was shot nineteen times and killed by four white New York City police officers, and Haitian immigrant Abner Louima was brutally tortured by New York police in 1997. But the racial disparities in policing appear to go well beyond isolated cases of abuse. Generally speaking, black people, particularly young black males, tend to have much worse experiences with the police than do white Americans. These experiences range from the annoying – frequent traffic stops for minor or imagined violations – to the fatal, as in the Diallo case. To some extent, racial disparities in citizen–police interactions are deliberate, as criminal "profiles" compiled by the police formally or informally employ race as one factor in identifying potential miscreants. In practice, race appears often to be a decisive element in whether a stop is initiated, or in how an encounter is handled. Nor is this an exclusively American phenomenon. In England and Wales in 1998, per 1,000 individuals of the specified race, 145 blacks were stopped by the police, 45 Asians were stopped, and only 19 whites were stopped.[10] Similar if less well documented disparities appear to exist elsewhere; in Russia, for instance, police are much more likely to stop individuals suspected of being from the Caucasus.

What is at the root of this phenomenon? Racist and brutal police? Yes, in part, and there is wide consensus that such bad cops should be rooted out and prosecuted for their misdeeds. But the overall problem isn't just bad cops. After all, most cops are not bad, while racial inequity in policing is both widespread and persistent. Rather, there are systemic forces that lead even good police to "do the wrong thing." In a sense, this observation is a basis for optimism. There will always be some bad cops, and if their behavior alone led to racial injustice in crime control, then even stepped up campaigns to identify and remove the worst offenders might not help matters much. But the systemic features that lead to racial inequity in policing can be changed in ways that provide some hope for qualitative gains.

Do widespread racial disparities in policing in the US actually exist? With respect to traffic regulations, for instance, are blacks and other minorities stopped by police more frequently, for a given level of violations of the law? Statistics on race, age, sex, and other information from traffic stops are not routinely collected.[11] But information that is available suggests wide racial disparities, in the US as in England. The Maryland State Police, in settling a lawsuit, agreed to collect racial information on traffic stops. "From January 1995 through December 1997, 70 percent of the drivers stopped on Interstate 95 were African Americans, while according to an ACLU [American Civil Liberties Union] survey, only about 17.5 percent of the traffic and speeders on that road were black."[12] Videotapes of stops for drug interdiction in Volusia County, Florida, also on I–95, indicated that blacks comprised 5 percent of the drivers, but 70 percent of those who were stopped.[13] Other statistics suggest that the war on drugs is waged primarily against the non-white segment of the population.[14] According to a report written by David Harris for the ACLU, "Today, blacks constitute 13 percent of the country's drug users; 37 percent of those arrested on drug charges; 55 percent of those convicted; and 74 percent of all drug offenders sentenced to prison."[15]

Racial disparities in policing exist; indeed, it would be surprising if they did not exist, since race is used as one of the indicators in criminal profiling. Are such disparities understandable, the result of scrupulous policing? While young black males are treated with more suspicion by the police, it might be argued that this is natural, because young black males cause a disproportionate amount of trouble, too. When attempting to prevent or solve street crime, police shouldn't devote much time to tailing elderly women (except perhaps as potential victims of crime) – young males are the likely perpetrators. Conscientious, unbiased policing would seem to require that police focus their suspicions on the most probable threats. By this reckoning, young black males should have more frequent and maybe even less pleasant police encounters than does the rest of the population.

As a seeming bolster to the notion that race-based policing is essential, an appeal might be made to the behavior of private citizens, as opposed to the police. When walking alone down the street at night, suddenly you notice some individuals walking towards you. If you perceive them as a threat, you may want to quickly take evasive action, such as crossing the street or returning to some more populated area. But you only have a few seconds in which to make this decision. The sole basis that you have for choosing your route is the small amount of information that you can visually gather, and your prior beliefs about likely and unlikely perpetrators. In a quick glance, you can only learn a few basic facts: the number of individuals, perhaps their size, their sex, their approximate age, their manner of dress, and their behavior. If the strangers are two elderly women, you continue on your way, rightly confident that you are not about to become a crime victim. If they are two young adult males, you might implement your evasion plan. You might be even more likely to take evasive action if they are two black males. You would not be alone in such a reaction. Here is what Rev. Jesse Jackson said back in 1993: "There is nothing more painful for me at this stage in my life than to walk down the street and hear footsteps and start thinking about robbery – then look around and see somebody white and feel relieved."[16]

So private behavior, in making judgments about potential criminality, discriminates on the basis of sex, age, race, and other factors. It seems unavoidable that when better information is not available – and in a chance meeting in the street, only a few characteristics will be observable – group reputations, even if mistaken, play a dominant role in determining private actions.

And group reputations can quite easily be mistaken. Few of us actually know how much more likely it is that we will be victimized by a black man than a white man, if indeed it is more likely – most crime involves victims and perpetrators of the same race. Nor would knowledge of crime statistics necessarily resolve the issue. If the police focus their crime-fighting resources on young black men, they will end up arresting such suspects more often than others, even if there is no sex or race based differential in the actual amount of crime. Group reputations for criminality might then yield the appearance of validity, even when they are actually mistaken.

Nevertheless, young men on average are widely and rightly believed to be more inclined to predatory violence than elderly women, and without better information, many people will respond to this perception. Such private actions based on group reputation by people who are not sexist nor racist cannot simply be condemned as inappropriate. Those who legally employ race as a signal of potential criminality, "like everyone, are caught up in a large tragedy that will require more than individual good will and bravery to resolve."[17]

Should good cops, then, behave as good private citizens often do? Perhaps surprisingly, the answer is: no. Police should, in general, not use race as a basis for deciding whom to watch, or, after a crime has been committed, whom to question or arrest on grounds of suspicion. This conclusion is not driven by some philosophical perspective that places a higher weight on racial equality than on crime control. Just the opposite: it derives solely from a concern with crime. As in many other policy arenas, the best long-term approach to crime control appears counterproductive in the short run.

Effective crime control in a democracy requires voluntary cooperation between the police and the citizenry. Voluntary cooperation requires trust. Race-based policing undermines trust. Reduced trust means lessened deterrence of crime, as minorities become unwilling to report crime – a not insignificant concern, given that approximately one-half of serious crime in the US is not reported to the police.[18] Further, hostility between minorities and the police creates an unwillingness to testify at trials, and, when serving on juries, an unwillingness to convict defendants.[19] This lack of cooperation, brought on by racial disparities in policing, reduces criminal deterrence.[20]

Beyond lowering deterrence, race-based policing also provides positive inducements to disobey the law. As noted earlier, when all young black males are thought to be and treated as criminals, a law-abiding black male cannot easily overcome this perception through his own virtuous behavior. The perception of criminality that is inherent in race-based policing prevents well-behaving minority youths from distinguishing themselves from those who are criminals. Being thought a criminal in any event, the payoff to law-abiding behavior falls.

The central problem is not bad or racist cops in an otherwise workable system. Rather, the problem is the hostility and distrust created among police and minority citizens. This pool of hostility between a group of citizens and the police is not the work of a single cop – especially a single good cop – or based on the activities of a single day. Rather, the pool of hostility is created by long-term, numerous interactions between the police and the citizenry. The activities of any single cop over a short period are essentially irrelevant in determining the size of the hostility "pool": they are literally a drop in the ocean. So when a conscientious police officer is doing his (or her) job, he ignores the effect that his actions have on the sea of hostility, because his actions make no noticeable difference. But the sea of hostility is in fact made up of unpleasant police–citizen encounters in the aggregate, despite the fact that any individual encounter, short of an obviously abusive encounter, is of little or no consequence.

Conscientious policing as described above may not only lead to a general mistrust of the police within a minority community, it also can hold rather severe adverse consequences for specific individuals. Police officers who use race and other suggestive but imperfect indicators unrelated to behavior in profiling potential criminals might "rationally" ignore the fact that the same indicators that lead them to make a stop will also lead other officers to do so, too. Thus their stop is often far from an isolated event for the individual in question, but just one in a continuing series of stops, as the famous "San Diego walker" case demonstrated: Edward Lawson, a black man, had been detained some fifteen times in the space of less than two years, often for walking in the "wrong" neighborhood.[21] Further, police actions to some extent serve as guides for the behavior of citizens. When private citizens see or learn about racial profiling by police, their own attitudes toward and treatment of minorities are likely to be influenced.

Race-based practices also harm police, even beyond the mistrust that such practices engender. While race-based policing makes it hard for law-abiding young minority males to distinguish themselves from law breakers, it simultaneously leads to a parallel stereotyping of police. Race-based policing generates an unfair perception that many or most police officers are at best insensitive to the concerns of minorities or, at worst, racists. So good and honest cops also pay a price from the countenancing of race-base policing, as they become perceived as rough equivalents to those few police whose motivations and acts actually are racist. And just as the pool of distrust undermines deterrence of criminals who needn't as strongly fear the community's wrath, bad cops can take solace from the reduced incentives good cops will have to cooperate with investigations of abuse.[22]

Race-based policing presents a familiar scenario, where rational individual behavior does not serve the social good. National defense, the paradigmatic example of what economists call a "public good," provides an analogy. Whether or not a particular individual pays his or her taxes has essentially no influence upon the amount of government military spending. Nevertheless, the amount spent on national defense depends on the aggregate amount of taxes paid. If tax payments were voluntary, we would expect too little defense to be supplied: people would recognize that their individual contribution would essentially not matter for the amount of defense provided to them, so they might as well not contribute. Unconstrained individual incentives do not serve society's interests with respect to public goods. Taxes, therefore, are not voluntary.

In the case of harmful activities, unlike public goods, the same type of analysis leads to an opposite conclusion. Citizen hostility towards the police is a "public bad," and individual police officers, acting rationally, will create or "supply" too much of it in the aggregate. Unconstrained individual incentives do not serve society's interests with respect to public bads, either, though here the problem is too much of a bad thing, as opposed to too little of a good thing.[23]

The remedy to the distorted individual incentives that characterize race-based policing is the same as with taxes: we must not allow the use of race in policing to be voluntary. For standard street and traffic enforcement, a stringent ban on race-based policing must be adopted.[24] The operational rule of thumb for police officers who are considering stopping or searching a black person (or potentially a Latino or another minority) should be: would I stop or search this person if he or she were white? If the answer is no, then the black person should not be stopped or searched, either, even if, for instance, the neighborhood is predominately white and blacks stopped in the area have been associated with crime in the past. Police "profiles" of drug couriers or other classes of criminals should not include race, even (as is currently done) as one of a panoply of characteristics.

Of course, if a description of a suspect is available, race should then be taken into account in attempting to apprehend the suspect. Even here, however, police must be careful to prevent using a description that includes race to cast too wide a net, or as a pretext for a stop unrelated to the crime for which the description was secured.[25]

Important questions remain about how to enforce a ban on race-based policing, and of course enforcement will not be perfect. But the standard in US federal law (*circa* 2002), which allows the police to use race not in isolation, but as one of several factors that determine their profiling of potential criminals, is likewise hard to enforce. In fact, evasion of the current standard cannot be prevented, as it is a simple matter to fabricate other, non-race-based factors to accompany race as rationales for police stops or searches. Perhaps a ban on race-based policing will also be easily evaded. But over time, if good police sincerely adopt it, the rule can alter the behavior of all officers, and reduce the pool of hostility towards the police that now exists among many black Americans.[26]

Because using racial indicators of potential criminality appears to be a rational approach for individual police officers (as for private citizens), a conscientious police officer who currently engages in raced-based policing is likely to believe that he or she is doing the right thing, something socially desirable. Adoption of formal rules prohibiting race-based policing will at least make it clear that society does not share that judgment. Race-based activity by police, then, can no longer serve as an open source of pride in a job well done, and this too can reduce the extent of race-based policing over time, even if the prohibition is hard to enforce.

Not all disparities in police–citizen encounters will be eliminated when race-based policing is no longer countenanced: policing high crime areas might require more stops than in other neighborhoods, for instance, and minorities are more likely to live in such neighborhoods. But minorities will also be the beneficiaries of this increased scrutiny, which will be more acceptable when it is not part of an explicit or implicit race-based policing strategy.

Outlawing race-based policing may require other changes. Possibly it might mean an increase in the number of police officers required to guard some neighborhoods. It may also mean stopping more citizens in the aggregate, encompassing a broader range than those who are habitually stopped today.[27] This latter measure would spread more widely the costs imposed by policing, and should not be viewed as necessarily a bad thing. It is easy to support certain laws and police practices if you are unlikely to be burdened by them. To those exempt from bearing the costs, almost any crime control policy will look beneficial, no matter how small its value in reducing crime. But will support for the many searches that take place in the name of the war on drugs, for instance, survive a broadening of the citizenry that is subject to such searches? A rule prohibiting race-based policing will not only serve the long-run goal of controlling crime, but will also help to protect, for all citizens, constitutionally guaranteed rights against illegal search and seizure.[28]

One area in which a prohibition on race-based policing might require supplementary measures is in traffic patrolling. The complexity of traffic laws guarantees available pretexts for race-based stops, and as a result differential traffic stops occasioned by race-based policing appear to be widespread.[29] But as traffic stops are more formal than street-to-street encounters, they can be more closely monitored. Videotaping stops (which already occurs in some jurisdictions), and the collection of statistics on the race of stopped drivers (which is now done by law in some states, and voluntarily by other police departments), offer means to ensure that strictures against race-based policing are not ignored.

The formal repudiation of race-based policing can be complemented with a strategy to enforce strict limits on the actions that the state can take in the absence of more compelling evidence of wrongdoing than noisy signals like gender, race, and age. In the drug search example, for instance, the searches can be limited to only a few minutes duration, and restrictions can be placed on the extent of their intrusiveness. Whether race-based policing is countenanced or not, there must be strict ceilings to what actions the state can take in the absence of information more incriminating than "suspicion" or group reputation. Otherwise, outrages such as the US internment of Japanese-Americans during World War II, or the mundane, daily outrages that some members of targeted groups are subjected to by police, will continue to be repeated.

In the long run, there is no trade-off between crime control and race neutral policing: more of one does not mean less of the other. Indeed, just the opposite. But the immediate rejection of race-based policing will not immediately reduce distrust between police and minority communities. The distrust was fostered over many years, and it will take sustained changes in police policy and behavior to reduce the sea of hostility. The time to make the change to race neutral policing, then, is when crime is relatively low. What the police have been doing right has helped to bring about the low crime rates that the US currently enjoys. Advantage should be taken of these low crime rates to change, now, what the police, generally in good faith, have been doing wrong.

6 Corruption

I once briefly borrowed a student's pen, idly commenting that it wrote very well. The next day, the student returned to my office and gave me two similar pens as a gift – "not a bribe," she said. At first I demurred, saying that I couldn't accept the pens, but eventually I acceded to her offer, perhaps not very graciously – and the pens really did write very nicely! Was this a corrupt act on my part? The student was not taking a class with me, but I was shortly to be among those responsible for evaluating her master's thesis, and I recognized at the time that I may have been called upon to write letters of recommendation for her when she applied for jobs.

Corruption is a form of rule evasion, and one that is frequently engendered by the potential to evade other rules. As a form of evasion, corruption shares many of the features associated with rule circumvention that have been noted in the previous chapters, including: the potential for corruption to be socially beneficial; the trade-offs associated with zero tolerance policies; the difficulty of drawing bright lines between corrupt and non-corrupt behavior; and treadmills of reform in response to corruption and their tendency to result in a complex system of rules. This chapter will highlight some of these similarities, as well as some of the differences, between corruption and other forms of rule evasion.

Defining corruption

> Corruption . . . 6. Perversion of integrity by bribery or favour . . . 7.
> The perversion of anything from an original state of purity.
> (Oxford Universal Dictionary, 1955)

Corruption involves evasion or avoidance of the rules or norms that govern how an office holder is expected to behave: "the misuse of office for private ends," in the words of economist Robert Klitgaard.[1] Corruption is not only evasive in itself, it can foster the evasion of other rules, as when bribery is used to purchase immunity from punishment for illegal activity. And like other forms of evasion, the evasion represented by corruption, as well as the further evasion that corruption promotes, needn't always be socially detrimental.

Corruption is usually associated with public office, but private office holders can behave corruptly, too. Occasionally corruption scandals are revealed within private organizations, as when automobile dealers bribe suppliers to receive shipments of fashionable cars that are in short supply, or when sellers collude with buyers in conducting their transactions underground to avoid sales taxes, or when professors accept pens from students! Private sector corruption cases have been the majority of the caseload in recent years for Hong Kong's exemplary corruption prevention and investigation commission, the Independent Commission Against Corruption.[2]

Given that corruption involves a misuse of office, identifying corrupt activity requires a delineation between legitimate and illegitimate uses of an office. While there are some uses of an office that are clearly legitimate, and others that are clearly illegitimate, there can also be a substantial gray area of questionable but not obviously corrupt activity: as with drawing distinctions via rules more generally, it is hard to establish a bright line distinguishing between proper and improper use of an office. When does the acceptance of a small gift become a corrupt act? Different people may judge a potentially corrupt endeavor against different and possibly contradictory standards: there are legal notions of legitimate uses of offices, but there are also ethical notions, as well as norms associated with ordinary practices.[3] (One reason why corruption appears to be widespread within countries undergoing fundamental changes is that in such places new norms are being adopted, and they can conflict with traditional practices.[4]) The legal standard of legitimate use of an office need not be any more precise than the others, particularly because the unobservable element of intent can play a role in determining whether or not an act is illegal.

It is easy to extend too far, however, the claims of uncertainty as to what constitutes a corrupt act. Gray areas are perhaps gray mainly to outsiders, or to those who require legal proof that a corrupt act has taken place. The parties involved probably know whether or not they are behaving corruptly, and one signal of this knowledge is the pains that they often take to conceal their questionable activities. Nuanced distinctions can be widely shared. In communist countries, for example, trading on personal connections was an integral part of day-to-day existence for many people. People in these societies often had a very sure sense of which dealings were legitimate – even if distasteful, illegal, or even immoral – and which were illegitimate, though to an outsider the distinctions would be hard to draw or even to understand.[5]

In both the private and the public sphere, the legal definition of corruption can be changed. Sometimes the definition is altered to formalize and legitimate previously corrupt or questionable behavior. In the US, corrupt corporate political contributions are no longer a major problem, because corporate Political Action Committees (PACs) have been permitted to openly make limited campaign contributions.[6] In other circumstances, previously legitimate (though questionable) behavior has been explicitly forbidden. Undisclosed gifts or payments ("payola") from record companies to disc jockeys in exchange for radio air-time, for instance, was made illegal in the 1960s in the US, though payola had been a standard music industry practice.[7] Another arena in which US law has been expanded to control questionable but once legal activity concerns "revolving doors." Employees of regulatory agencies, upon leaving their jobs, not infrequently took up employment with the firms they previously had been charged with regulating. Similarly, some former US Representatives lobbied their erstwhile Congressional colleagues on behalf of business clients. In both of these cases, the new employment could be a payoff for favorable treatment by the employee in his or her previous job. The potential for future jobs to compromise the integrity of employees in their current positions, therefore, has been countered by the adoption of waiting periods. Prior to the expiration of the waiting period, the ex-employee cannot legally switch to certain proscribed forms of new employment.

Though both a broadening or a tightening of controls can be a response to perceived corruption, the overall global trend seems to be towards a stricter view of what uses of a public office are deemed legitimate. According to researchers Frank Anechiarico and James B. Jacobs, authorities on corruption control in the US "have radically expanded the definition of corruption to include the appearance of conflict of interest, failure to disclose financial interests, misstatements on job applications, unauthorized use of government telephones, leaving work early, accepting favors and gifts, and entering into public contracts with morally tainted private companies."[8] In any event, not all of the existing legal distinctions are easy to understand: undisclosed music industry payola to disc jockeys to air certain songs is illegal, but payments by recording companies to music stores to feature prominently certain releases remain legally permissible.

Measuring corruption

As with other types of illegal or informal activity, corruption is not amenable to precise measurement. While newspapers are often filled with stories related to corruption, it cannot be taken for granted that an increase in the amount of corruption that is revealed implies an increase in the amount of corruption that actually exists. Nevertheless, there are methods to gauge the extent of corruption over time and in various locations. One popular approach is to survey individuals engaged in international business transactions, asking them to rate countries on the extent of corruption. The collected responses are then aggregated into an index of corruption. I am typing these words in Moscow, capital of a country that has performed poorly in such ratings in recent years, and where some forms of corruption are so evident and mundane that they are not particularly newsworthy.

While such forms of measurement are not likely to offer a reliable guide to the absolute amount of corrupt behavior in a society, they do offer a route to comparing the extent of some forms of corruption across countries. Even for this limited purpose, however, indices derived from "expert" opinions are rather crude. The experts may base their opinions on reputations for corruption, which need not be reliable or could reflect previous, though not current, conditions. Or business people might extrapolate from those few cases with which they have first-hand knowledge, or let their knowledge about the overall economic or political conditions color their specific assessment of corruption. Different people might hold different notions of what constitutes a corrupt act; were there complete agreement on the definition of corruption, there would still be the problem of offering an overall assessment given that corruption comes in many forms. Some types of corruption might be more prevalent in one country than in another country, while for other types of corruption, the situation could be reversed. Even within a country, some governmental departments might meet the highest legal and ethical standards, while others are fantastically corrupt. And even within a department, not all types of corruption need be equally prevalent. Consider the types of corruption once identified as existing within the Philippines' tax collection agency, the Bureau of Internal Revenue (BIR):[9] (1) speed money (payments to expedite activity); (2) extortion; (3) collusion to reduce taxes; (4) embezzlement; (5) fraud; (6) delaying remittances; (7) personnel scams; and (8) undermining internal investigations. Human ingenuity is no less prolific in dreaming up corrupt activities than it is in devising other forms of evasion and avoidance.

Principals–agents–clients[10]

There are three actors who are relevant players in most potentially corrupt settings: (1) the central or higher level authorities or government, or more generally, the "principal"; (2) the bureaucrat (the "agent") who implements the policies of the center; and (3) some "client" who interacts with the agent. One common example of this trichotomy involves the federal government (principal), the tax service or some individual tax auditor (agent), and a taxpayer (client). In the "pen" example, the school authorities are the principal (the principal is the principal?), while the teacher (yours truly) is the agent, and the student is the client. Typical cases of corruption involve the agent illegitimately electing not to deal even-handedly with all clients. Such unequal treatment has itself been offered as a definition of corruption: "intentional non-compliance with the arm's length principle aimed at deriving some advantage for oneself or for related individuals from this behavior."[11] The Weberian view of a fully developed bureaucracy, alternatively, is where jurisdictional areas are ordered by rational rules, where there is "a discharge of business according to *calculable rules* and 'without regard for persons.'"[12]

Notice that many of the forms of corruption that existed in the Philippines' BIR represent violations of the arm's length principle in the dealings between tax inspectors and taxpayers. Personnel scams and the undermining of internal investigations do not have a direct connection to taxpayers; these types of corrupt activity involve a different application of the principal–agent–client framework, where both the agent and the client are officials within the agency. But these forms of corruption themselves are largely the result of the opportunities for tax auditors to make corrupt earnings in their encounters with taxpayers: except for embezzlement or other misappropriation of funds, which an official might engage in unrelated to any connections with a client, most common forms of corruption have a ready interpretation within the principal–agent–client framework.

When is corruption likely?

What determines the overall extent of corruption in a society? Compliance with rules in general is determined by many factors, of course, some of them broad cultural considerations: Germany, for instance, is claimed to be a relatively rule-abiding society. As for factors that are specific to corruption, Robert Klitgaard has put forth the following heuristic equation: Corruption = Monopoly + Discretion – Accountability.[13] The notion is as follows. If there are many potential suppliers of some license or permission sought by a client, any individual agent will have little scope for seeking a bribe, as the client faced with such a demand could go somewhere else. Hence, the greater the "monopoly power" of an agent, the more likely that corruption will be present. Similarly, the more scope an agent has, within his or her official duties, to help or harm clients, the more likely that this discretion will be "sold" through a corrupt transaction. And a lack of accountability to higher authorities or the public (the principal) shields officials from negative consequences as a result of corrupt behavior. Further, the worse the rules or the greater the number of impediments to private activity – providing monopoly power and discretion to agents – the greater the demand to evade the rules by corrupt means. One reason that there appears to be substantial corruption in developing and post-socialist countries is that in these societies, the rules applied to regulated clients, and perhaps even the internal rules governing the behavior of officials, are themselves generally less conducive to promoting overall societal welfare than are the rules in other settings.

In praise of corruption

> "I suppose you gentlemen of the Navy are wholly opposed to corruption," observed Raffles.
>
> "Corruption, sir?" cried Jack, "I love the word. Ever since my very first command I have corrupted any dockyard or ordnance or victualling board officer who had the shadowiest claim to a traditional present and who could help get my ship to sea a little quicker and in slightly better fighting-trim. . . . I believe it paid hands down, for the service, for my ship's company and for me. If I only knew the ropes here, or if I had my purser or clerk, both experts in the matter at a lower level, I should do the same in Batavia, saving your respect, sir, and do it on a far larger scale, being far better provided now than I was then."
>
> (Patrick O'Brian,
> *The Nutmeg of Consolation*[14])

One of the definitions of corruption quoted previously associates corruption with perversion from "an original state of purity," as in the usual rendering into English of a charge against Socrates, that of "corrupting" the youth of Athens.[15] The desirability of corruption depends on whether the relevant alternative is indeed a state of purity, or rather something less hallowed. The general rule of evasion applies to corruption; namely, the worse the laws or their implementation, the more valuable corruption is likely to be.

Consider those types of corruption that pave the way for rule evasion by clients. Note first that in a direct sense, as long as they voluntarily choose the path of corruption instead of following the rules, both the agent and the client must believe themselves to be better off from their corrupt activity. Third parties, potentially including the principal, also could benefit from the corrupt trans-action: e.g. the corruption might license a business that generates benefits for consumers, or provides jobs better than those the workers could have acquired in the absence of the corruption. Of course, it is also possible that third parties will be harmed by a corrupt transaction, as when bribery allows environmental degradation to take place by inducing non-enforcement of regulatory controls. In overall terms, whether corruption that promotes rule evasion is beneficial or not depends on whether the rules that are being evaded are generally inappropriate barriers to economic activity, or efficient regulations required to internalize the social costs of self-interested behavior.[16]

In other words, the potential social benefits of rule breaking by means of corruption are similar to those of evasion more generally. At the risk of needless repetition, we can briefly characterize the sources of such benefits, here, and in Table 6.1: corruption allows flexibility in rules; because rules are sometimes mis-guided and always incomplete, such flexibility can be desirable. Good rules can be made more responsive to individual circumstances via corruption, while bad rules can be circumvented entirely. In the case of rules that are written and otherwise enforced in an even-handed way, violations of the arm's length principle can add discriminations, and perhaps in an efficient manner. For example, informal softening of some taxes through corrupt means may allow valuable, but relatively marginal, small-scale economic activity to take place, when complete taxation would result in its socially unfortunate demise.[17] Or, speed money can give officials the incentive to allocate their time to what really are the most pressing tasks. Alternatively, if the rules are not written or enforced in an even-handed way, corruption may be a means for socially-discriminated-against groups to buy "equal" access to government goods and services. In the case of bribes paid to officials to avoid fines for wrongdoing, the malfeasor might be indifferent between a bribe and the same size fine, while from a social viewpoint, the bribe might be less expensive, if it avoids a costly trial or the use of other administrative machinery.[18] Bribe income might cause agents to value their jobs more highly, making it easier for principals to induce agents to perform well. And as with other forms of evasion, visible corruption has some chance of bringing bad rules to the attention of policy makers, who can then improve the rules – though the corruption itself may limit their incentive to do so.

Table 6.1 Some potential consequences of corruption

Positive features	Negative features
Allows (even good) rules to be more responsive to individual circumstances: increases flexibility.	Increases horizontal and vertical inequality (undermines fairness, morality).
Provides exemptions to regulations, taxes, possibly in an efficient manner.	Selects against honest people, foreign firms, small firms, and new firms.
Allows bad rules to be circumvented.	Allows breaking of rules even when it is not efficient; increases incentives to commit violent crime, or to pollute, for example.
Provides incentives to officials to work hard, and increases the control of principals over the behavior of agents.	Undermines economic statistics.
Lowers administrative and other costs; for example, a bribe might be socially less costly than the same size fine.	Serves as an inferior substitute for efficient reforms.
If visible, the corruption provides information about the quality of laws, and promotes efficient reforms.	Engenders costly efforts to control corruption.
Increases access to the government for some socially marginalized groups.	Encourages government officials to set up and maintain inefficient roadblocks to secure bribes.
	Creates uncertainty as to what the rules really are; engenders instability in the effective legal environment.
	Breeds cynicism, and undermines the establishment of the rule of law.
	Reduces tax revenues, potentially leading to increased rates on those who pay, or to higher inflation.
	Drives businesses underground through the need for unrecorded income to pay bribes.
	Diminishes incentives to reduce costs, innovate, etc., as connections become more important than efficiency for business success.

Not all corruption is aimed at the evasion of other rules; there is also corruption in the sense of misused discretion, violation of the arm's length principle. From a legal standpoint, patronage or nepotism may not be corrupt, even if in some cultures they are ethically suspect. If the president has the right to nominate whomever he pleases for attorney general, he could nominate his brother, despite there being candidates more highly qualified on some objective grounds. In situations with a good deal of discretion, violations of the arm's length principle might be impossible to verify – even for those who are engaged in the violation!

How can a judge be sure that he or she is not favoring or disfavoring a friend who appears before the bench? In situations in which adherence to the arm's length principle is viewed as particularly important, auxiliary rules can be introduced to protect against its violation: judges might be required to recuse themselves from cases involving personal friends, eliminating the appearance of impropriety, or universities might adopt a rule barring two members of the same family from teaching in the same department, as a crude but effective way to ensure that family status does not play a role in faculty hirings.[19]

Surely some patronage and nepotism is socially desirable. Consider an example from the history of the British navy. An important component in rising through the ranks in the eighteenth century was an officer's "interest," the connections and pull he had with politically influential people. To attract qualified sub-ordinates and to maintain order on board, an officer needed to demonstrate that he could deliver benefits to his followers. As a result of insufficient connections, some able officers were left behind, while mediocre but better-connected officers might be promoted instead. This sounds like the making for potentially very costly corruption, but one modern scholar of the British navy summarized the system *circa* 1760 as follows:

> So the patronage system was not perfect; to work at its best it needed patrons of the right temperament, and it needed a strong lead in the right direction. But it is difficult to see what other system was possible in the eighteenth century, and far from clear that any method since devised has identified and promoted merit any more efficiently.[20]

With respect to the definition of corruption as "the misuse of public office for private ends," such forms of nepotism need not represent a misuse, nor, in the aggregate, need they serve only private ends. Allowing an official some leeway to bestow favors as he or she pleases can improve the morale and performance of the official, and provide the possibility that the benefits themselves will be distributed in a manner that reflects localized information, unavailable to the principal. In the long run, more able people will be attracted into a profession that has some scope for discretionary distribution of benefits. The value of such nepotism in part explains its pervasiveness, even in areas where it might be considered potentially damaging: star faculty members, for example, are often recruited by bestowing upon them the "right" to fill other faculty positions, in the sense that their recom-mended candidates for those posts will be nearly assured of being offered a job. Private businesses often view nepotism – for instance, hiring friends and relatives of existing employees – as a sound business practice, helping to ensure employee loyalty, morale, and exertion. There is little or no empirical evidence suggesting that civil service employment produces better results than political appointments in government agencies.[21]

Challengers to the political leadership in corrupt societies often adopt an anti-corruption message in their campaigns, and perhaps make some highly publicized revelations and at least superficial changes when they come to power. But not infrequently, widespread corruption soon returns, suggesting that the initial opposition was not so much with the system of corruption, but with the incumbent beneficiaries, or that there is an inherent compulsion towards corruption. Indeed, at some level, nepotism is quite natural: why should office holders treat their friends and relatives in an arm's length manner?[22] Unequal treatment can have a significant constituency, so much so that Max Weber emphasized the tension between a rule-oriented bureaucracy and a democracy consisting of individuals who favor personal considerations in decision making.[23] According to the famed American journalist Walter Lippmann, "an entirely objective view of political life at its base where political organization is in direct contact with the population, would show that corruption in some form is endemic." Lippmann suggested that "organizations like Tammany, which bind together masses of people in a complex of favors and coercions, are the ancient form of human association. They might be called natural governments."[24] But this is not to say that all corruption should be welcomed, or even tolerated.

Costs of corruption

"You were in jail?"
"Only for a few days. Bribery"
"Bribery? Who did you bribe?"
"No, the problem was I hadn't bribed anyone. They were very upset."
(Tibor Fischer, Under the Frog[25])

Despite some benign and even popular aspects, "corruption" generally carries a negative connotation. This connotation in part may derive from the fact that while the ends may be desirable – such as the avoidance of useless regulations – corrupt means are not viewed as a legitimate path to secure those ends. When seeking their own benefits through corrupt activities, individuals prefer to use euphemisms, such as "greasing the wheels" or Captain Aubrey's "traditional present," to downplay the sordid aspects of such behavior.

The general distaste for corruption is also fueled by the fact that often the ends that it serves are not so benign. The positive aspects of corruption outlined above all have negative counterparts, in keeping with evasive behavior generally. Increased rule flexibility is more likely to be bad, if it is good rules that are being made more flexible through corrupt means. If the rules are evenhanded in theory and in legitimate implementation, corruption will add elements of unfairness, and there is some evidence that it increases income inequality.[26] The incentives to work hard provided by the potential to receive bribes can generate an incentive to purposely slow things down, in order to extort a bribe. Providing favored treatment to those who pay a bribe might require less-than-fair treatment for others, so that an official's behavior in the aggregate does not make plain the existence of bribery.

Rather than creating a dynamic that leads to improved rules, corruption can motivate law makers to adopt and maintain inefficient rules, precisely to increase the opportunities for corrupt earnings; government investments, for instance, might be channeled into large-scale but socially wasteful construction projects from which kickbacks can be obtained, as opposed to potentially more valuable but less corruption-prone areas such as primary education.[27] Individuals might skew their choice of occupation in a socially detrimental way, basing their decision on the possibility of corrupt earnings, or alternatively on the avoidance of victimization by corrupt officials. Corruption, like other types of evasion, can serve as an imperfect substitute for, and therefore delay, a beneficial formal reform.[28]

The illegality of corruption and the acts made possible through corrupt means can undermine respect for rules more generally, particularly among those charged with enforcing the rules. Police or tax officials who flout the law by coming to voluntary agreements with some "clients" – perhaps, following Lippmann, in a "natural" way – might then find it easier to coerce other clients who have no autonomous interest in corruption: the toleration of bribery can lead to a problem of extortion. The familiar difficulty is that of drawing and enforcing bright lines: it is hard to permit the good kind of corruption, while simultaneously forbidding the bad kind, even if you could establish a clear distinction between the two types. Further, in a system where corruption is widespread, nearly everyone is behaving illegally in his or her dealings with government bureaucracies. As a result, everyone is vulnerable to selective (or arbitrary) enforcement, and insecurity will be as widespread as corruption.

While visible corruption might prove informative to policy makers about the quality of their rules and enforcement regimes, the informal rules established by corruption would seem to generate more uncertainty than a system of adherence to the formal rules.[29] How can a person develop rational plans if the rules are unclear? Even where the existence of extensive corruption is commonly known, the corruption itself is not particularly visible. Corrupt acts are hidden almost of necessity, and it is difficult, as the fictional Captain Aubrey discovered in Batavia (now Jakarta), for an outsider without connections to operate in a corrupt system. The reliability of economic statistics can also suffer from corruption, as with other forms of evasion. What is the actual, as opposed to the legislated tax rate, if businesses must pay bribes to various government officials, or if bribery of tax inspectors paves the way for widespread tax evasion? And generally the payment of bribes cannot be officially recorded in a business's accounts; the business will then need a source of unrecorded income, and is more likely to operate in the underground economy when large bribe payments are required, further distorting standard measures of economic activity.

Cascading

The toleration of low levels of beneficial or relatively unobjectionable corruption can promote more corruption that is less benign. Beyond the inability to enforce bright-line distinctions between good and bad corruption, other sources of positive feedback in corruption exist. If some firms are prospering through corrupt means, their competitors will be pressured to secure the same advantages for themselves. (In the end, then, all could pay bribes, without any of the firms receiving a net advantage.[30]) If a bureaucrat sees that all of his or her colleagues are accepting bribes, he or she will be more likely to take a bribe. Indeed, if the corruption is sufficiently institutionalized, it might be necessary for the bureaucrat to take bribes, in order to meet the informal – but no less real – requirement to pass some of the corrupt earnings up the chain of command, and official salaries will tend to be low in recognition of the opportunities for illicit earnings.[31] Over time, non-corrupt individuals will find that they have a comparative disadvantage in this line of work, and as they seek cleaner pastures, corruption will become even more the norm within the original bureaucracy.

Because corruption, like other forms of rule evasion, tends to be hidden, individuals will generally have poor information over the actual extent of various types of corruption. Still, they will have subjective perceptions or beliefs about the extent of corruption, and these perceptions can influence reality. Potential "demanders" of corruption, such as individuals apprehended by the police for minor crimes, are more likely to offer bribes if they believe that bribery is common. "Supply creates its own demand," a classical economic dictum known as Say's Law, has largely been discredited in modern macroeconomic theory.[32] Nevertheless, a variant of Say's Law would seem to apply to corruption: the perception of supply creates its own demand.[33] A familiar illustration is stories of individuals traveling abroad who are quick to offer bribes to foreign police – though the same individuals might never consider attempting to bribe a police officer in their native country – solely on reputations for police corruption. And as noted above, potential "suppliers" are more likely to become corrupt if they believe that it is the social norm, and that all of their colleagues are corrupt: the perception of supply creates its own supply, too.[34] As with other forms of evasion, the perception of an increase in corruption can be self-fulfilling.

Corruption and growth

A common concern is that the negative features associated with public sector corruption will undermine economic growth: certainly many developing countries appear to be more corrupt than richer countries, and more systematic empirical evidence points to a negative relationship between corruption and growth.[35] But the official rules and their implementation also tend to be worse for fostering growth in developing than in developed countries, suggesting a comparative advantage to a corrupt ordering in those settings. As the political scientist Samuel Huntington once suggested, "In terms of economic growth, the only thing worse than a society with a rigid, overcentralized, dishonest bureaucracy is one with a rigid, overcentralized, honest bureaucracy."[36] With so many other social and governmental problems in developing countries, it is hard to isolate the role that corruption plays in influencing economic growth. And there are some countries that appear to be rife with corruption, including China and South Korea, that at the same time have recorded sustained periods of phenomenal economic progress.

Nevertheless, it is likely that on average, and in the long run, high levels of public sector corruption retard economic growth, relative to a low-corruption setting. Why? One reason is that corruption may exact political costs, generally hindering the functioning of government. Huntington, who suggested that there is a relative disadvantage to a non-corrupt but rigid bureaucracy, also noted that the virtues of corruption were confined to small-scale instances.

> A society which is relatively uncorrupt – a traditional society for instance where traditional norms are still powerful – may find a certain amount of corruption a welcome lubricant easing the path to modernization. A developed traditional society may be improved – or at least modernized – by a little corruption; a society in which corruption is already pervasive, however, is unlikely to be improved by more corruption.[37]

Widespread corruption tends to undermine governmental responsiveness to the overall preferences and welfare of its citizens.[38] (This tendency is predicated on the assumption that in the absence of corruption, the government would be reasonably attuned to the welfare of its citizens. If the government is not so attuned, then corruption may be the means whereby citizen preferences get taken into account by government officials.) Officials will see their own rewards as being tied to the possibilities for corrupt earnings; instead of being responsive to broad societal welfare, then, government officials are likely to acknowledge only the narrow interests that reward them most directly. From the point of view of corrupt officials, a system of widespread corruption generated by inappropriate rules will appear to be a very satisfactory substitute for a formal reform that would serve society better, but reduce or eliminate corrupt earnings. Huntington's "honest bureaucracy" might be worse in the short term, but will generate pressures to change in the long run that will be attenuated in a corrupt bureaucracy, since those best placed to make the requisite changes – the corrupt bureaucrats – are among the major beneficiaries of a corrupt *status quo*. Tolerating widespread corruption in an otherwise woefully inefficient bureaucracy presents another variety of the dilemma of expediency: there is a tension between what appears to be effective and reasonable behavior in the short run and desirable long-run outcomes.

Corruption and organization

For a given level of corruption, the extent to which the system of corruption is organized and stable is an important determinant of its overall social effects.[39] The generalization here is that the greater the organization/stability, the lower the short-run social costs. Corruption in stable, single party political machines is often extensive, but not necessarily all that bad. In stable settings, one can be certain of what office holders require payments, and those officials will be coordinated so as not to charge "too much." (Indeed, strict penalties might be brought to bear on bureaucrats who are either too corrupt or insufficiently corrupt.) Organization provides information and predictability. Recall Captain Aubrey's difficulty in getting his ship repaired in a place he did not know well. A more organized system of corruption would have allowed him to learn the requisite information – whom to pay, and how much – relatively quickly, and also provided more assurance that the corrupt payments would actually result in expediting the work. A stable setting allows trust to develop, so that bribe payers can be relatively certain that they will get what they pay for, and not be subject to extortion down the road. The organization of corruption is akin to the formalization of red light running in Bogota: not a first-best situation of good rules honestly enforced, but a situation markedly preferable, in the short run, to the alternative of bad rules and disorganized corruption.

Further, the types of activity that are associated with organized corruption tend to be less socially costly than those that are associated with random corrupt acts. Lawrence Sherman, in a study of US police forces in the 1970s, looked at many of the trade-offs presented by various forms of corruption and anti-corruption policies:

> Consider the types of corruption that are defined as more or less organized. The more organized types of corruption include protection of prostitution, gambling, and violations of the liquor laws. The less organized types of corruption include burglary committed by the police officers, police thefts from arrested persons, and the 'fixing' of crimes as serious as murder. The types of corruption committed by lone police officers may often be more serious than those types committed by several police officers in cooperation. While it may be a more serious general community problem to have the law put up for sale than to have individual police officers committing crimes, the specific crimes policemen initiate are usually more serious than the crimes they are paid to ignore.[40]

Organized corruption, then, is likely to be preferable in the short run to the alternative of disorganized corruption. But just as widespread corruption undermines the responsiveness of government and hence the incentive to reform the rules that are being evaded through corrupt means, the organization of corruption undermines the impetus to implement serious anti-corruption measures. This barrier to reform is due in part to the lower social costs entailed by the organization of corruption, and in part to the strengthening of those interest groups that benefit from the corrupt system. While better in the short term than the alternative of disorganized corruption, organized corruption decreases the potential to move to an even more preferred alternative. The tolerable is the enemy of the good.

Corruption scandals do break out, of course, and they can lead to attempted reform of the corrupt agency. Scandal can overcome the usual bureaucratic inertia by undermining the *status quo*: "a bureaucratic system will resist change as long as it can; it will move only when serious dysfunctions develop and no other alternatives remain."[41] Scandal provides the perception that there will be significant efficiency gains from reforming the corrupt department.

A corruption scandal in an agency will typically be met with new restrictions, attempts to increase accountability or to decrease discretion. Whether there will be any long-lasting effects is less certain. According to Sherman's analysis of police scandals, the size of the scandal is critical: small scandals, those that do not define the entire agency as corrupt, are less likely to leave a long-term impact than are large scandals, which can precipitate major and effective changes.[42] But even multiple significant scandals and the host of new rules that they generate do not guarantee that certain types of governmental activities are less corrupt today than they were one hundred years ago:

> scandal may lead the media and the public to conclude that corruption is rampant. When time passes without scandal, the media and public may conclude that corruption is under control. . . . But such inferential reasoning is unsatisfactory. The occurrence or absence of scandal tells us little. The rate of corruption may be constant, and the appetite of the media and the public for corruption scandals may oscillate.[43]

Comparative dynamics of evasion and corruption

When the political economy of reform was discussed in Chapter 2, it was argued that wide-scale evasion can promote desirable policy reform, while small-scale evasion often serves as a substitute for formal changes in the rules. It has here been suggested, however, that both small-scale and widespread corruption tend to serve as a substitute for reform. But if widespread evasion leads to reform, and if widespread corruption can be a means by which widespread evasion is allowed to persist, shouldn't widespread corruption promote reform, too? Why should there be a distinction between the effects of widespread evasion and widespread corruption?

One reason why significant levels of corruption and evasion tend to have different propensities to lead to policy reform has already been mentioned: the responsiveness of government. The example of the building and razing of the Berlin Wall indicated that the extent to which large-scale evasion prompts improved policies – as opposed to simply changed policies – depends on the mindfulness of the government to the preferences of citizens. As widespread corruption directly undermines the responsiveness of government to overall societal welfare, this force for efficiency is diluted or destroyed.

Widespread evasion of rules often presents a rather obvious policy reform that can improve matters: namely, legitimizing (or perhaps regulating differently) the evasive activity. Such was the case of the red light running in Colombia. A given regulation governing private economic activity generally doesn't strike at the heart of a socio-economic system. If the regulation is widely evaded, then, legitimizing the evasion by rescinding the regulation has an opportunity to make most people better off – even if it is not the best of all possible policies – without threatening the fundamental integrity of the system. Legal recognition of widespread corruption, however, is neither so obviously available nor so likely to offer an improvement. Consider, for instance, a corrupt political system with pervasive vote buying and kickbacks. To legitimize current practice by legalizing vote buying might make the vote buying easier to implement, but it also represents a surrender of any pretense of normal democracy. Further, the liberalization that might be appropriate under widespread corruption is not of the corrupt activity itself – the acceptance of bribes by government officials, say – but rather of the rules that require governmental approval of private activity, such as export licensing. That is, widespread evasion of a rule often presents a direct remedy in the form of liberalization or reformation of the rule, while such an approach is but an indirect remedy for widespread corruption, as it is not the corruption itself but rather those rules that provide the opportunity and incentive for corrupt behavior that may be in need of reform.

Nevertheless, governments may implicitly condone widespread corruption as a byproduct of tolerating evasion, and they might tolerate the evasion as a way of learning about the effects of potential reforms. The Chinese decollectivization of agriculture in the late 1970s, as noted in Chapter 2, took place in defiance of central government regulations. In this case, the bribery and corruption that paved the way for the informal marketization of agriculture eventually set the stage for the official endorsement of decollectivization.[44]

Corruption in business

Recall the gift of two pens that I mentioned at the beginning of this chapter. Was it corrupt of me to accept the pens? In my defense, let me mention that it was unusual: in the past I have generally refused equally guileless offerings. With hindsight, I believe that there were two main factors that contributed to my accepting the pens: the absence of one or both of these factors would have made it much more likely that I would have been steadfast in my refusal. First, the bestowal of pens took place in Moscow, and I believe (wrongly?) that the refusal to accept would be more likely to be considered rude in Russia, than the acceptance would be considered corrupt – there are cultural differences in definitions of corruption. Second, the gift giver was a graduate student, and at least in my experience relationships with graduate students are less restrained by formalities than those with undergraduates. Had the student who proffered the pens been an undergraduate in the US, I would have refused, or at least so I tell myself – and I suspect she would have been less likely to make the offer in the first place.

The acceptable level of potentially corrupt behavior is not merely an academic question, of course. Private firms must make these determinations as well: in fact, one of the differences between private firms and governments is that private firms really do have a choice as to how much corruption to tacitly permit, whereas democratic governments are under some pressure to root out any corruption that comes to light.[45] A former student who became a manager at a lending institution once told me (no bribes involved) that in his office, the official policy was that any employee caught making personal long-distance telephone calls at work would be fired. Nevertheless, he sometimes rewarded exceptional performance with implicit tolerance of such phone calls, and viewed this as helpful to the organization. In terms of the "misuse of office for private ends," his behavior was not corrupt, for though it was indeed a misuse of office according to the firm's rules, it was not motivated by the potential for direct private gain.

Consider a similar story, related by sociologist Melville Dalton.[46] A manager of a soda fountain in a chain drug store consistently had far higher profits than managers of fountains at other, nearly identical stores in the chain. She achieved these extraordinary profits perfectly honestly, and through her own diligence. It might be thought, therefore, that she was more handsomely rewarded than her colleagues, conceivably received a promotion, or was moved to other stores to improve their performance. Such a notion is partially correct. Since her contract involved some profit-sharing (once a certain level of profits was attained), the manager in question did receive more monetary compensation than other managers. Simultaneously, however, her situation was made so difficult, partly by innuendoes of cheating, that she resigned her position within two years.

The reason for the woman's extraordinary profit performance was that she was "too honest." She did not give free food and drink to other store employees, herself, or to friends, a practice that was common and expected throughout the chain. This lack of corruption was also the reason for her undoing, as these informal perks smoothed the overall functioning of the drug store. Dalton explains her manager's view:

> The store manager regarded her as a failure because she did not understand what he could not tell her – that her margin of profits was too high and that some social use of materials, not theft, was expected. In his mind, she was too little concerned with the system's internal harmony, and too devoted to formalities.[47]

Again, the gratuitous distributions of food in the other stores were not necessarily corrupt, to the extent that they served the firm's interest. Why were the formal rules not amended to permit some explicit scope for such food distributions? The roadblock to codifying "some social use of materials," presumably, was that such exceptions could not easily be written and enforced in a sufficiently discriminating and bright-line manner.[48] Simply handing $5 or $10 worth of food each week to every employee would not serve the firm's interests – the food must be distributed in a way that provides appropriate incentives, and is widely perceived as fair. Distributions to employees who worked particularly long or hard, or who took on an unpleasant task, or who had experienced a difficult personal event, might raise morale and make the firm, as well as the workers, better off. But an attempt to codify such discriminating rules would probably fail to create sufficiently bright lines. As a result, the formalization of some beneficial corruption would present too many opportunities for detrimental corruption. The actual rules at the drug stores, therefore, remained at odds with the written rules, but those charged with enforcement could not openly say so: "she did not understand what he could not tell her."

Eerily similar to the Dalton account is a story emanating from the former Soviet Union, indicating that corruption in business is not solely a byproduct of exploitative capitalism.[49] During one of the periodic anti-corruption campaigns, a particularly corrupt (or at least high-profile) Moscow food store – creatively named Food Store Number Five – was given a new manager to clean things up. The new manager was chosen for the post because of his deserved reputation for personal integrity. In his new job, however, this decent man's refusal to engage in any illegal or outside-the-plan activity meant that within a very short period of time his shop was no longer adequately supplied. He was faced with the dilemma of having to choose between either running his store effectively, or not engaging in corrupt transactions: he could not do both in Soviet circumstances. His resolution of the crisis was to tacitly permit his assistant to engage in all the wheeling-and-dealing needed to receive supplies, while remaining above-the-fray himself.

Rule complexity

It was noted in Chapter 4 that rule complexity within government bureaucracies is often criticized for resulting both in poor decisions and in high cost. The adoption of complex rules in public organizations can be driven by fear of corruption, by concern over violations of the arm's length principle. Someone who feels that he is badly treated within a private bureaucracy often can rather easily "exit" (in Hirschman's terminology), by taking his labor or custom elsewhere. And if the firm feels that permitting the possibility of unequal treatment is important for other purposes, it will tolerate some "corruption," as noted above. But in dealings with government bureaucracies, the exit option is less available; not surprisingly, then, "voice" plays a larger role for those who have a grievance with the government. Nor does the government have the same latitude to tolerate corruption as do private businesses. The government can hardly tell an aggrieved client, unable to secure a government service without a bribe, that perhaps he was treated unfairly, but that a few such individual injustices are the cost of getting the system as a whole to work well. Rather, the government is quite naturally under pressure to adopt what amounts to a zero tolerance policy towards visible corruption. The response by the government to an incident of revealed corruption, then, is likely to include new rules that are meant to further limit discretion and encourage equality of treatment.[50]

Added to this pressure from clients to generate more rules is the internal dynamics of government bureaucracies themselves. Government agencies are often charged with handling difficult social problems such as crime or drug abuse that they perhaps can ameliorate, but certainly cannot solve. A bureaucracy faced with an unrealizable objective will tend to substitute an objective that is within its power to achieve, and in particular it can promote the fairness of its own internal procedures.[51] So both client pressure and bureaucratic dynamics promote government rule complexity aimed at limiting discretion and corruption.

Anti-corruption measures tend to cause rules to proliferate. "New corruption controls do not displace old ones; rather, they supplement them."[52] But more rules do not necessarily bring enhanced control or better outcomes. The treadmill of corruption reforms and the resulting rule expansion can lead, as with other types of evasion control, to the perverse consequence of creating new channels for corruption.[53] Government administrators can avoid civil service rules – often adopted precisely to combat patronage – by hiring temporary employees or through other stratagems.[54] Privatization, sometimes promoted as an anti-corruption measure, can also be used to avoid anti-corruption controls. A "corrupt" practice like nepotism, for instance, will be more readily countenanced in the private than in the public sector. Privatization of a formerly government-conducted activity can lead to increased "corruption," then, but corruption of a less socially incendiary variety, as it no longer involves public employees.

Combating corruption

Revelations of governmental corruption are likely to lead to more rules aimed at increasing accountability and limiting discretion. One way to promote accountability is to augment the transparency of government operations.[55] Independent audits or performance reviews can be institutionalized, for example, and officials can be required to disclose their financial interests. Broader mandatory disclosure rules, such as the US Freedom of Information Act, can limit government opacity. Another element of the standard "accountability" response to a perceived increase in corruption is to identify and prosecute venal officials, and, if the crackdown is serious, to bring severe punishments to bear. China, for instance, periodically executes officials found guilty of corruption.

There undoubtedly is some merit to the standard anti-corruption approach. The penalties actually imposed on corrupt officials in many countries generally are quite low, typically not going beyond dismissal, so raising these penalties (though short of execution, I would hope) is often sensible. Nevertheless, there are some problems with implementing an off-the-shelf crackdown on corruption. First, it is very hard to measure changes in corruption, since so much of it never comes to light. How will success of an anti-corruption campaign be assessed – by fewer arrests or by more arrests for corruption? Second, charges of corruption frequently are baseless, and without adequate safeguards for defendants, a stepped-up crusade against corruption could become little more than a way of settling political scores, or even be used to persecute those officials who, in the eyes of their colleagues, are insufficiently corrupt. This is particularly true if the starting point is one of very widespread corruption, and if the crackdown is applied retroactively. Then, the discretion to "legitimately" target almost anyone will lead to the appearance that those who are prosecuted are not the worst offenders, but those with insufficient political clout. Third, and perhaps more important, there are benefits associated with some forms of corruption, as already discussed. A crackdown may do a poor job in discriminating between reductions in the bad and the relatively good types of corruption.

Corruption tends to have many of the qualities that make it an inappropriate candidate for zero tolerance policing, despite the pressure on democratic governments to be intolerant of any visible corruption. (Recall the discussion of zero tolerance policies in Chapter 3.) First, corruption frequently is widespread, and likely to remain so even in the face of strict enforcement. Second, offenses vary greatly in terms of their social costs, and some of them are even beneficial. Third, corruption is not precisely defined, so well-intentioned people will have to monitor their activities very closely to avoid inadvertent offenses.

The recognition that corruption will not be eliminated, even by a severe crackdown, often fosters futility-style reasoning. Corruption, like the poor, will always be with us, or moneyed interests will always hold disproportionate sway in politics, are the sorts of laments one hears. The fine study on music-industry payola referred to earlier concludes: "Long before we had television, or radio, or records, the music industry had payola. It still does. It always will."[56]

Accepting that corruption will not be eradicated is not equivalent to suggesting that policy reform cannot be valuable. Once again, the alternative to a zero tolerance-style crackdown is a "harm reduction" strategy. Here, the focus is not so much on reducing corruption *per se*, but on reducing the social costs of that corruption that does take place.

There is an area of overlap between a crackdown and a harm reduction strategy, of course. Some forms of reducing corruption also are likely to reduce the social costs of corruption. Encouraging a free press, free elections, an independent judiciary, and a legislative branch with some oversight over the executive branch, as well as promoting a civil society that has oversight over government more generally: these represent alternative routes to increased accountability, beyond enhanced penalties and augmented transparency. Such forms of corruption control are good at targeting socially detrimental corruption, because unlike beneficial corruption, socially costly corruption frequently has tangible victims with incentives to complain, if they can do so in a manner that provides reasonable assurances against reprisals.[57] Free and competitive elections do not ensure that venal officials will not be elected and re-elected; nevertheless, fair and secret balloting makes it likely that the social costs of that corruption that does take place are relatively minor, because those officials who engage in particularly costly corruption will have difficulty getting re-elected. The corruption of the poor – trading their votes for economic advantage such as patronage jobs – can then be used to control the efforts of wealthy individuals to convert their cash into political power, the corruption of the rich.[58]

Fostering competition is important in limiting monopoly power and the extent of corruption. In overall terms, a competitive system involves fewer restrictions on private economic activity, and hence fewer opportunities for corruption.[59] The extent to which wealth is available and distributed widely outside the state sector (and without direct dependence on the state sector) serves as a limit to corruption – individuals can avoid the government's dominance over the availability of desirable opportunities, and ambitious young people needn't turn to the public sector for advancement.[60] Laws can be improved or eliminated to reduce bureaucratic obstacles to business, decreasing both monopoly power and the discretion of officials. Such changes can often be accomplished through minor alterations in rules and procedures; for example, internal regulations can prevent regular police officers from enforcing laws against minor vices, when enforcement of such laws provides frequent opportunities for corrupt behavior.[61]

Limiting discretion, cultivating the independence of private wealth generation from direct state activities, and increasing competition and transparency, however, are not miracle cures for corrupt bureaucracies. Discretion, it has been noted, can itself be fostered by an array of opaque or confusing rules, even if the rules themselves were introduced to try to limit discretion and control corruption. While there may be a general predisposition for increased transparency to lead to better government, the example of Dalton's drug store indicates that it needn't always be the case, in part because rules cannot be tailored sufficiently finely.[62] And while the availability of wealth outside of the state sector can serve to limit corruption by undermining the monopoly power of the state, private wealth can also be used to try to suborn governmental activities or procedures. Attempts are made, therefore, to prevent wealth from controlling processes where it is believed to have a negative influence, as in the judicial system, or in government more generally. For example, the votes of citizens cannot legally be sold, and to help enforce the restriction, secret balloting is employed, so that compliance with any agreement to sell one's vote would be difficult to ascertain. The philosopher Michael Walzer has suggested that limitations are put on wealth accumulations to help enforce prohibitions against types of behavior that might be termed corrupt:

> If we succeeded absolutely in barring the conversion of money into political power, for example, then we might not limit its accumulation or alienation at all. As things are, we have strong reasons to limit both of these – reasons that have less to do with the marginal utility of money than with its extramural effectiveness.[63]

Policies that would be appropriate in a world of rule-abiding angels may be ill-advised in a world peopled by, well, people. And government officials are people, too. The potential for corruption, therefore, must be taken into account in designing public policy; indeed, this is the real key to limiting the social costs of corruption. Powers of officials must be restrained to reflect the possibility that powers will be corruptly misused. Nevertheless, considerations of corruption are often paid little heed at the stage of policy development: "the more usual practice is to choose the policies that would be best *if* the whole bureaucracy were dependable, and then to deplore its corruption, and condemn it for the failure of the policies chosen."[64]

US campaign finance reform[65]

Money influences political outcomes. Large campaign contributors expect and receive favored consideration for legislation that promotes their interests, or advantaged treatment by regulatory agencies that must answer to political authorities. Excessive influence by monied interests in a democratic political process threatens to informally convert the government from a democracy into a plutocracy.

The straightforward way of dealing with the problem of disproportionate influence of monied interests on political activity is to prohibit the trading of legislative votes or favors for campaign contributions. The direct and explicit sale of a legislative vote for a campaign contribution is indeed illegal.[66] But it is a simple matter to arrange a *quid pro quo* without resorting to open bribery.

The impotency of anti-bribery laws to combat the leverage of money on the political process, combined with other perceived weaknesses of the campaign funding system, has led the US (and other democracies) to enact various other regulations. (And here, as in other areas where the formal law is insufficient, public opinion and scandal can serve as a potential supplement to legal restraints.) Controls on private contributions to US political campaigns date from the early twentieth century, but comprehensive restrictions were not enacted until the 1970s, and then primarily for federal, not state, elections. Rules govern both the spending and solicitation of funds by candidates and parties, as well as the allowable contributions by individuals, corporations, labor unions, and political action committees (PACs). Prior to changes pending in early 2002, individuals legally can contribute up to $1,000 per candidate per election, up to $20,000 annually to the federal accounts of a national party committee, and up to $25,000 in the aggregate for annual federal contributions. A "multicandidate" PAC is permitted to contribute up to $5,000 to a candidate per election, and $15,000 to a national party committee. The rules are somewhat different for presidential campaigns, which can receive public funds if they meet certain criteria, including an agreement to limit campaign spending in primary elections. Contributions in excess of $200 received by candidates, party committees, or PACs, must be disclosed.[67]

A 1976 Supreme Court decision, *Buckley* v. *Valeo* (424 U.S. 1), precludes many types of restrictions on campaign finance as being incompatible with the First Amendment. The Court distinguished between campaign *contributions*, which are given over to a party or a PAC, say, with no control by the contributor on how the funds are spent, and campaign *expenditures*. Contributions are more prone to *quid pro quo* corruption or the appearance of such corruption, the Court reasoned, while simultaneously the "speech value" (and hence the extent of First Amendment shelter against regulation) is more tied to the existence of the contribution than to the amount contributed. Regulatory limits on campaign contributions, therefore, are not as problematic for protecting First Amendment interests as are expenditure limitations, according to the Court. Attempts to restrict expenditures face a further hurdle, too: they are invalid on grounds of vagueness unless the restrictions apply solely to "expenditures for communications that in express terms advocate the election or defeat of a clearly identified candidate for federal office."[68] The *Buckley* decision indicated that "preventing corruption (or guarding against the appearance of corruption) is the only rationale that will justify any restrictions on campaign finance."[69]

(Incidentally, the *Buckley* decision included an endnote in which the Court listed some forms of wording, such as "vote for" or "vote against," that would constitute express advocacy. The suggested wording can be seen as an attempt by the Court to provide bright lines in what otherwise would be murky boundaries between "express advocacy" and other forms of political speech that are exempt from regulatory jurisdiction.)

Those controls on campaign finance that have survived constitutional scrutiny have been undermined by various avoidance strategies. Some types of avoidance were expected and either explicitly or implicitly condoned by the rule makers. Other forms of avoidance appear to have been unanticipated. Further, enforcement of campaign finance rules was designed to be lenient.[70] Civil violations are patrolled by the Federal Election Commission (FEC), whose six members are divided evenly between Republicans and Democrats; the FEC cannot directly impose penalties on campaigns that it deems to have violated the rules.

Among the forms of avoidance have been exceptions explicitly written into regulations as to what constitutes a "contribution": donations of time and limited travel funds, for instance, are not counted as contributions. One less foreseen avoidance strategy is that groups that can bypass the designation of a "political committee" are not subject to restrictions on money raising and spending, even when the expenditures are related to federal elections.[71] As in the case of S&L regulation, federalism presents opportunities for avoidance: state-chartered political committees can circumvent the federal restrictions, and as national political parties have both federal and state-level functions, creative melding of the two roles can loosen the federal restrictions. The two most important forms of avoidance of campaign finance rules have come to be known as "soft money" and "issue advocacy."

Political parties cannot solicit or accept contributions above the limit (or from prohibited sources, which include corporations, labor unions, and foreigners) when the funds are aimed at influencing federal elections. But contributions that are not for this purpose are not so restricted – they form "soft money," funds that are outside the main federal regulatory structure.[72] Political party committees therefore have separate non-federal, soft money accounts, for which they can solicit funds free of most federal restraints (though disclosure of the source of the funds is still required). The purposes for which soft money can be spent by political parties are regulated, but the joint federal and state roles provide room to maneuver.[73] Allocation formulas developed by the FEC, for instance, govern the extent to which expenses such as voter registration drives can be paid for with soft as opposed to hard money. Following the creation of the soft money loophole in 1979, the two major national parties collected $19 million in soft money in 1980 – a figure which ballooned to $463 million for the 2000 election cycle.[74] Expanded notions of what activities can be paid for with soft funds have led seasoned political observers such as journalist and author Elizabeth Drew to conclude that "The distinction between hard and soft money has become a fiction."[75]

The Supreme Court's *Buckley* decision has been the source of the other major loophole, "issue advocacy." Expenditures can be controlled, according to *Buckley*, only if they "expressly advocate" the election or defeat of a candidate in a federal ballot, given that the attempted controls meet all the other constitutional requirements. Political advertizements that avoid such direct electoral appeals can therefore be paid for with contributions that are not subject to federal constraints and disclosure rules. Issue advertizements for the 1999–2000 election cycle were estimated to have cost approximately $509 million.[76] Soft money can be utilized for issue advocacy advertizements undertaken by party organizations, while corporations and unions also can sponsor issue advocacy campaigns.

Soft money and issue advocacy have combined with other forms of avoidance to render the current controls on campaign finance largely ineffective. "The legal framework to curb campaign finance has become little more than an annoyance, not a real constraint on the behavior of the contestants."[77] By 1996, there were "effectively no limits on how much money could be raised and spent in a campaign, and the limits on how it could be raised were rendered meaningless."[78] Once one party or candidate unearthed successful avoidance strategies, rival parties and candidates had little choice but to mimic the circumvention of the intent of the controls.

Widespread avoidance of campaign finance laws, then, is generating pressure for reform – though some popular proposed reforms are diametrically opposed to one another. ("It is as if *Buckley* were rotting from both sides and the only question is which way it will fall."[79]) One set of proposals aims at "closing the loopholes" and tighter enforcement; the more comprehensive reforms within this set include the banning of soft money in its entirety, and full public funding of campaigns. Alternative reform proposals in the other direction call for near complete deregulation of campaign finance. Some proposals involve elements of both strategies, stricter but more narrowly focused regulation: tighter restrictions over the permissible uses of soft money, for instance, can be combined with increased allowances (above the current $1,000 per candidate per election for individual donations) for hard money contributions.

Not surprisingly, the choice among reform proposals turns largely on the extent to which the revised regulatory structure could be avoided or evaded. While full public funding would seem to nearly eliminate a candidate's demand for private contributions, private money might still be able to wield significant and potentially even corrupting influence: wealthy PACs could still fund their own political advertizements, for instance.[80] Complete deregulation, which leaves intact the potential for the excessive influence by monied interests that provides the rationale for regulations in the first place, also involves some enforcement issues. Deregulation proposals are typically teamed with disclosure requirements, so that voters will have reliable information concerning to whom a candidate is beholden. But some forms of influence, such as issue advocacy, could fall outside of the disclosure requirements, diluting the public information that could control abuses in an otherwise *laissez-faire* system. Ongoing state-level experiences with various campaign finance regulations might provide evidence of the best direction in which federal reform should proceed.

Major contributors might be among those who favor stricter controls on campaign finance. The flip side of contributors receiving political favors is that those who do not contribute can be disfavored. While the usual fear is that contributions can have the appearance and functions of bribes, it is also the case that sometimes bribes are extorted, implicitly or explicitly. Even if there is no extortionary angle, contribution competition has some of the features of an arms race, where large expenditures are made without changing the relative position of the rivals. Stricter controls on campaign finance, from this perspective, are like an arms control agreement.

Whatever type of federal campaign finance reform is undertaken – and it looks as if campaign finance has entered a "treadmill of reform" – the influence of private wealth on public policy will not and arguably should not be eliminated. Harm reduction strategies, then, can make a positive contribution. The central idea here is that there should be limits on how a candidate can reward a major contributor.[81] Transparency in the legislative process, and media oversight of egregious attacks on the public fisc for private benefit, can play the increased accountability role that is useful in all areas of corruption control. But increased accountability can be teamed with reduced discretion by elected officials, particularly in the regulatory sphere.

The Savings & Loan crisis illustrates the problem. S&L owners were heavy campaign contributors in the 1980s: "between 1983 and 1988, more than 160 political action committees (PACs) representing savings and loans poured almost $4.5 million into House and Senate campaigns."[82] Why was the S&L industry so involved in politics? It appears that the S&L industry was interested in promoting leniency in the adoption and enforcement of regulations with their contributions. The Keating Five, those legislators who seemingly helped S&L owner Charles Keating postpone a showdown with regulators, collectively had received some $1.4 million in campaign contributions from Keating.[83] Why should regulators be subject to pressure on specific rulings from individual Congress people – as opposed to Congress as a body – when making regulatory decisions that are within their delegated responsibilities? Curtailing the ability of legislators to provide such services would help limit the payoffs that elected officials could provide to contributors. One possibility would be to remove all constituent service currently undertaken by representatives to a separate agency.[84] A historical precedent of a rule change limiting the scope for corruption was the Pendleton Civil Service Act of 1883, which led to the replacement of many political appointees in federal jobs with civil servants.[85]

Finally, recall that the larger goal, presumably, is good government, not the elimination of corruption or the appearance of corruption. Abolishing discretion would also end corruption – it would produce clean government, but not good government. Single-minded campaigns against government corruption threaten to confuse the means with the end, while the definition of a corrupt act can always be further extended. These considerations again suggest that a strategy of harm reduction would be preferable to an intense zero tolerance campaign waged against corruption or the appearance of corruption.

7 Evasion and the demise of the Soviet Union

> ... it is the ultimate aim of this work, to lay bare the economic law of motion of modern society
>
> (Karl Marx, Preface to *Das Kapital*)

The most momentous policy changes in recent decades have been the economic and political transformations in the formerly socialist countries. The largely peaceful collapse of the USSR, which for many decades had stood as the military and ideological challenger to Western capitalism, represents one of the most extraordinary events in political history. Why did Soviet socialism give way to Russian capitalism? Any sufficiently general theory of policy transformation should be able to offer an effective post-mortem of the defunct USSR.

The USSR's economic failure in comparison with Western market economies is given a leading role in almost all accounts of Soviet collapse, and rightly so. Soviet-style central planning proved itself incapable of keeping pace with Western capitalism in terms of the average standard of living, at least if living standards are measured by the availability and quality of consumer goods. The most compelling evidence for this claim comes from comparisons between the two Germanys, Koreas, and Chinas after decades of central planning in one of their respective incarnations.

Economists and others have analyzed why decentralized markets and private ownership tend, in the long run, to produce better economic outcomes than central planning: the primary advantage of market systems appears to be their ability to generate and disseminate information about consumer preferences and relative scarcities through the price mechanism, simultaneously providing incentives to respond to this information.[1] While central planning has some advantages in terms of mobilizing resources towards a known and widely shared goal – and hence market systems typically employ more planning elements during wartime – when goals are more diverse and decisions have to be made about where to place new investments, the information and incentive shortcomings of planning become more pronounced. Given limited resources, what goods should be produced? Over the course of decades, markets and decentralized decision making revealed themselves to be superior to central planners at answering the "what to produce?" question.[2]

While relative economic failure almost always plays a central role in expla-nations of the Soviet collapse, there remain many elements of contention among analysts trudging through the ruins of the USSR. For instance, the "what goods to produce" explanation offered above is not universally accepted, and other causes of poor Soviet economic performance have been advanced. One deep divide is over the issue of inevitability.[3] Some explanations for the Soviet collapse suggest that, given the economic inefficiencies of central planning relative to capitalism, the demise was inevitable. It is unclear, however, whether lagging living standards of necessity lead to a systemic collapse, irrespective of the causes underlying poor economic performance. Soviet socialism lasted more than sixty years, and its legacy included some impressive economic achievements. Even if claims of inevitable Soviet doom are correct, it would still be nice to know how the inefficient Soviet system, as opposed to all the other inefficient systems one could dream up, remained viable as long as it did. An alternative strand of analysis of the Soviet collapse relies on "mistakes were made" logic. In these explanations, the socialist system was fundamentally viable, even if it could not keep pace in terms of average living standards with Western market economies. The collapse, from this point of view, was due more to poor central planning than to central planning *per se*, with potentially avoidable errors – such as an over-allocation of resources to the military or excessive geo-political commitments – eventually undermining the Soviet system.

The sorcerer's apprentice

> Louis XV did as much to weaken the monarchy and to speed up the Revolution by his innovations as by his personal defects, by his energy as by his indolence.
>
> (Alexis de Tocqueville,
> *The Old Régime and the French Revolution*, 1856[4])

As a proximate cause of Soviet demise, analysts from both schools of thought implicitly invoke the tale of the Sorcerer's Apprentice, with Mikhail Gorbachev in the title role. Temporarily left in charge of the moribund Soviet economy, the apprentice Gorbachev tried various approaches to improve matters, with little success. Eventually, he decided or stumbled upon *perestroika* (restructuring), the unleashing of some market elements, though he intended to limit the scope of the market forces to the fairly narrow bounds consistent with what was left of Marxist-Leninist ideology and a primarily planned economy. Alas, the market forces multiplied, escaped from the formal bounds, and in their uncontrollable explosion swept both the Soviet economy and its last caretaker from the stage of history. There was no sorcerer able to return in time to restore order; instead, the International Monetary Fund showed up.

Again, versions of the Sorcerer's Apprentice approach to Soviet demise have wide currency, being shared even among those with otherwise incompatible appraisals, among those who welcome and those who revile the changes. The difference between the views of the "doomed" and "mistake" schools can be recast in terms of whether Gorbachev had a choice, or whether eventually some fledgling sorcerer would have had to open the floodgates of markets.

How does a focus on the dynamics of evasion and reform explain the collapse of the Soviet economy? The Sorcerer's Apprentice logic remains intact, with rule evasion serving as both the impetus towards the initial partial marketization, and the source of the positive feedback that prevented the market forces from being successfully contained within the confines of a centrally planned economy. This argument is developed in more detail below, but a summary is as follows. First, informal and illegal economic activity was needed to fill in the gaps and correct the mistakes of central planning; in this sense, the black market kept the centrally planned system afloat, and partially – but only partially – substituted for a formal reform. Second, underground private economic activity generated the conditions that made limited market-oriented reforms likely. Finally, following the partial liberalization, an unavoidable surge of quasi-legal capitalism undermined the remnants of the planned system and paved the way for an official transition to capitalism. Such an account suggests that some Gorbachev would have had to arise as the unwitting apprentice: better planning could have delayed, but not prevented, the demise of Soviet-style socialism.[5]

Rule evasion within the planning system

> There we have the old régime in a nutshell: rigid rules, but flexibility, not to say laxity, in their application . . . It might almost be said that under the old régime everything was calculated to discourage the law-abiding instinct.
>
> (de Tocqueville[6])

Central planners are people too. As such, they are woefully limited in their ability to obtain accurate information about the workings of a vast and complex economy, to formulate coherent instructions, or to ensure compliance with their dictates. And so, while centrally planned economies are full of rules, regulations, and commands, many of these strictures are misguided. Simultaneously, such economies are also brimming with evasion of their rules, activity that forms much of what became known as the "second economy."[7]

The inherent rigidities of Soviet central planning virtually required informal or illegal activity, even for state-owned enterprises to meet their plan targets.[8] Many goods were illegally traded outside of the plan, and such behavior was generally tolerated and to some degree even officially encouraged. Price controls could be evaded by bribes, whether monetary or in-kind. Theft of state property from the workplace was common enough that it became an accepted practice, virtually a standard part of compensation, and such theft was not viewed negatively by Soviet citizens.[9] All told, there was considerable private economic activity, often sheltered within the confines of state-owned firms, despite the illegality that drove it underground. Over time, economic crime influenced planner decisions. For instance, official salaries were lower in occupations that provided good opportunities for second economy earnings; in effect, planners offered lower official wage rates to offset theft or bribe income.[10] Professor Gregory Grossman, a leading Western analyst of the Soviet economy, provided this assessment in 1977:

> the second economy, grafted onto the present institutional setup in the USSR, is a kind of spontaneous surrogate economic reform that imparts a necessary modicum of flexibility, adaptability, and responsiveness to a formal setup that is too often paralyzing in its rigidity, slowness, and inefficiency. It represents a *de facto* decentralization, with overtones of the market.[11]

The general rule (as it were) of rule breaking applied to economic crime in the Soviet economy: some rule evasion was desirable, and some was not. Some Soviet criminal activity furthered plan fulfillment, improved state-owned enterprise performance, or filled productive and distributional gaps within the official economy. Simultaneously, however, some second economy behavior hindered plan fulfillment and lessened central control; much of the theft from the workplace, for example, probably was of this nature. (Whether plan fulfillment was actually beneficial for the overall Soviet economy, as opposed to satisfying the stated objectives of the planners, is another matter, and one that can by no means be taken for granted.)

Why was such extensive economic crime tolerated in the totalitarian USSR? As already suggested, one reason is that some rule evasion was necessary for central planning to work at all – working to the rules would have been a particularly effective job action for the Soviet proletariat – and it was impossible to countenance this "desirable" evasion without opening the door to evasion that was less beneficial. A related reason is that, given the conditions created by central planning, the overall impact of the second economy was probably to impart "a necessary modicum of flexibility" and to increase average living standards. The costs of a serious crackdown would have been large, increasingly so as the second economy assumed a more important role in the overall economy. In many instances, politically powerful people were the primary beneficiaries of the extra-plan activity: the pyramid of graft led to extensive accumulations at the top. One Kremlin insider noted that following the death of Konstantin Chernenko (Gorbachev's immediate predecessor as general secretary), the desk drawers and safe in his Kremlin office were found to be stuffed with cash.[12]

Informal and illegal activity in the Soviet Union was accompanied by the standard informational penalty, the undermining of the integrity of official economic statistics. But the costs of informational erosion tend to be much higher in a centrally planned economy than in a market economy, because central planners presumably require extensive and accurate data, both to formulate future plans and to assess the fulfillment of previous plans. An unfortunate irony of central planning is that it leads to informal activity which creates inaccurate statistics, which in turn makes the next plan bear less relationship to reality, thereby increasing the incentive (and the necessity) for further informal and illegal activity, and so on.

Not surprisingly, Soviet economic crime apparently increased over time. While reliable data are quite limited, of course, most observers have concluded that the Soviet second economy expanded noticeably throughout the Brezhnev era, and by the late 1970s it was estimated to provide approximately one-third of the income of urban households.[13] The increase in second economy activity was in a sense a gradual economic reform, as Professor Grossman indicated. Still, illegal markets are no match for legal ones, and Soviet living standards could not keep pace with those in Western market economies.

Perestroika-era reforms

> During his entire reign Louis XVI was always talking about reform, and there were few institutions whose destruction he did not contemplate before the Revolution broke and made an end of them. But after eliminating from the constitution some of its worse features he made haste to reinstitute them; in fact, he gave an impression of merely wanting to loosen its foundations and leaving to others the task of laying it low.
>
> (de Tocqueville[14])

Then the apprentice, Mikhail Gorbachev, emerged as general secretary in 1985. He tried a few reforms to jumpstart his ailing economy, but to little effect. Eventually, Gorbachev latched onto *perestroika*, a series of measures which essentially placed a somewhat greater reliance on market forces, though within the confines of a predominantly planned economy. A major portion of *perestroika* was aimed at legitimizing the private economic activity that already took place, *sub rosa*, in the USSR. The 1986 Law on Individual Labor Activity legalized household-level business, but continued to prohibit the hiring of non-family members. The 1988 Law on Cooperatives allowed unrelated individuals to enter into business together, though there were still many restrictions on the type of business and the hiring of labor. The Law on State Enterprises (effective January 1988) officially ended plan targets, but they largely were replaced with functionally similar "state orders," while above-plan production was liberalized. Taken together, these measures were in significant measure an explicit recognition of what had long been a *fait accompli*: widespread evasion of the old rules led to the codification of permissible exceptions. This codification is a specific instance of the more general political economy of evasion: widespread evasion of rules (particularly bad rules) promotes their partial liberalization, as the pre-existing evasion implies that there will be few people who are negatively affected by the explicit loosening. But there can still be significant gains to an official liberalization. The benefits accrue in the form of the elimination of the necessity to behave with stealth when engaging in the previously illegal endeavors. Changing the rules so that existing underground activities become above ground lowers the costs of conducting the activities.

Positive feedback

> Thus the social order overthrown by a revolution is almost always better than the one immediately preceding it, and experience teaches us that, generally speaking, the most perilous moment for a bad government is one when it seeks to mend its ways.
>
> (de Tocqueville[15])

How did the limited reforms of *perestroika* lead to the demise of central planning? Evasion, yet again. *Perestroika*-era measures that largely were aimed at legalizing second economy activity and improving the performance of state-owned enterprises – most particularly, the Law on Cooperatives and the Law on State Enterprises – simultaneously provided new loopholes that allowed managers to increase their claims on state funds, while decreasing the taxes that they had to remit back to the central government. While the previous constraints on private economic activity had been widely evaded, they nevertheless prevented a complete marketization. The plan remained dominant, and managers and government ministry officials had to present a plausible case that their plan was fulfilled. In liberalizing existing activity, however, the *perestroika*-era reforms could not establish bright, enforceable lines between the permissible and the impermissible, with the result that the central planning system soon eroded away.

Following the *perestroika* reforms, claims on the state budget were increased by the new option for state-owned enterprises to deal with private cooperatives. In their pure forms, such dealings were legal, but it proved impossible to police purity. An enterprise could purchase fictional services from a cooperative owned by some subset of its managers and employees, and the state would pay for the services. Or, the enterprise could sell some of its output to a cooperative at the low prices fixed by the state (and produced with state-owned inputs), and the cooperative could then resell at much higher free market prices; i.e. the state was subsidizing the private profits of cooperatives. Simultaneously, as part of the market incentives that the *perestroika* measures were intended to introduce, enterprises were allowed to keep larger percentages of their profits and foreign currency earnings, leading to sharply decreased tax collections. In essence, *perestroika* made it easier for enterprise managers to privatize their revenues, while continuing to shift their costs onto the state.

The result of higher state expenditures and lower revenues was an increased government budget deficit. (The state budget had already been badly damaged by the anti-alcohol campaign initiated in May 1985 – taxes on alcohol sales were a major component of state revenues, and the remittances declined as the campaign cut official alcohol purchases by more than 50 percent between 1985 and 1987.[16]) The budget deficit was monetized, causing significant inflation. At this point, a positive feedback loop was initiated. The inflation increased the gap between the fixed state-sector prices and prices on the informal market. The larger price gap in turn increased the incentive to divert goods out of the state sector, a process that was facilitated, quasi-legally, by the *perestroika* reforms. Entire factories, nominally state-owned, were diverted into private hands by various channels of "spontaneous privatization."[17] The increased diversions led to still more opportunities to socialize costs while privatizing benefits, which served to increase the government budget deficit further, leading to more inflation, a larger gap between state and free-market prices, and so on.

The expanded market activity intended by *perestroika* inadvertently lowered the costs and increased the benefits of evading the remaining state controls, undermining the state sector and the official price controls, in advance of official privatization and price liberalization. Note that the next steps, of formalizing the movements to a market economy, then became easy: once evasion was sufficiently broad, price liberalization and official privatization no longer represented a "big bang." Rather, they simply ratified the existing situation; for example, most Russians were already paying market prices for many goods, prior to the ending of price controls, because the goods were unavailable in the state sector.[18] But once again, the necessity to behave in a clandestine and informal fashion when diverting goods and assets to the private sector used up considerable real resources, which could be redeployed following legalization. There are substantial gains to be had from switching from widespread illegal market activity to widespread legal market activity.

Was it inevitable?

> . . . for never was any such event, stemming from factors so far back in the past, so inevitable yet so completely unforeseen.
>
> (de Tocqueville[19])

The Sorcerer's Apprentice legitimated the market forces that had previously exerted themselves subterraneously, opening the way for a cascade of private activity that undermined the planning system. Was this pattern inevitable, or could a better-trained or luckier apprentice have salvaged Soviet central planning?

There are essentially two alternatives to the route that Gorbachev chose. First, an apprentice could have initiated *perestroika*-style reforms, but kept tighter control on the bounds of the market activity: the quasi-legal spontaneous privatizations could have been stopped, perhaps, and diversions from the state sector could have been more effectively policed. In other words, the line between legal and illegal economic activity could still have been shifted, perhaps without becoming as blurred as it in fact did become. The second alternative available to an apprentice consisted of better performance within the planned sector itself: improved quality, better work discipline, increased output, etc. Or, some combination of these two basic measures could have been tried.

Streamlined central planning was surely not an attractive option, however, and it may not even have been a feasible one, given that "further perfecting" of the planning mechanism had been a nearly continuous process for many decades. Gorbachev himself initiated many such tinkerings within the planning system. The anti-alcohol campaign, the *gospriemka* reforms whereby presumably autonomous quality control officers were placed in enterprises, and the brigade system in which small groups of workers could sub-contract in ways that improved their incentives: these were just three reforms promoted during the Gorbachev era that were aimed at improving work discipline, product quality, and overall efficiency. Decades of experience with similar reforms ended with the same old problems of low quality, high cost, and poor work discipline reasserting themselves, and the Gorbachev-era reforms were no more successful.[20]

Still, there was the alternative of *perestroika*-style reforms, but with improved implementation, to prevent the new legal private activity from giving rise to an expansion of quasi-legal activity. Surely some further steps along these lines could have been taken, in terms, say, of auditing state-owned firms' transactions with cooperatives more closely. Such a crackdown on quasi-legal behavior, however, would have itself required significant resources to implement. Further, those whose cooperation would have been necessary to implement the crackdown at reasonable cost often were those who stood to benefit, directly or indirectly, from the evasion. As a result, any crackdown, like the periodic anti-corruption campaigns during the Soviet era, would have been half-hearted at best.

By the late 1980s, even a serious desire to enforce the restrictions on private economic activity might not have been sufficient. *Glasnost'* (openness), the political twin to *perestroika* during the late 1980s that liberalized internal political discussion, provided Soviet citizens with improved information about capitalist economies. Much of this information compared favorably with first-hand information about their own economy, so movement in the direction of Western market economies gained appeal among Soviet citizens. Further, the traditional means of controlling the economy rested upon the authority of the Communist Party of the Soviet Union (CPSU). The Party's economic incompetence was growing increasingly clear, however, while it remained tied to a Marxist-Leninist ideology that had lost almost all of its enchantment. Given these circumstances, and the fortunate unwillingness of the Party to employ Stalinist methods, the longstanding deference to the Party line was undermined. As the CPSU lost its authority, any hope of corralling market forces within the legal bounds of *perestroika* was also lost.

More important, however, is that the restriction of market forces within the limits initially envisioned by *perestroika* would have done very little to improve the fundamental flaws in Soviet central planning, particularly the wasteful production of low-value or nearly useless goods. A centrally planned economy can be a stable institutional setting for decades, though it spawns abundant rule-breaking. A market economy likewise can be stable. But market socialism hybrids do not appear to offer the same potential for stability, in part because of the difficulty in drawing bright lines between legitimate and illegitimate activity, so that there is pressure to move towards markets or towards planning.[21] The larger the planned sector within a market socialist hybrid, the greater this pressure for movement one way or the other is likely to become – and in the USSR, the planned sector dominated the economy. The economic disadvantages of central planning then favor an eventual evolution towards markets, at least with a government sufficiently responsive to citizen preferences.[22]

A law of motion of socialism

> Capitalist enterprise is the child of evasion . . .
>
> (Sir John Hicks[23])

Following Marx, let me summarize with a "law of motion" of socialism based on rule evasion. Centrally planned economies, often effective at mobilizing resources towards a clear goal such as winning a war or industrializing with known technologies, have a very difficult time innovating, in adjusting production in ways that cannot be anticipated. Further, official price controls and state owner-ship limit the information available to planners about relative scarcities, and diminish the incentive and ability of private citizens to respond appropriately to such information as exists. Over time, therefore, an economy that adopts central planning will face increased resource misallocations, and see its average living standards begin to slip relative to market economies that started from similar conditions. To reduce resource misallocations and to lessen the gap in living standards, central authorities will tolerate growing illicit market activity.

The authorities may engage in occasional tepid crackdowns, but it will even-tually become obvious that these do not solve the problem, and probably make matters worse.[24] The crackdowns themselves become less desirable as the second economy grows in relative importance, and as the service sector – where the comparative advantage of markets over planning is particularly acute – becomes more extensive. Eventually the second economy will grow to such a point that its legalization will offer substantial efficiency gains through lowered transactions costs, with relatively minor distributional consequences, since the distributional consequences are brought to bear informally prior to the official reform. Central planning suffers from an internal, evasion-based contradiction.

If there is any merit in this argument, the second economy played a funda-mental role in maintaining and then destroying Soviet socialism. Yet most academic analyzes of the Soviet system paid scant attention to the second economy. The focus was rather on the official economy and even official statistics, with the second economy acknowledged, but sidelined – much like rule evasion in Western policy analyzes. Further, note the different roles played by small-scale as opposed to wide-scale rule evasion in the USSR. When it remained of moderate size, the rule evasion represented by the second economy tended to serve as a substitute for official reform, and to prolong the system. As it grew, however, the second economy paved the road to a partial liberalization which recognized existing evasion. By further obscuring the line between public and private property, this partial liberalization then led to widespread evasion, which itself induced a major policy change: the end of central planning in the Soviet Union. The experience of Soviet socialism, then, can serve as a stark reminder of the power of evasion to stimulate major policy reform.

By essentially postponing radical economic transition until widespread evasion left it little choice, the USSR started its economic transition under conditions that were much less favorable than in countries (such as the then Czechoslovakia) that embraced reform at an early stage, before widespread evasion made the transition inevitable. One component of this unenviable starting point derives from the positive feedback mechanism associated with evasion of the partial liberalizations of market-oriented reforms in a generally centrally planned system: some evasion (such as spontaneous privatization) leads to higher budget deficits, causing inflation and a greater gap between state sector and free market prices, increasing the incentive for additional evasion, and so on. But the "and so on" means that a centrally planned economy that has radical reform thrust upon it by evasion has developed a very high rate of inflation and probably significant foreign debt as well. Russia's price liberalization in January, 1992, for example, took place only after months of near-hyperinflation and state shops that were largely bereft of goods.[25] A second reason that evasion-led reforms result in a poor starting point for economic transition is that evasion itself is unconcerned with consistency. Widespread evasion almost necessitates partial or complete liberalization of the evaded rule, but it does not provide the same impetus for changes in complementary rules – changes that might be required for the liberalization to result in improved social outcomes. Liberalization is not equivalent to deregulation, and the regulations that might make liberalization successful might not be as obvious as the need to liberalize.[26] Further, in the rush to liberalize, there is limited time in which to devote much thought to the requisite complementary measures. For these reasons, while widespread evasion promotes radical reform, generally it is not wise to wait for evasion to force the hand of policy makers.

China and the law of motion of socialism

China is still officially a socialist country. Does the "Law of Motion of Socialism" – the gradual acceptance of illicit market activity, followed by its legitimation – apply to China as well as to Russia? Or has China managed to evade the "Law"?

Market activity certainly has become legitimized in China. Most employees work in the non-state sector, which produces a majority even of industrial output.[27] The extent to which illegal private economic activity, particularly in agriculture, preceded the official reforms has already been noted. The major remaining economic element of socialism in China is the still significant scope of state-owned industry. All in all, however, the Chinese experience appears to be consistent with the proclaimed general dynamics of socialism.

Nevertheless, the outcomes of reform in China and Russia have been quite different. While measures of economic activity deteriorated significantly during the Russian transition, China has enjoyed virtually unprecedented growth since 1979. Attempting to account for the gulf between the market-oriented reform experiences in Russia and China has been a major preoccupation of transition researchers in recent years.

Many important factors can be pointed to that account for much of the differential in transition paths.[28] China was a much poorer and overwhelmingly rural country at the initiation of its reforms, while Russia was burdened with a significantly larger sector of inefficient industrial enterprises. (Even in relatively successful reform-era China, the state-owned industrial sector continues to be very problematic for economic transition. But this sector does not dominate the Chinese economy, as it did in the USSR.) Central planning was not nearly as developed in China as it was in Russia, in three senses. First, planning in China encompassed only a small fraction of the goods that were part of the planning profile in the USSR. Second, the length of time that the full-fledged planning system existed was much shorter in China (beginning about 1953) than in the Soviet Union (beginning in the late 1920s). Third, much of the planning that did take place in China was conducted at the sub-national level, i.e. there was more reliance on regional planning and less reliance on central planning than in the Soviet Union.

But another important difference between Russia and China has been what might be termed "organization." China developed a system of reform – the "dual track" system – that allowed for an orderly transition between planning and markets.[29] Furthermore, the continuing control of the Communist Party in China has meant that the system of corruption could be rather well-organized there as well, generating the usual advantages that organized corruption presents in comparison with disorganized corruption.[30]

The dual track system of China involved the creation of a legal market sector, coexisting in parallel with a controlled or planned sector; over time, the controlled sector declined in relative importance, while the market sector grew. For example, the planned portion of industrial output (in value terms) fell from 91 percent of total industrial output in 1978 to 5 percent in 1993.[31] China used the dual track approach in many different areas of the economy, including such key areas of reform as price liberalization, enterprise restructuring, and foreign exchange operations.[32]

In essence, the dual track system systematized the law of motion of socialism. Rather than implicitly permitting more and more illicit market activity over time, the dual track system progressively legitimized what would have otherwise been growing illegal activities. (The dual track pricing system, however, initially was a spontaneous development, like the household contract responsibility system, first tolerated and then endorsed by the authorities.[33]) The disadvantages that illegal markets have over legal markets, then, were largely avoided in the Chinese transition.

The simultaneous existence of a controlled track and a parallel, market track creates incentives to divert goods from the controlled sector to the market sector, or simply to ignore or underfulfill the plan. Indeed, it was precisely such "diversion" that was legitimated over time by the increased reliance on the market track. How can this diversion be prevented from occurring quickly and massively, eviscerating the planned sector, as happened in the USSR in the early 1990s? It is with respect to promoting the continuing "integrity" of the plan that the Chinese Communist Party played a useful economic role during transition. Communist Party officials could use their authority to ensure that the controlled track fulfilled (or gave the appearance of fulfilling) its prescribed duties. The shrinking of the relative importance of the planned sector during the transition process could then take place in an organized way. Further, the siphoning of resources out of the controlled sector by corrupt means could be managed in a more orderly fashion, when it was clear who had the authority to approve such siphoning, and hence who had to be compensated.[34] The corruption itself was limited by the need for the officials to provide some evidence that the plan was being fulfilled.

While the Chinese Communist Party maintained its control over the levers of power during the economic reforms of recent decades, there has been a substantial decentralization of that power. The implementation of economic policy, never as centralized as in the USSR, has also been further decentralized. Many of the gains in China in recent years represent not so much the superiority of markets over plans as the superiority of decentralized planning over centralized planning[35] – though much of that superiority is itself due to the greater need for limited-budget localities to respect market forces. The system of corruption has also been decentralized, and thus made more accountable to local conditions.

In Russia, in contrast, Communist Party control broke down, and the state sector was eviscerated via goods diversion and spontaneous privatization. As a result, Russia's *de jure* liberalization occurred in a highly inflationary, highly disorganized environment. A plethora of bribe demanders, official and otherwise, continues to plague the workings of Russia's market economy. China was able to find an alternative not available to Gorbachev, a *perestroika* that allowed a partial, gradually increasing liberalization, with enough central control to prevent a full-scale, illicit marketization.

In other ways, however, the comparison between Russian and Chinese reforms does not appear so favorable to China. The USSR simultaneously endured the collapse of its one-party political system, the loss of most of its empire, and the abandonment of its centrally planned economy. These monumental changes occurred largely peacefully, and for many Russians they led (even in the early 1990s) to a better quality of life, which included new freedoms such as unrestricted foreign travel and the right to criticize the government, as well as some un-measured economic gains such as the near elimination of queues to purchase consumer goods. While China's measured economic growth greatly surpassed Russia's growth in the last decades of the twentieth century, the relative stability in China might be largely illusory. The forces of political pluralism in China are not absent, even as they are suppressed. For a while, perhaps, high economic growth can serve to mollify the desires of many Chinese for more political freedom, and widespread corruption can allow some economic freedoms to be purchased. Eventually, however, China's one-party state will have to address the gulf between its official Marxist/Maoist ideology and the political demands of a populace grown more prosperous through a nearly unrestrained embrace of capitalism. One of those demands will be for a reduction in the very type of corruption that in the past helped to smooth the path for the successful economic reforms, and for increased political accountability more generally.

Post-Soviet corruption and organized crime

Radical market-oriented reforms in Russia did not exactly call a halt to economic crime. Indeed, all indications have been of a massive increase in rule evasion, in many different dimensions of Russian life, and in particular in corruption and organized crime. Many analysts attributed the disappointing performance of the Russian economy in the 1990s to the crime and corruption-ridden post-Soviet environment. Do organized crime and corruption in Russia continue to be a stumbling block for successful reform?

The term "mafioso" is bandied about quite loosely in Russia; it can be used to identify any business person, any government official, any criminal, any rich person who does not sufficiently hide his wealth, or even anyone the speaker does not care for. What makes a criminal organization a mafia? Following Diego Gambetta's study of the Sicilian mafia,[36] I will consider a mafia member to be someone who engages in the private (non-state) provision of protection, and further, I will employ "organized crime" as a synonym for mafia activity. The protection can be offered against other would-be protectors, petty criminals (e.g. protection against theft), contracting partners who might be tempted to renege on a deal or not pay a debt, or, in the worst case of pure extortion, protection against the protectors themselves. Mafia members may be involved in a host of legal and/or illegal endeavors, but it is the provision of protection that distinguishes a mafia from, say, a ring of thieves. Of course, private protection can be provided by Western-style security firms, too, so to differentiate between a mafia and such a security firm, a further condition is required: the difficulty of exit. A security firm can be fired by a client and another hired in its place with little difficulty; mafia protectors generally cannot be replaced at a client's whim. A saying associated with entry into Soviet Military Intelligence (the GRU) applies just as well to dealing with the mafia: it's a ruble to get in, but two to get out.[37]

The phrase "the Russian mafia" is often used in ways that suggest a unitary and relatively well-structured organization along the lines of the Sicilian mafia – an analogy that is quite misleading. What exists in Russia is thousands of "organized criminal groups," most of them consisting of just a handful (often two or three) members, and with no overarching hierarchy. The heroic Italian anti-mafia crusader Judge Falcone noted the difference between the Sicilian and the Russian mafias before his assassination in 1992, in terms that largely remain applicable:

> Even if the Russian Mafia (and those of the other countries of the ex-Soviet bloc) do pose serious problems . . . in the East an organization comparable to Cosa Nostra does not exist. Without doubt the collapse of state and ideological structures will inevitably cause a growth in illegal trafficking and criminality, but the criminal organisations of the ex-Soviet Union, for the moment, are above all a phenomenon of generalized administrative corruption. There is no sense in calling something a Mafia when it is not . . .[38]

Corruption and some forms of organized crime are intimately related, often in a complementary fashion. Corrupt officials can ensure that the state does not interfere with mafia organizations (or that the state selectively interferes with a rival to a favored mafia group, say, or a reluctant client of that group), and they can channel state procurements towards mafia clients; mafia revenues can be donated to the election campaigns of corrupt officials, or to illegally undermine the integrity of balloting. By establishing a long-term, repeated relationship with the government, organized criminal groups can combine with corrupt officials to find the best ways to manipulate the system to their mutual benefit.

In some respects, however, the state and the mafia are substitutes, and even competitors. Known connections with high-ranking government officials can provide a business with disproportionate access to public protection (i.e. access to police and the courts can itself be partially privatized), and organized criminal groups might be deterred from approaching potential clients so protected. In the extreme, whether they cooperate or compete, it might be very difficult to differentiate government officials from mafiosi – an overlap that frequently is noted in the case of Russia.[39]

Back in the USSR

Widespread evasion in the pre-reform setting must be borne in mind when appraising how much of the corruption in the reform years represents an increase over the pre-existing levels. Consider, then, the illegal sector in the Soviet pre-reform setting. As we have discussed, the extensive restrictions on private economic activity and the shortcomings of the planned economy created a large demand for illegally produced goods and services. Illegal activity then created its own demand for private protection, since the official state channels of protection (police, contract law) were not available to those behaving illegally. (For a similar reason, organized crime in the West tends to be most prevalent in illegal sectors, such as narcotics, prostitution, and gambling.[40]) The monopoly on power established by the CPSU, enshrined in the Soviet constitution and implemented via control over the police, judiciary, and all important economic posts (the *nomenklatura*), made state officials, operating informally, the natural providers of that protection. That is, there was a close affinity between mafia activity and official corruption, and bribes tended to flow up the CPSU hierarchy. Here is one description of the system of protection for illegal economic activity in the Soviet Union:

The patron, often some official, grants his permission, or at least his forbearance, and extends some measure of conditional protection. The client pays in cash or kind, and not infrequently buys his way into the particular niche. Indeed, second economy operations of even modest size require multiple and periodic payoffs – to administrative superiors, party functionaries or secretaries, law-enforcement personnel, innumerable inspectors and auditors, and diverse actual or potential blackmailers.[41]

Recall the Klitgaard equation indicating determinants of corruption: Corruption = Monopoly + Discretion – Accountability. Communist Party officials had a monopoly on power, almost unlimited discretion over what they could choose to overlook, and little accountability for their illegal actions. Corruption was promoted further by the system of central planning. First, there was significant demand for corruption by illegal economic actors, whose activity was itself fostered by the extensive controls and weaknesses in the official sector. Second, price restrictions and generalized shortages implied that legal markets were not the mechanism that was employed to allocate scarce goods and services. As a result, state officials throughout the hierarchy, from truck drivers and retail clerks to state ministers, frequently had control over determining who would receive desirable commodities. The alternative to resource allocation by legal markets, in many cases, became corrupt allocation in illicit markets.

As with other types of crime, the systemic corruption and protection payments in the USSR were understood widely, but not acknowledged officially. Individual incidents of corruption would be reported in the Soviet press (often when it was to the political advantage of the rulers, as when some of Brezhnev's associates were discredited following his death), but the extent to which corruption permeated the system (indeed, almost defined the system) went unreported.[42] For many years, the second economy was not a legitimate research topic for Soviet economists.

Glasnost', perestroika, and economic crime

With the advent of *glasnost'* under Gorbachev and the further liberalization of the press under Yeltsin, crime and corruption became major topics for public discussion, and there often were novel incentives to offer sensationalized accounts. Even had there been no increase in the amount of corruption or mafia-style activity, this liberalization of the media would have resulted in heightened perceptions of economic crime. Furthermore, media revelations of corruption during a systemic reform have an intensified impact on people's perceptions, because the relevance of information gleaned from experience with the old system simultaneously is devalued.

It is not unusual for analysts to note the distinction between crime and the perception of crime, though such notice is often rather perfunctory, a minor qualifier in interpreting crime statistics and social concerns with crime.[43] In transitional circumstances, however, partly because of the suppressed situation pre-reform, the role of perceptions is greatly enhanced. And perceptions can influence reality: as noted earlier, widespread perceptions of an increase in economic crime are, to some degree, self-fulfilling.[44]

The reform era in Russia liberalized more than just the media, however. There also was an extremely far-reaching liberalization of private economic activity, from cooperatives to individual enterprises and to Western-style firms. Entirely new markets, such as the financial market, developed – bankers, who often have access both to substantial funds and to information concerning wealthy firms and individuals, became favored targets for business-related crimes – and other markets grew from primitive roots in the underground economy.

The market-oriented reforms were incomplete, however, and the partial nature of the reforms led to increases in economic crime. The reforms were partial in three senses. First, taxes and restrictions were extensive enough that it was almost impossible, as many Russian business people would testify, for a business to obey all the laws and still earn a profit.[45] Second, local governmental officials retained considerable discretion over what the rules were, and over who could do what. Government control of the local commercial real estate market provided one important lever to manipulate private businesses, for instance, and multiple approvals and licenses were necessary to receive local services.[46] Third, the public provision of protection, in terms of both police and business law, was inadequate. The result of the extensive, yet incomplete liberalization was a surge in the demand for corruption and private protection, for which there was a ready supply. In early 1997, there were 9,800 officially registered private security firms in Russia, with some 155,000 employees.[47]

Such partial reforms would provide fertile soil for economic crime anywhere, but Russia was particularly susceptible. Corruption frequently is associated with the excess profits that accompany artificial scarcities arising from anti-competitive government policies, such as import licenses or price controls. The provision of protection (a good that has a strong natural monopoly element) in itself creates "protection rents," which can flow to organized criminal groups or the state.[48] But another source of super-normal profits is natural resources, which can fetch prices well in excess of the costs of extraction. Russia is uniquely well-endowed with natural resources. Liberalization of foreign trade during transition increased greatly the potential for those with access to resources to capture huge profits through exporting. Not surprisingly, a good deal of alleged corruption and criminal activity has been associated with such resources: for example, there are frequent references to the aluminum mafia, the tin mafia, etc., and the far eastern parts of Russia, which are home to many of the resources, appear to harbor extensive organized criminal activity. Russia's bounty of natural resources, which probably prolonged the lifespan of the Soviet planned economy by years, combined with the decentralization of power and access to world markets to provide a major impetus to economic crime during the transition.

Costs and benefits of corruption and organized crime

While substantial economic crime existed prior to the transition, there is much truth to the perception that corruption and organized crime increased in Russia during the 1990s. The nature of these activities also went through an important transformation. Most notably, the organization and stability of corruption and protection in the old regime collapsed with the CPSU, leaving contending protection agencies and uncertainty over whom to pay. One result has been a massive increase in violence. Just as illegal drug markets are most dangerous during turf wars that establish precedence, competition to replace the former CPSU monopoly has greatly increased the costs of economic crime in transitional Russia. The extreme economic uncertainty that characterizes the transition also has raised the costs of economic crime: private protection agencies behave as if the future existence of either their own organization or their clients is doubtful, creating a situation closer to extortion than to that characterizing Western security firms.[49] Homicide statistics provide one measure of the increase in violent activity. In 1996, there were approximately 29,700 premeditated murders or attempted murders in Russia, compared with 15,600 in 1990: an increase of more than 90 percent.[50]

The distribution of the costs of economic crime also changed during transition. Foreigners, new businesses, and small firms are at a relative disadvantage in operating in a high-corruption, mafia-infiltrated environment. In illegal markets, establishing a "connection" typically is much more difficult than in legal trans-actions; therefore, those who are not already well-connected face higher obstacles to doing business. One result is that old relationships are favored relative to new business ties, militating against precisely the sorts of changes in business practices intended by reform. In transitional economies, furthermore, new firms and, to a degree, foreign investors are important elements of growth, so discouraging these actors is particularly detrimental.[51]

In the preceding chapter, Table 6.1 (p. 96) indicated that corruption entails both costs and benefits. The main benefit of corruption is that it allows business people to avoid or evade bad laws and regulations. While the rules governing private economic activity in transitional Russia are much more conducive to economic growth than they were in the pre-reform setting, the incomplete nature of reform still leaves a good deal of room for socially beneficial corruption. Of course, other forms of corruption, such as bribery of the police that allows violent criminals to operate with impunity, are far from beneficial, and it may be impossible to tolerate "good" corruption without simultaneously providing a green light to "bad" corruption.

Despite the conditions that tend to raise the costs of mafia-style activity during the transition, organized crime also provides some benefits. Successful mafia groups actually do provide protection, and as noted, that protection needn't merely be against their own threats. Mafia protectors with sufficiently long time horizons are in some sense partners with their clients, often making the mafiosi willing to provide services that increase their clients' profits, such as contract enforcement, debt collection, and dispute resolution – nor do these services necessarily involve strong arm tactics. For many, if not most Russian businesses, security represents a normal business expense, but it is not an overwhelming concern. Even firms with foreign investment do not tend to see the mafia as an important obstacle to business.[52] If the feasible alternative to mafia protection is effective, publicly provided protection – good courts, police, and contract law – then an increase in organized crime is almost certainly economically and socially detrimental. If, however, effective public protection is unavailable, then the presence of a mafia can be, on balance, a positive development, and can reduce the uncertainty facing a business, at least in the short run.

The heightened level of violence presents an enormous cost. Abstracting from the violence (if that is possible), however, the overall economic impact of corruption and organized criminal activity in Russia is not so obvious. The difficulty in making a definitive pronouncement ("corruption is bad") is that the relevant alternative in Russia is far from a well-oiled, market-style system. But such a pronouncement isn't required, either. Much of the concern over economic crime is aimed not at static calculations of costs and benefits, but rather at the influence that mafia-style activity and corruption will have on the course of transition. Does Russia run the risk of becoming mired in a long-term, high economic crime equilibrium? How salient is the concern that "Palermo may represent the future of Moscow"?[53]

The danger clearly exists. Officials growing wealthy off corrupt incomes have little reason to push for liberalizations that will reduce their illicit gains, and they may even seek to establish more roadblocks that business people will pay to avoid. It often is quite difficult to break away from a situation of high corruption; a police officer who would like to stop taking bribes, for instance, might still be expected to pass a share of the bribes to his superiors, and honest people will find police work less attractive than it is to those willing to accept bribes. (The officer's formal pay, in fact, may be quite low, in anticipation of the informal routes to higher income.) And as noted, one characteristic of organized crime is that its clients in general cannot exit from the relationship at will. Further, the extent and visibility of corruption and organized crime, even beyond their actual costs, can induce cynicism in the population. If the way to individual economic success in Russia frequently involves, as before, illegal or immoral behavior, then in this dimension at least, reform can appear to be a rather futile endeavor.

Nevertheless, there is room to hope that Russia is not condemned to high economic crime in perpetuity. One reason for this (somewhat) optimistic assessment relates to the very disorganization of the current crime scene; while the disorganization, as we have argued, is likely to raise the social costs of economic crime, it simultaneously suggests that the "criminals" cannot easily operate as a coherent political force, capable of stalling further reform. Consider the comparison with the pre-reform system. The Communist Party was very well-organized, with a monopoly on power virtually unequaled in political history, with control over the mass media, and with representatives in every nook and cranny of Soviet society. Further, CPSU officials frequently were the beneficiaries of illicit incomes that flowed from that power. Nevertheless, the CPSU was unable to prevent the loss of its power and the onset of massive economic reform. Could the 9,000 "organized criminal groups" in transitional Russia be more effective?

A second reason to believe that economic reform need not be permanently stalled by the profit-seeking behavior of corrupt officials is that such officials often do quite well in a liberalized environment – and particularly when they are helping to shape the rules of the new market regime. Evidence for this contention has been accumulating throughout the Russian reform era. The former *nomenklatura*, by and large, has been financially successful despite the extensive liberalization. There is a significant overlap between the skills that were required to get ahead in the Soviet system (which, after all, included a large illicit market) and those that are rewarded in a market economy.

A third reason to suspect that there will be continued pressure to lower economic crime is just the unpleasantness of it all. Business people and politicians in the current Russian environment often have had to dirty their hands in the course of their activity, but they are not proud of it, nor is that the environment that they want their children to inherit. And while individual exit is not easy, widespread incentives to legalize the business environment make the possibility of an evolution to more regular markets far from impossible, particularly in legitimate businesses (as opposed to illegal drugs, for instance). Further, much of the illegal activity was associated with one-time opportunities, such as the "primitive capitalist accumulation" of spontaneous privatization.

In stable settings, the extent of corruption depends on past levels of corruption.[54] A transitional environment has the advantage that perceptions of previous behavior have less weight in affecting current decisions. Corruption of the old planning apparatus needn't lead people to believe that a new organization such as the State Tax Service or the Tax Police will be equally corrupt. Transition, and the new institutions that accompany transition, offer a slate that may not be perfectly clean, but at least is not as discredited as the previous system.

Fourth, like any evasion, widespread and visible corruption provides information to policy makers regarding where the rules and their associated enforcement regimes are not compatible with providing incentives to individuals to comply. This information then suggests that the rules or their enforcement should be changed. This may sound like meager compensation for economic crime, but it is preferable to no compensation. And the provision of such information is more pressing in a transitional setting, where policy makers have little familiarity with regulation of legal private economic activity.

Fifth, and finally, many of the steps that are necessary components of a transition to a market economy, such as privatization and price liberalization, also would seem to serve as anti-corruption measures in the long run. Such complementarities arise from non-essential reform-related measures, too. For example, Russia's interest in joining the Organization for Economic Cooperation and Development and the World Trade Organization will involve additional domestic liberalizations, as well as the adoption of explicit anti-corruption policies.[55]

What should be done?

Russia actually has two economic crime problems, what economists would call a "stock" problem and a "flow" problem. The stock consists of the accumulated economic crime during the transition; the flow is the additions to that stock in the future. The approaches to reducing the flow, to reducing the future incentives for corruption and organized crime, are standard and widely understood, and in part they relate to completing the partial reform measures that led to the increase in economic crime in the first place.[56] Further liberalization and rationalization of the tax code are needed to allow profitable private businesses to operate legally. Also required is a brightening of the line between public and private firms. Laws should be improved to reduce bureaucratic obstacles to business, while on the supply side, the discretion of officials can be reduced simultaneously with an increase in accountability. The public alternative to private protection, particularly the provision of contract law and improved police protection, also is part of the solution.

Harm reduction measures can also be implemented to reduce the costs, not simply the quantity, of economic crime. To reduce the costs of organized crime, "effective time horizons" can be increased (that is, a less present-focused orientation can be fostered) via macroeconomic and political stabilization. (Indeed, without political and macroeconomic stability, there will be many other problems more pressing than economic crime.) Macroeconomic stabilization in Russia has been slow in coming but after the financial crisis of August 1998, it appears to be well along. Political stabilization has also been precarious at best, given such conditions as the parliamentary–presidential battle in 1993, the poor health of President Yeltsin through the mid to late 1990s, and the murder of democratic icon Galina Starovoitova in November, 1998. The costs of the crime that does take place can also be reduced via increases in accountability arising from a free press, an independent judiciary, and a watchdog legislature.

One element of anti-corruption and anti-organized crime measures that is indispensable is a real commitment by leaders to seriously undertake such campaigns. Such commitment is surprisingly hard to come by, in part because the leaders themselves often emerge at the top without completely clean hands, and in part because the commitment can be both socially and personally costly. Analysts of the Sicilian mafia frequently suggest that its long-term vitality is in part illusory, because of the absence of a sustained state campaign to combat the mafia. Despite the frequency of public announcements of anti-corruption campaigns, it is still an open question whether top political levels in Russia are committed to the rule of law, much of which involves limitations on their own powers, particularly when the current deviations from legality are more likely to serve than to harm the political leadership's direct, short-term interests.

The temptation to signal commitment to an anti-corruption platform is to deal with the stock of past economic crime, as opposed to the potential flow of future corruption. The problem with attempting to suddenly punish past crimes in a system of widespread corruption is that you cannot punish everyone. Anyone who is punished, then, can plausibly (and perhaps even accurately) claim that they are being singled out for political reasons. There is bound to be little reason to believe that those who are targeted are somehow more guilty than others who are not targeted. When the crackdown also inhibits the working of a free press, one of the established bulwarks against corruption, then it is doubly ill-advised.[57] And yet this appears to be the approach that is being taken in President Putin's Russia.

The retribution for some previous crime and corruption comes at the expense of providing improved incentives for the future. Because the sudden zero tolerance crackdown deals with the past, and in an obviously biased manner, the deterrence that it might provide against forthcoming misbehavior is undermined. When starting from a situation of widespread violations, the better strategy is to invoke an even-handed harm reduction policy for future crime (one that might employ some elements of targeted zero tolerance), while providing an official or unofficial amnesty for all but the most egregious past offenses.[58]

8   Gun control

"If you outlaw guns, only outlaws will have guns." Logically impeccable, this bumper-sticker truism indicates the extent to which arguments against gun controls rely on the potential for regulations to be evaded. Beyond the evasion of gun controls themselves, firearm policy is affected by murders, robberies, and other violations of criminal laws. An increase in crime can prompt stricter firearm controls, as occurred in Britain following the March, 1996 massacre of sixteen schoolchildren and their teacher in Dunblane, Scotland. Alternatively, crime can serve as a rationale for a relaxation of gun laws; a wave of state-level liberalizations of statutes regulating the concealed carrying of firearms in the US since the mid-1980s is in part a response to heightened levels of crime.

The debate about gun control also is replete with claims of futility and perversity, many of them based on evasion. One common claim is encapsulated in what might be called the "futility syllogism": gun controls apply, by definition, only to the formal market; criminals acquire their guns through informal means; therefore, gun controls will not pose any barrier to criminal acquisition of firearms.[1] The syllogism can also be put into the service of the perversity argument: if the controls make it harder for law-abiding citizens to acquire guns, then criminals will be less deterred, so gun controls aimed at reducing crime will actually increase it.

The rhetorical power of the futility syllogism is impressive: it suggests that supporters of gun controls are not just misinformed, but that they are unreasonable or even irrational. Were the syllogism correct, opponents of gun control would have a very persuasive case. But the syllogism is not correct, as I will demonstrate below. Gun control, whether advisable or not, is not illogical.

Evasion and the choice of preventive v. punitive controls

The main rationale underlying firearm control is evasion of the criminal laws. If people were angels, or if would-be murderers and robbers were sufficiently deterred by the threat of punishment, then there would be few murders or robberies, with or without firearms, and there would be little to gain from controlling guns.[2] Gun control, like blood alcohol content restrictions on drivers, regulates an "input," when the direct public interest is with an "output," violent crime or reckless driving.[3] The availability of cheap and effective output (or punitive, *ex post*) controls, in many circumstances, obviates the need for preventive, *ex ante* controls.

Those who argue against gun control, therefore, often propose as an alternative an enhanced deterrence strategy, in the form of more certain and/or more severe punishment for individuals who criminally misuse guns. But the general notion that effective punitive controls eliminate the need for preventive regulation is not immediately applicable in this instance: even if all murderers were caught and dealt with harshly, and even if there were no potential for guns to be involved in suicides, accidents, or non-fatal crimes, some gun controls might still be sensible.

The argument is simple: murders impose enormous personal and social costs, and even swift, severe, and sure punishment would not eliminate all murders. Some murderers will not forgo their activity by the certainty of punishment; indeed, murder-suicides are not uncommon, and someone contemplating such a route will not be dissuaded by official punishment. Other murderers may fail to be deterred if they are unable to make the expected judgments concerning their actions and the threatened punishment, because of diminished mental capacity, or because they are children, or perhaps because they are temporarily enraged or intoxicated. This point is widely accepted, at least implicitly, as many people who generally oppose gun controls nevertheless support restrictions on gun sales to children and the mentally unstable. In short, even with perfect *ex post* enforcement against crimes, there is still a case for preventive gun controls. Further, all else equal, the worse the *ex post* enforcement, the stronger that case is – and real world enforcement, of course, is far from perfect. Gun suicides and accidents offer a further rationale for preventive gun controls.

But what type of preventive controls might make sense? Controls can be distinguished on the basis of types of gun (handgun v. long gun, say), or on other characteristics such as magazine capacity or rate of fire. Certain technological features such as safety devices or trigger locks can be required, and others, such as automatic firing mechanisms, can be banned. Location is another factor on which controls can turn, as in laws against possession of firearms on school grounds or on commercial airliners. Restrictions can be based on characteristics of the user or purchaser; felons and children, for instance, often face stricter controls. And the firearm-related behavior that is regulated can also vary: controls can be placed on sale, purchase, possession, concealed carrying, required training, brandishing, or firing, among other activities.

There is a general principle that underpins firearm regulation: all else equal, controls are best placed on those firearms, users, and potential applications that present the highest social costs relative to their benefits. Thus typical controls include prohibitions on sales of automatic weapons (among the most dangerous firearms), restrictions on gun possession by convicted felons (among the most dangerous users), and bans on the firing of guns on downtown streets (among the most dangerous applications). Guns with a wide range of beneficial uses, such as shotguns, tend to be governed by a more relaxed regulatory regime.

The general principle of applying stricter controls to the most socially costly weapons, users, and intended uses, however, must be modulated in practice by the efficacy of the controls themselves. Some restrictions may be fairly well enforced at low cost, whereas others may be widely evaded or their hoped-for benefits unrealized, even if substantial resources are put into their enforcement. An ideal firearm regulation aimed at reducing the social costs of crime would pose a substantial barrier to criminal acquisition and use of guns, not unduly inconvenience legitimate gun users (though various approaches can be taken as to what constitutes legitimate gun use), and be inexpensive to implement and enforce.

Varieties of anti-control arguments

While preventive gun control is not illogical *a priori*, and while better criminal justice would not in itself eliminate the rationale for gun controls, these points only establish a case for the theoretical possibility that some gun controls, following the general principle suggested above, might make for sound public policy. As a practical matter, gun controls might not work.

There are three main channels that could lead to the ineffectiveness of gun controls. The first channel involves an avoidance response: perhaps it is the case that even if gun regulations prevent criminals (or potential suicide victims) from procuring a gun, they will simply carry out their deeds with different weapons.[4] A second channel involves evasion, the basis for the futility syllogism outlined above: it is possible that given the existence of a black market for guns, controls will prove little or no barrier to criminal acquisition of firearms. A related argument is that while controls might pose some obstruction to firearm acquisition by high-risk users, the same controls will also make it more difficult for low-risk users to acquire guns, and the new balance of forces could result in increased crime. The third channel that could undermine the case for gun controls is based not on the notion that restrictions have no benefits, but rather that the indirect costs of gun controls are too high to justify the benefits: this is an example of what Albert Hirschman called the "jeopardy" argument. One common "jeopardy" argument is that gun controls, by disarming the citizenry, could lead to the destruction of democracy, as potential governmental tyrants who gain control of the police and military would no longer have to fear an armed uprising of the masses.

Balloon effects: weapon substitution

Action films are full of scenes of weapon substitution. Temporarily denied access to a firearm, James Bond will have no trouble finding some other means, ranging from fists to futuristic gizmos, to overcome the bad guy. Furthermore, the bad guys in these films are particularly strongly motivated to wreak mayhem. A control that prevented them from acquiring guns would only lead to more poison gas or space-based lasers or hired goons.

It is sometimes argued that even in real life, such weapon substitution under-mines the rationale for gun controls. The argument is that potential criminals are highly motivated (akin to movie bad guys), and that, prevented from acquiring guns, they will use knives, or fists, or something, to commit crimes: by whatever means necessary. It is the intent of the criminal, according to this logic, and not the choice of weapon, that determines the social costs of violence.[5]

Research into this issue, however, has yielded a reasonably clear conclusion: there is a substantial "instrumentality effect" to firearms, to the extent that the use of a firearm as opposed to a knife, say, in an otherwise similar attack, greatly increases the probability of a fatality.[6] This accords well with intuition, of course: most of us would rather face an assailant who is armed with a knife than one armed with a gun, and would rather face one who is armed with a slingshot than one armed with a knife. There are no guarantees, of course, as Goliath found out, but on average, firearms are more lethal than other types of weapons commonly employed in run-of-the-mill violent encounters. And while some murderers and robbers are indeed highly motivated, and will pursue their goal by any means necessary, this is not the case for all of them.

From the point of view of would-be criminals, firearms offer significant advan-tages. Guns are a cheap (given their current availability in the US, that is) and effective way to project power in a discriminating way at a distance, and they can pose a significant threat even in the hands of someone with no special skills. Alternative weapons are either difficult to use in as threatening a manner at a distance (this is the case with knives), or are less discriminating (grenades, for instance), or tend to require special skill either to manufacture or to deploy effectively (bombs). Guns are therefore the weapon of choice in a variety of settings, including robberies in public areas and drive-by attacks. Therefore, gun control measures that are successful at reducing gun availability to high-risk users would also stand a good chance of reducing the social costs of violence, though the probability of such an outcome would also depend on the effect of the controls on low-risk users.

Let me add one final point concerning the instrumentality effect associated with guns, which I characterized above as being "reasonably clear." Empirical demon-stration of an instrumentality effect is guaranteed not to satisfy some critics of gun controls, because it is impossible to measure the actual intentions of potential criminals or of those contemplating suicide. It may be that those individuals who are most intent on inflicting harm upon others or themselves choose to acquire a gun for that purpose; indeed, some gun acquisition is undoubtedly driven by such determination. Then, higher death rates associated with guns could simply be due to these stronger motivations, and not to any inherent dangerousness of firearms relative to other weapons. Research into the instrumentality effect has done what it can to try to take into account differing motivations. Investigations have been conducted into robberies, for instance, because it appears that the death of the victim generally is not the intention in robberies, even when someone is shot or stabbed in the course of the encounter. But taking into account the exact intentions of criminals cannot be done in an absolutely precise manner.

Nevertheless, the best evidence and our intuitions coincide: guns are simply more dangerous than most other weapons employed in everyday violent situations. Many gun control opponents implicitly concede this point in their characterizations of the singular effectiveness of guns for defensive purposes.

Substituting to more socially costly firearms

Given the operational problems with bombs, grenades, chemical weapons, etc., it is extremely unlikely that your typical robber or murderer will switch to these weapons if prevented from acquiring a firearm. Some may use weapons that appear to be less socially costly, such as knives or strong-arm tactics, and others might exit the business altogether.

Within the category of firearms, however, are a wide variety of weapons that differ in terms of caliber, rate of fire, magazine capacity, and so on. These weapons also differ in terms of their utility for socially approved purposes (such as hunting, for instance), and their usefulness for crime. A preventive gun control might impact one type of gun more than another, either by design – the assault weapon ban in the US, for example – or simply as a byproduct of individual choice in a regulated environment. Gun controls could cause weapon substitution, not just to knives, bombs, or fists, but also to other types of firearms.

Such substitution is particularly likely when the control is aimed specifically at only one segment of the firearm market, such as handguns, or perhaps low-quality, Saturday-night special-type handguns. An argument commonly mustered by anti-control forces is that strict controls on handguns could result in increased criminal use of shotguns, or perhaps even sawed-off shotguns.[7] Because shotguns and sawed-off shotguns are extremely lethal at close range, if such a switch occurs, the social costs of crime could increase following the institution of effective handgun control.

While it is true that shotguns are extremely dangerous weapons at close range, they are more difficult to aim and to fire rapidly in confined areas, and so it is not clear that they would prove more socially costly when substituted for handguns. But accepting that shotguns (or rifles) are indeed more deadly, the strength of the argument that a handgun-specific ban will lead to more carnage depends on how frequently this type of substitution to a more socially costly firearm actually takes place, and there is no reason to expect that the answer will be the same in all places and at all times. Certainly there are other aspects of shotguns, such as their limited concealability relative to handguns and restricted magazine capacity, that make them fairly poor substitutes for handguns in some types of crime. There seems to be little *a priori* reason to think that such a substitution will be common, or more likely than a switch to low-powered airguns or even combs concealed in a menacing fashion in a jacket pocket.[8] Britain did not see any noticeable shift towards long gun crime following the post-Dunblane handgun ban.

Concern with substitutability within the class of firearms raises the question of how to choose the best mix of preventive firearm controls. Once again, there is no reason to expect that this mix should be the same at all times and at all places. The existing stock of firearms, and its distribution among specific guns and users, is an important determinant of the type of substitutions that might occur, from a regulation applying either to a limited class of firearms or to guns more generally. But there is also no reason to expect that weapon substitution will undermine any specific gun control proposal. Rather, given the instrumentality effect, the expectation (at least for a control that applies broadly across the class of firearms, or that is aimed at particularly dangerous weapons) is precisely the opposite: weapon substitution may reduce the benefits of a control – relative to what would occur in a hypothetical world in which there is no possibility of substitution – but the control will still tend to lead to substitutions that reduce the social costs of violence. The main reservation against accepting this conclusion at this point is the possibility of differential substitution possibilities and preferences between "good guys" and "bad guys," an issue that will be explored further below.

Evasion and the firearm futility syllogism

So much for avoidance. But what of evasion? Recall the firearm futility syllogism: gun controls apply, by definition, only to the formal market; criminals acquire their guns through informal means; therefore, gun controls will not pose any barrier to criminal acquisition of firearms.

The logic behind the futility syllogism is faulty. First, many criminals (at least in the US) do acquire guns through formal channels. But even accepting that they do not, the conclusion of the syllogism does not follow from the premises. Gun controls aimed at the formal market can (and do) influence the informal market. Further, some measures can be adopted to suppress the informal market directly.

Given the existence of a black market, can a gun control actually reduce firearm availability to criminals? The notion that it cannot reflects either a belief that regulations will not raise the effective price required to secure a gun illegally – evasion is free, essentially – or that criminals have a completely inelastic demand for guns, i.e. that they will pay any price for a firearm. (This "price" includes non-monetary elements such as the effort required to find a gun supplier or the probability and length of a prison sentence.) In other words, either would-be criminals do not notice the controls, or they notice them but do not care, being extremely highly motivated, movie-type bad guys.

The extreme versions of both the inelasticity claim and the avowal that controls cannot raise black market prices are clearly false: the relative infrequency of criminal acquisition of guns in prison, for example, shows that controls can greatly inconvenience firearm procurement, and that this inconveniencing – which brings on a much higher effective price – causes the quantity of firearms acquired to fall. Evasion of strict firearm regulations is not free, and the costs such regulations add to gun acquisition are sufficient to deter some people. Otherwise, all current regulations, such as bans on gun ownership by felons, bans on extremely dangerous weapons such as bazookas, and metal detectors at airports, should be abandoned.

For less intrusive controls such as a certification system for legal sales, the extent to which black market prices are raised is less clear, and furthermore, undoubtedly depends on the specific control, the enforcement regime, and the overall regulatory environment. Nevertheless, black market prices for guns appear to be higher in the US Northeast, which has relatively strict controls and lower gun prevalence, than in many southern states, where guns tend to be both more common and less regulated. Also unknown is the extent to which a moderate rise in the effective price occasioned by a control will cause criminal demand to change – though as with almost any other commodity, it is likely that a higher effective price will reduce the quantity demanded. Youths, with their generally low incomes and perhaps a disinclination to persistence, might be especially sensitive to higher effective prices for firearms. One interview study of juvenile offenders in metropolitan Atlanta found that the majority had come across their first gun in a passive manner, without planning to do so.[9] Places that have a higher overall prevalence of firearms, and hence are likely to have a more flourishing black market, tend to have a higher percentage of crimes committed with firearms, as might be expected given a non-negligible responsiveness to price in the criminal demand for firearms. Guns are much less prevalent in Britain, for instance, than in the US, and whereas about 70 percent of US murders are committed with firearms, less than 10 percent of British murders involve guns.[10]

Good guys and bad guys

As noted above, a further anti-control argument is that firearm regulations that reduce availability to criminals might increase the social costs of violence, if the regulations also serve to disarm law-abiding citizens. An obvious initial point that is nevertheless sometimes overlooked is that there is no clear and lasting demarcation between good guys and bad guys. Children or convicted felons may be responsible gun users, whereas many adult gun murderers have no prior convictions. Individuals can become drunk, enraged, temporarily insane, careless, or despondent, and they might misuse guns under such conditions even when they are normally reliable. This is not to say that the presence of a gun will entice an otherwise upstanding citizen to suddenly go on a violent rampage, but rather that gun misuse is not confined to some habitually criminal class. Perhaps a better distinction than good guys v. bad guys is low risk v. high risk users, keeping in mind that this terminology is itself shorthand for what actually is a continuum of types differentiated by their likelihood to misuse a firearm.

While the presence of a gun won't turn an upstanding citizen into a murderous maniac, in many instances gun carrying will alter a person's behavior. Feeling newly secure after acquiring a firearm, a person might be more willing to travel through dangerous neighborhoods, or be slightly more self-assured in encounters with groups of youths, perhaps. Much of this changed behavior has no major social ramifications. But matters can be taken further, to the point that the gun owner could be said almost to be seeking out an appropriate opportunity to brandish or fire the weapon. Geoffrey Canada, drawing on first-hand experience, provides an excellent description of this phenomenon. Canada purchased a gun for security when habitually walking nearby a group of violent teenagers in the Bronx in the early 1970s. "When I look back on the power the gun had over my personality and my judgment I am amazed," Canada writes.[11] Instead of trying to keep a low profile and to avoid the gang when possible, he began to take an openly defiant stance, "prepared to shoot to kill to defend myself." Upon reflection, Canada elected to get rid of the gun: "I knew that if I continued to carry the gun I would sooner or later pull the trigger."

At any rate, the relevance of the argument that a differential impact on low-risk and high-risk users can cause a gun control to have a perverse effect will turn, again, on the actual control envisioned, the ease with which it can be circumvented, the overall regulatory environment, and the extent to which criminal behavior is altered by a change in the number and distribution of firearms. Many gun controls, such as mandated background checks or increased scrutiny of dealers, impose few costs on legitimate purchasers. Controls can have multiple effects, so that a perverse outcome in one dimension could be an acceptable price to pay for the desired effect in another dimension. A control that eliminated 95 percent of all firearms from low-risk and high-risk users in equal proportions, for instance, might make residential burglary a safer and more attractive occupation, while at the same time decreasing the social costs of street crime.[12]

That the environment matters is made clear by a comparison between the US and Britain. In the US, some 40 percent of all households own guns, and many of these presumably do so for defensive purposes.[13] Accordingly, the perversity argument against gun control – which shares with the futility argument the implication that, if correct, it would call for the elimination of existing controls – is commonly made. In Britain, alternatively, guns are not considered to be a legitimate means of private defense, in that an individual will not be granted a permit to legally purchase and possess a firearm for the purpose of personal protection. Proposals for stricter gun controls in Britain, therefore, are generally not attacked on grounds that they will perversely cause the costs of violent crime to rise, because privately owned guns are not supposed to be a deterrent to crime in Britain, anyway.[14] And indeed, street criminals in Britain already have a very high level of assurance that their intended victims are not armed with guns (though perhaps some communities fall outside this general pattern), so stricter gun controls that further disarm low-risk users are unlikely to provide much of a marginal advantage to street criminals.

Jeopardy: Hitler favored gun control

The third type of anti-gun control argument is that gun controls impose costs, perhaps indirectly and only paid in the long term, that are much more significant than any crime-control benefits that might be associated with firearm regulation.

In the US, where these "jeopardy" style arguments are common, the claimed costs of gun control run the gamut from oppression of the gun enthusiasts' sub-culture, to paving the way for the destruction of liberty. Sometimes even the Hitler card is played in these debates: Germany confiscated guns during the Nazi era, following Weimar-era gun registration.[15]

While an ideal gun control would draw a bright line between high-risk (i.e. prohibited) users and others, as a practical matter, many controls that would be effective at keeping guns away from high-risk individuals also impose greater burdens on law-abiding citizens. Some of the costs that are pointed to by purveyors of jeopardy-style arguments are quite specific, and should undoubtedly be taken into account in designing firearm policy. For example, the enforcement of some preventive gun controls requires police efforts that lead to a loss of privacy. While regulations such as instant background checks are not very intrusive, others, such as house-to-house searches, would be another matter entirely, and in the extreme could bring on a police state.

Violating a preventive gun control, as opposed to committing a criminally violent act, is a victimless crime. Many illegal gun transfers, for example, take place between consenting adults. Lacking a victim to register a complaint, police enforcement against illegal firearm activity requires proactive efforts that could range from the innocuous (encouraging people in the community to provide tips) to the intrusive (stop and frisk campaigns). Undercover sting operations involving fake buying and selling might also be part of a proactive enforcement arsenal. While such operations could be relatively well-targeted at suspected high-volume sellers or those who supply youths, undercover stings can also cross the line into police entrapment. As with enforcement of other types of victimless crimes, there is the potential for police corruption in the enforcement of preventive gun controls.[16] Another enforcement issue that arises in combating the informal firearms market is the difficulty of ensuring the safety of the police, their informants, and their undercover agents against armed opponents.

Other costs sometimes associated with gun control are more speculative. For example, it has been argued that privately owned firearms are an important component of a distinctive US sub-culture, and that gun controls are "a form of 'cultural genocide.'"[17] Why regulations (short of wide-ranging bans) need destroy the gun culture is unclear, to say the least. It could be argued just as persuasively that sensible regulations would enhance gun culture, and lend it wider appeal. Similarly, the notion that gun controls cast aspersions on the decency of gun owners, the vast majority of whom are upstanding citizens, is no more compelling than the claim that the licensing of automobiles and their operators calls into question the decency of drivers.[18] This is not to say that such jeopardy-style concerns are not genuine, or that they can be dismissed out of hand. But the costs that they point to are generally too conjectural to justify as a basis for firearm policy.

A further speculative cost of gun controls is featured in jeopardy-type arguments of the "slippery slope" variety.[19] The proposed gun control isn't so bad in itself, the argument might go, but it creates conditions that will lead to stricter controls with onerous consequences in the future: a treadmill of reform will be initiated that leads to bad outcomes. Registration of handguns, for instance, might be viewed as being a first step towards government confiscation of handguns at a later date, as the British experience (discussed in more detail below) has shown. Again, there is some substance to such a claim, for indeed registration would make confiscation easier to implement, and undoubtedly there are gun control advocates who are hoping for just such a progression. But slippery slope arguments also suggest a certain irrationality in future democratic decision making: today's reform will make us choose bad reforms later. Given such capriciousness in legislative activity, how can we be confident about the suitability of any governmental decisions today, whether they be pro- or anti-gun control?[20]

The Second Amendment

Perhaps the most important of the jeopardy-style arguments against gun control is that an unarmed population would have no protection against governmental tyranny. Beyond the Hitler analogy, this concern is often pointed to as being the basis for the Second Amendment to the US Constitution, which reads: "A well regulated Militia, being necessary to the security of a free State, the right of the people to keep and bear Arms, shall not be infringed." Here, clearly, is a jeopardy concern that cannot be casually dismissed. But how should it be taken into account with respect to a given firearm regulation, which might contribute to the constitutional intentions, as stated in the Preamble, of ensuring domestic tranquility and promoting the general welfare? It probably is the case that a would-be dictator would find it in his or her interest to restrict the private ownership of guns. But simply because a policy would be useful for a dictator does not mean that a similar policy cannot be beneficial in a democracy.[21] Otherwise, such government policies as social security or maintaining a strong military might also be considered inappropriate in a democracy.

The meaning of the Second Amendment is the subject of continuing debate, most notably concerning whether the right to arms is an individual or a collective right (i.e. only applies to citizens as members of a militia). As with other constitutional protections, however, the right to keep and bear arms is not absolute, and no federal gun control measure has ever been found unconstitutional by the US Supreme Court on Second Amendment grounds. The argument that the motivation for the amendment is to prevent governmental tyranny would be most salient for sweeping measures, such as an attempted ban on private firearm possession. It is generally recognized that other controls, such as restrictions on ownership of bazookas, or on the firearm ownership rights of children and felons, are not inconsistent with the tyranny concern underlying the Second Amendment.[22] Nevertheless, opponents of US gun controls frequently invoke the Second Amendment, and it could be interpreted in future court decisions to rule out some restrictive legislation.

Note that even if future gun controls were ruled invalid on Second Amendment grounds, these controls might still be desirable: "most people . . . would not be impressed by the argument 'I admit that my behavior is very dangerous to public safety, but the Second Amendment says I have a right to do it anyway.' That would be a case for repealing the Second Amendment, not respecting it."[23]

The unwholesome side effects of gun regulations present legitimate concerns, and care must be taken in designing gun policy to minimize the potential for undesirable consequences. Jeopardy, however, is not a concern specific to stricter preemptive gun controls. The current system of US gun regulation has side effects of its own, as would a system of fewer restrictions. The current regulatory regime, for instance, contributes to a pattern of gun misuse that puts many US citizens' lives in jeopardy, creates a climate of fear, and makes many public spaces in-hospitable or worse, providing some impetus towards suburbanization and a privatization or even a cocooning of lives. The liberty that many fear is put at risk by gun control can also be threatened by a proliferation of firearm violence.[24]

A summing up

The futility, perversity, and jeopardy arguments against gun controls are not devoid of logic, which explains their continued appeal. But they do not apply to all controls in all places at all times, and in their extreme versions they are wrong in most instances. Gun controls will not work perfectly or without cost, but they can work, and in the right direction. Rule evasion matters – but so do rules. The next few sections look at how both firearm rules and their evasion do matter with respect to the social costs of violence, informed by the differential experiences of Britain and the US.

Gun prevalence and evasion[25]

The examination of common anti-control arguments presented above indicates that a new gun control need not be an exercise in futility or perversity, nor need it be contaminated by unacceptable side effects. The balance of direct costs and benefits, however, might be unfavorable to the proposed control, and even suggest that existing controls should be repealed. Faced with widespread criminal evasion of gun laws, for instance, legitimate users might welcome a relaxation of gun regulations to enhance their defensive capabilities, or they might even begin to evade the existing restrictions themselves. The sort of positive feedback that characterizes arms races between nations can also fuel an outbreak of evasion of domestic gun laws: criminal acquisition of guns leads to better arming of their potential victims, leading to further criminal acquisition or perhaps more powerful weaponry, eliciting further counter-response, and so on.

As noted earlier, such positive feedback or epidemic-style phenomena tend to exhibit a threshold phenomenon: if evasion of gun laws is sufficiently small, it will remain small, but if for some reason evasion rises above a certain (or rather, an uncertain) threshold, it can spiral upward to a much higher level as more and more individuals find it in their interest to obtain and perhaps to use a firearm.

An increase in the number of firearms alone does not necessarily imply that an increase in the social costs of violence will follow, despite the instrumentality effect associated with firearms. The impact of more guns will, to a significant degree, depend on the characteristics of those who acquire the additional guns, as well as on the overall environment. Nevertheless, in broad terms, there seems to be a positive correlation between the number of guns and violent death[26] – an unsurprising conclusion, given the instrumentality effect of guns. Further, secondary markets (fueled by thefts of guns, for instance) redistribute some firearms from low-risk to high-risk users, so increases in the stock of firearms owned by low-risk individuals need not be socially benign in the long term. But it is possible for high gun prevalence to be accompanied by either low levels of gun violence (as in Switzerland, for example), or by high levels of gun violence (as in some parts of the US). What is difficult, however, is for a country to maintain a low prevalence of firearms as firearm violence grows to a significant level, because of the positive feedbacks described above: with gun violence growing, both low-risk and high-risk individuals will find gun ownership increasingly attractive.

As in other "balance-of-power" situations, it may be the transition phase to high gun prevalence when violence is most common, whether on the scale of a neighborhood or a nation. When the new, high gun prevalence "equilibrium" is established, public protection and private self-protection will presumably have adjusted in ways that limit the advantages that can be gained by initiating armed encounters. Such adjustments, which might include moving to a new neighborhood or never leaving home after dark, can themselves be quite costly, even ignoring the transitional violence. And if the "equilibrium" is disturbed in a high gun prevalence setting, then gun violence could once again spurt upward. In short, a country (or neighborhood) that is in a low gun prevalence setting is likely to find itself well-served by avoiding the violence-induced transition to high gun prevalence, even if, once established, the high gun equilibrium is itself not appreciably more violent than the starting point.[27]

Positive feedbacks and threshold effects hold implications for appropriate policies, with respect to firearms as well as in other instances. Interventions in high gun violence areas must be massive enough to reduce prevalence below the threshold. Smaller interventions will have no long-run impact. Another implication specific to the threshold view is that temporary measures can nevertheless have long-term consequences, if they can induce a switch from the high to the low gun-ownership environment. In a community that is near the threshold, small interventions can have large and lasting effects, if they provide the requisite marginal impetus towards the low-gun society. The utility of these general observations in practice, however, is likely to be very limited, given the impossibility of actually identifying a clear threshold level of violence, even when the existence of forces engendering positive feedback is unmistakable. In relatively closed settings, however, such as in airports or schools, an enforcement regime of credible zero tolerance is feasible, and given the potential for positive feedback in firearm prevalence and violence, may well be desirable.

Responding to perceived increases in firearm crimes

Both the US and Britain responded to higher gun crime throughout the twentieth century by enacting stricter controls on some of the most dangerous types of firearms. The British response, however, was much more wide-ranging – recall the post-Dunblane ban on private ownership of handguns, for instance – and as a result the stock of firearms in Great Britain has been decreasing rather steadily during recent decades.[28] In the US, while automatic weapons and "assault weapons" have become strictly controlled, legal access to other types of guns remains comparatively much more liberal. A few million more firearms are added to the US stock every year, and in many states, rules regulating the concealed carrying of firearms have been significantly softened. In the mid-1990s, the 200 million or so firearms in the US exceeded the British stock by a factor of 100.[29]

In Britain, those who wish to obtain a firearm legally must first acquire a certificate. Among other requirements, they must demonstrate that they have good cause for possession of a firearm, and they also must show that they have made provision to store the firearm safely. Personal protection does not constitute a legally acceptable rationale for firearm ownership, even for those individuals who routinely handle large sums of money or valuables. In the US, alternatively, legal owners generally do not have to indicate any reason for firearm acquisition, nor demonstrate provision for safe storage, and gun possession for personal protection is common.[30]

The difference between the US and British responses to increased firearm crime can largely be traced to differences in the level of such crime and to the availability of firearms. British firearm crime has been only a small fraction of US firearm crime in the second half of the twentieth century – in 2000, there were more than 10,000 firearm murders in the US, compared with 62 in England and Wales – and firearms seem to be considerably more accessible to high-risk users in the US than in Britain.[31] While the relevant policy question in Britain is how to prevent an outbreak of evasion of criminal and gun laws, in the US the issue is how to deal with the existing epidemic.

Britain's difficulty in trying to maintain a low gun crime, low gun prevalence society is that such a situation can be unstable. An increase in gun ownership or violence by certain groups (drug dealers, perhaps) can initiate the positive feedback leading to a high evasion society. To reduce the potential for such a dynamic process to unfold, people require strong assurances that other people whom they encounter will not be armed with guns. Strict firearm controls, to the extent that they can support the reasonable belief that others do not have guns (or that if they do have guns, there is little to fear from them), can help prevent transition to the high evasion situation. Signals of forceful policing against those who carry firearms, and against illicit providers of firearms, can help to generate this belief, when combined with low levels of gun crime.[32] The limited carrying of firearms by British police officers also plays a role in keeping forces of positive feedback in check.

The wide support in Britain for the stricter gun laws instituted following the Dunblane massacre is indicative of extensive interest in maintaining a low gun prevalence society. The relatively small extent of firearm ownership previously prevailing in Britain implied that only a small minority of people would be directly hurt by the stricter controls, and many of them were partially compensated when the newly prohibited handguns were bought and destroyed by the government. Further, as firearms have not been legitimate weapons for personal protection in Britain in recent decades, there was almost no concern that the new laws would lead to more violence against the law-abiding population.

The existence of high levels of firearm violence in some areas of the US, however, creates a much different policy environment. Stricter policing alone is unlikely to generate much assurance that others are unarmed, at least in high prevalence areas, in part because the black market in such areas is likely to be larger and more difficult to suppress. For the same reason, a British- style ban on handguns or the delegitimation of firearm acquisition for personal protection would not be appropriate policies under current US conditions. Somewhat paradoxically, the imposition of stricter controls could be more beneficial in low gun crime areas than in areas marked by high levels of firearm violence. Given its relative dearth of firearms, Britain can pursue a zero tolerance-type policy against gun violence and illicit gun possession with a significant degree of credibility – an approach that is not available in much of the US, which has to look to other measures to limit the harms from high gun prevalence and misuse.

The current high gun violence situation in the US has increased the perceived need by some law-abiding citizens to own and carry firearms for personal protection. In recent years, many states have liberalized their laws governing the conditions under which citizens can legally carry concealed firearms. The impact of these regulatory changes on crime rates is a hotly debated issue, related to the more general – and no less controversial – question of the extent and effectiveness of firearm use for defensive purposes.[33] Irrespective of how these research issues are eventually decided, however, the liberalized concealed carry laws are not unreasonable responses when individuals find themselves in a high gun violence environment. Nevertheless, these laws themselves may hinder an eventual transition to a low gun violence setting, both through arms race effects and through the supply of black market guns via diversions from the legal stock.[34]

Weakening the link between gun prevalence and availability to high-risk users

In the US, the virtually unregulated secondary gun market provides youths and felons relatively easy access to guns. For this reason, futility-type arguments against general gun controls are significantly more compelling in the US than in Great Britain, contributing to gun proliferation by making it very difficult in some areas to offer reasonable assurances that others are not able and willing to use firearms. Any proposed gun control looks to many law-abiding citizens like an arms control treaty with an enemy, where the enemy neither has the intention nor faces the compulsion to abide by the terms of the treaty. Strict British-style gun control, therefore, is unlikely in the US, and the country will almost certainly remain a high gun prevalence society, at least for the foreseeable future.

But as we have seen, high gun prevalence need not lead to high levels of firearm crime, though at a broad level firearm proliferation is positively correlated with the extent of firearm crime: a correlation that appears to be particularly strong with respect to American youths.[35] Given that the US will remain a high gun prevalence society, then, regulatory policy should be aimed at weakening the link between overall gun prevalence and the availability of firearms to high-risk users.

How do those high-risk users, including felons and youths, who are prohibited from gun ownership under current law, acquire firearms? Only recently has fairly detailed information on this question become available.[36] For the most part, it appears that it is "leakages" from the legally owned stock of guns that supply criminals, as opposed to direct smuggling of guns from abroad or home manufacture, say. Many of these leakages occur without the consent of the previous owner: about 500,000 guns are stolen in the US each year. Others take place unwittingly, in the sense that a legal owner who is selling a gun may not know (or may be indifferent to the fact) that the buyer is in a prohibited class. Firearms dealers are licensed and regulated in the US, but non-dealers can sell used guns with almost no oversight. There are also unlicensed dealers, those whose transactions in firearms are of such a scale as to require a license, but who illegally remain outside the licensing system. Some of these illegitimate dealers engage in gun running, purchasing guns in states with relatively lax controls and illegally reselling them in states with stricter regulations. Drug dealers, who find guns to be an almost necessary tool in plying their illicit trade, sometimes diversify their underground economic activity by trading in guns.[37]

Licensed dealers, who legally can receive firearms through the mail and who can order a wide assortment of guns, are in a privileged position if they choose to operate illicitly. Indeed, rogue dealers appear to form an important segment of the underground traffic in guns. Sometimes such dealers knowingly sell to "straw purchasers," those who acquire a gun for the purpose of transferring it to someone else who cannot make a legal purchase himself or herself. Some individuals operate as straw purchasers on a one-time or small-scale basis, while others might engage in such transactions repeatedly, perhaps to supply guns to urban gangs. Gun shows, which bring licensed and unlicensed dealers together with prospective buyers, provide a forum in which guns can be illegally trafficked with relative ease. Further, small-scale informal transfers can take place through a wide variety of markets, including classified advertizements or over the Internet.

Given the multiple channels of illicit supply, guns are readily available in the US to prohibited users such as many felons and youths. Nevertheless, this ready availability does not seem to apply across the board. In one survey of individuals who had been arrested for crimes in urban areas, only slightly more than half said that guns could easily be obtained illegally, and a much lower percentage (37 percent) indicated that they could acquire a gun within a week.[38] Even the relatively permissive gun regulations in the US impose a degree of restraint on the ability of some prohibited users to expeditiously acquire a firearm. Evasion of existing gun laws may not be an expensive proposition, but it is not free.

To weaken the link between overall gun prevalence and availability to high-risk users, attempts should be made to reduce the most common channels of illicit supply. Of course, many criminals will still be able to acquire firearms, and no doubt other supply routes will increase as those that are now most common are more strictly controlled. Nevertheless, it should be possible to raise the costs of firearm acquisition by high-risk users significantly, with minimal impact on the availability of firearms to law-abiding citizens, given that the current system often puts little barrier in the way of criminal firearm acquisition.

The most obvious step towards preventing leakage of firearms from low-risk to high-risk individuals is to pay more attention to the secondary market, which in the US is, *de facto*, largely unregulated. Gun shows, classified advertizements, and many other means allow people to exchange firearms informally. As in Britain, secondary sales could be subject to regulatory provisions similar to those demanded of official dealers; implementation of such regulation could be facilitated by requiring private transfers to be registered through the existing licensed dealer network. (The 1994 Youth Handgun Safety Act, prohibiting private transfers of handguns to youths just as such transfers by official gun dealers were already prohibited, provides one example of an extension of primary-market regulation to the secondary market.) An important complement to such an approach to limiting the black market involves increased scrutiny of dealers, to discourage off-the-books sales to prohibited high-risk purchasers. Scofflaw licensed dealers traffic a disproportionate amount of illicit guns in the US, so large gains would seem to be available by monitoring the behavior of dealers more closely.

The substantial amount of firearm theft in the US, together with the approximately 1,000 fatal accidents each year, suggests that safe storage requirements for legal gun ownership could profitably be introduced, though some provision might have to be made for the considerable numbers of Americans who believe personal protection requires them to keep a loaded and unlocked firearm close at hand.[39] Theft might also be dissuaded through some encouragement to "personalized" firearms, which can only be fired by the designated owner, identified by a fingerprint or a special ring.[40] Spillovers from drug law changes could also be important in the firearms market. Diminished illicit drug transactions would reduce a major component of demand for informally acquired firearms, and simultaneously narrow a channel for black market firearm supply.

Suggestions such as these for new firearm regulations in the US are sometimes countered with a futility argument that implicitly invokes both evasion and rule complexity. The argument notes that there are 20,000 gun laws (or 30,000, or some other large number) already on the books in the US, and that everything the bad guys do with their guns is already criminal – what could possibly be the value of more rules? The answer is that irrespective of the number of rules, the firearm regulatory regime in the US has major, built-in inadequacies that make it too easy for prohibited users to acquire firearms. The fact that secondary sales by non-dealers are essentially free of regulation, and that gun shows provide a forum for a large number of unregulated and often illicit sales, renders evasion of the existing rules easy. Barriers (imperfect as they will be) can be raised against this evasion, without substantially increasing the burden placed on legitimate gun purchasers. The existing regulatory structure has large holes, holes that cannot be filled solely by stricter enforcement of the existing laws. Filling these holes makes sense, whether there are 30 or 30,000 laws already on the books.

Weapons of mass destruction

I suggested above that restrictions on bazookas were widely accepted and generally thought consistent with the US Second Amendment, though perhaps it is worthwhile asking why. Why should law-abiding citizens not be allowed to own any weapon they desire, including atomic bombs? The extreme versions of the arguments that are frequently invoked against gun control would seem to apply equally well to nuclear weapons: it is better just to punish people who misuse them; criminals will ignore any restrictions on nuclear bombs anyway, or substitute to biological or chemical weapons that are more deadly; the government has atomic weapons so the only way to counter the potential for tyranny is for private citizens to have the bomb, too; etc.

The reason that such arguments appear silly when applied to atomic weapons, even though they are seriously advanced by intelligent commentators in the context of gun controls, is that most people do not actually believe the extreme versions of such arguments, and they implicitly accept the general notion that all else equal, controls are most appropriately applied to those weapons, users, and intended applications that present the highest social costs relative to their benefits. *Ex post* controls, punishing the bad guys after they "misuse" an atomic bomb, simply are inadequate. A single atomic weapon has the potential to inflict massive death and destruction, and given the very limited or non-existent benefits of private uses of atomic weapons, strict *ex ante* controls are called for.[41]

An aside on the Cold War

During the Cold War, the predominant US security concern was with Soviet nuclear weapons, and vice versa. Once the Soviets acquired their nuclear capability, there was no possibility for the US to impose *ex ante* controls on the USSR, and again, vice versa, though some people held out hope for defensive measures that would render harmless the other side's nuclear weapons. But the day-to-day hope was that deterrence, through the credible threat of a massive retaliation should a nuclear attack take place, would be sufficient to preclude any first use of strategic nuclear arms. As a result of the need to make retaliation credible, both sides had to respond to any increase in the other's nuclear capability with more nukes of their own, and an arms race inevitably ensued. An agreement to hold the line at low levels of weapons, given the general state of mistrust between the adversaries, would have been extremely vulnerable to evasion or the presumption of evasion by the opposing side. The US and the Soviet Union therefore moved from conditions of low to high prevalence of nuclear weapons, such that each ended up with enough nuclear weapons to destroy the other many times over.

Large stockpiles of nuclear weapons by the US and the Soviet Union presented some dangers that were greater than existed with low stockpiles, even with no difference in the overall military balance: as with firearms, high prevalence tends to be more problematic than low prevalence. First, the greater the number of weapons, the higher the probability of a launch occasioned either by accident or by some rogue element within the military, and the higher probability of a non-launch, domestic accident or explosion. Second, the outcome of an all-out war would have been more damaging the greater the number of weapons; with the tens of thousands of weapons possessed by each side, the possibility of a post-attack "nuclear winter" that would destroy all life on earth was raised by some scientists. Third, though probably least important, the immense inventories were more expensive to create and maintain.[42] As a result, once the arms race had already produced enormous stockpiles, arms control measures were attempted and even enacted between the US and the Soviet Union. These treaties were tremendously complex and controversial, largely because the potential for evasion or avoidance had to be controlled by extensive verification procedures. But the treaties that limited weapons did not take place until there was already huge "overkill" in the nuclear stockpiles, so that even one side's cheating on the negotiated limits would not have proved fatal to its adversary.[43]

There were myriad nuances to the delicate nuclear situation during the Cold War. One was that many analysts believed that, with respect to conventional weapons, the Soviets had superiority in the European theater. If this were indeed the case, a Soviet invasion into West Germany, for instance, potentially could not be stopped except by tactical (battlefield) nuclear weapons. But would the US use such weapons to protect Germany, if their use meant that US cities would then be destroyed by Soviet nuclear weapons? (Though of course, it was also unclear if the Soviets would respond with strategic nuclear arms, knowing that their bombs would lead to retaliation by the US.) It was in the US interest, therefore (and, in the curious logic of arms races, probably in the Soviet interest, too), to try to create a bright line distinguishing tactical nuclear weapons from strategic ones, so that the use of a tactical nuclear weapon would not be seen as inviting or even requiring a response with strategic atomic bombs. In this way, the threat to use tactical weapons would gain credibility, and serve as a better deterrent against a Soviet advance into Western Europe.

Nuclear weapons have led to two other "bright lines," one intentional, one that arose more-or-less unintentionally. The latter is the distinction between nuclear and conventional weapons, irrespective of their firepower. Thanks to more than fifty-five years without a hostile nuclear explosion, the use of an atomic weapon in a military conflict would be clearly, qualitatively different from the use of otherwise equivalent conventional weapons.[44] (For other reasons, the use of chemical or biological weapons is also viewed as being qualitatively different.) The long period of non-use appears to have made those countries with nuclear capabilities extremely reticent about using them – and rightly so – though one hostile use might completely change this situation. Both the US and the Soviet Union abandoned conventional wars against non-nuclear opponents despite the superpowers' nuclear weapons arsenals.

The other bright line is between military and non-military applications of atomic power. They are not technologically distinct: advances in civilian use of nuclear energy, for instance, make it easier to gather the radioactive material necessary to make a bomb, and research and development efforts often have dual, military and civilian, uses. The Nuclear Nonproliferation Treaty and its collateral agreements, however, attempt to draw and enforce the military v. civilian distinction – as well as a distinction between states that already had manufactured and exploded a nuclear bomb by 1967, and those that had not – with promises to aid the civilian atomic energy program of non-nuclear weapon states, and to negotiate "in good faith" to achieve nuclear disarmament. (Indian critics of this line-drawing have referred to the policy as "nuclear apartheid."[45]) And while the preventive controls on the transfer or development of nuclear weapons technology have been remarkably (though not fully) successful for decades, evasion threatens the long-term viability of the treaty: despite monitoring provisions, some signatories, including Iraq and North Korea, have been able to advance clandestine nuclear weapon programs, and non-signatories (including India, Pakistan, and Israel) have made successful efforts to acquire nuclear arms.

In terms of the number of nations that possess nuclear weapons, it is possible that the world is now facing a transition from a low to a high nuclear arms "equilibrium."[46] And once this transition occurs, especially if the taboo against the use of nuclear weapons is broken, it is hard to know where it will or should stop, as still further proliferation may be stabilizing. If India has nuclear weapons then it might lead to greater stability for Pakistan to have them, too, in one of many examples that spring to mind.[47] Once *ex ante* controls have failed, deterrence is all that is left to prevent a determined but hopefully sane leader from launching a nuclear attack.

Terrorists

Nations are one thing, and small terrorist groups or even a disgruntled individual are something else entirely. They may be beyond deterrence, as Thomas Hamilton was when he attacked the schoolchildren of Dunblane, intending his own suicide as well. Or they may rightly recognize that it is far from certain that they will be apprehended after a murderous attack. Lacking a state actor that officially takes a military action, the victimized nation may not know whom to retaliate against following a terrorist attack, thereby weakening deterrence. A lone, undeterrable maniac with a gun or a conventional bomb can present terror enough, but what if weapons of mass destruction are available to such a person? This prospect is sufficiently harrowing that some preventive, *ex ante* measures are clearly necessary to limit the possibility of an attack with weapons of mass destruction by terrorist groups or lone maniacs.

Controls and the inherent difficulties and expense of manufacturing nuclear weapons have apparently and thankfully kept atomic bombs away from terrorists so far, though the break-up of the Soviet Union has heightened concerns that the availability of these weapons has been substantially enhanced. Chemical weapons are easier to manufacture than nuclear arms, but are not simple to handle and to deliver in ways that result in large numbers of casualties, though they certainly are capable of mass destruction. Not all attempts to deploy such weapons are sure to have as few fatalities as the 1995 nerve gas release in the Tokyo subway. But it seems as if "biological weapons combine maximum destructiveness and easy availability,"[48] as well as being difficult to detect. If so, then a single madman, instead of killing hundreds or perhaps thousands of people with a conventional bomb, could kill millions with some biological agent such as anthrax.

Preventive controls on biological weapons are therefore justified, and most nations have banned them by the 1972 Biological Weapons Convention (though evasion of this treaty is a significant issue). But if a lone madman can without too much difficulty secure and deliver a biological weapon that can kill millions, enforcing the ban on nations will prove to be insufficient. Intelligence gathering and the infiltration of terrorist groups will have to be increased, and perhaps even more drastic measures will be necessary. The threat to civil liberties that some people see in firearm regulations could become much more severe if an attack with a biological weapon is the event to be forestalled.[49] The precise measures that are appropriate will depend on the actual ease of acquiring and deploying biological weapons. If the capability and the intention to acquire and use these weapons is sufficiently large, however, the unpleasant trade-off between civil liberties and defense against terrorists will become more acute, and more agonizing, in the future.

Postscript: The future is now. The preceding paragraphs on terrorism were written prior to the events of September 11, 2001, which, alas, have made the trade-offs between civil liberties and defense much more palpable.

Conclusions

Economics has earned its reputation as the dismal science in part because economists are fond of pointing out hidden costs. The benefits of most economic activities are relatively obvious, while the sacrifices tend to be a bit more obscure. When the government erects a building, the benefit, the finished product, is there for everyone to see. The costs, though, are veiled – some businesses did not hire additional workers, the ice cream store down the street did not expand. Economists specialize in revealing these opportunity costs, and messengers of bad news have never been highly regarded.

As consistent contrarians, however, economists are likely to emphasize the benefits of those activities in which most people see only harm. The direct social costs of theft, for example, are judged by most economists to be small, since a theft involves a transfer of resources from one person to another: the victim's loss is at least partly compensated for by the thief's gain.[1] While economists are unlikely to argue that theft, or dictatorship, or slavery are socially optimal, they are more likely than others to point out that these activities or institutions are not quite as bad as they seem. One could explain much of the behavior of economists, it would appear, by asking how one could go about making oneself unwelcome at the average dinner party.

Rule breaking generally has a negative connotation, so my duty as an economist has been to sacrifice personal popularity by highlighting the benefits of evasive activity. I hope that I have succeeded in doing so – at least the diminished popularity part seems to have worked out – without unduly minimizing the significant costs that can also arise from rule evasion. I have started from the premise that disparate areas of policy making, from campaign finance reform to S&L regulation, from zero tolerance to gun control, are linked in that they are permeated by the formation and reformation of rules in the light of potential and actual evasion. Public policy is as much about the breaking of rules as it is about the making of rules. The two are intertwined in a complex web.

The general inquiry presented in the previous pages has attempted to untangle, however slightly, the web connecting evasion to reform. Some of the threads of that web have been identified. Small-scale evasion tends to substitute for explicit policy reform. Massive evasion prompts reform, and often reform for the better, in a type of unintentional civil disobedience. The success of evasion-induced reforms, however, can require alterations in complementary policies, and the requisite alterations might not be as obvious as the need to replace the evaded rule. Corruption is less well-endowed with the reform-inducing properties of other modes of exit from rules: government officials, those ultimately responsible for changing the rules, might have their personal interests closely tied to the existing corruption. Potential evasion and avoidance often are invoked as arguments against reforms, on the grounds that such forms of exit would render reforms impotent. Nevertheless, the conditions under which reform futility is likely are rather limited – those arguing against a reform in terms of futility might actually fear the reform precisely because it would not be futile.

So rule evasion matters. But armed with this realization, and with some guidelines about how evasion matters, what new or more emphasized considerations should policy makers attend to? When considering a reform, policy makers must understand that their rules will shape the behavior of fallible and disobedient humans – humans who may have interests much opposed to simple compliance with the strictures delivered by law givers. While perfect foresight cannot be expected from policy makers, attention should be directed towards potential channels of avoidance and evasion of the new policy. Can minor changes in the proposed policy, perhaps involving a partial liberalization, or closing a loophole for avoidance, prevent circumvention of the policy or channel it into less undesirable directions? Can the most costly types of rule evasion be curtailed through changes in the enforcement regime? Which path towards improved outcomes will be most sustainable, formal changes in the rules or informal changes in enforcement? Might it make sense to tolerate more circumvention of the policy, in exchange for lower social costs associated with those evasions that do take place?

Policy makers must also remember that enforcers are drawn from the sea of fallen humanity, too. Does the policy call too deeply upon scarce reserves of integrity on the part of enforcers? Is corruption made too tempting? Does the policy endow a simple act or failure to act on the part of an individual enforcer with the power to induce a sizable bribe? Can the incentives for corrupt behavior be reduced, perhaps by increasing transparency, or by limiting discretion, without compromising the goals of the policy?

When faced with increased evasion of an existing policy, policy makers must revisit these same issues. The reflexive response to evasion is dismay and calls for stricter enforcement. The reflective response is to ask what can be learned from the extent and the nature of the rule circumvention that is taking place, and then to use that information to mold better policies. Is the evasion tolerable, or can evasion be directed into forms that would be consistent with overall policy objectives? Can a noticeable dent be made in the evasion through low-cost means, perhaps a short-term crackdown or get-tough rhetoric? Does the potential for positive feedback in evasion render even a small amount of evasion a matter of concern, one worthy of a significant policy shift? Has corruption of enforcers undermined their interest in socially desirable reforms? Should a blind eye be turned to forms of corruption that are not directly socially damaging?

Evasion of constraints has been with us since the beginning, when Eden's one rule was broken. Banishment from a world of plenty is a steep price to pay for a single act (or two acts) of noncompliance. We can take some solace in the recompense, however meager, that rule breaking now provides, in the form of exerting pressure for better public policies.

Notes

Introduction

1 The Colombian story was reported on the BBC World Service, February 17, 1998. See http://news.bbc.co.uk/hi/english/world/newsid_57000/57304.stm (accessed March 21, 2002).
2 It is far from clear that a crackdown on robbery would be a preferable option. First, it might be very costly to employ enough police to make for a significant deterrent at every traffic intersection. Second, the police might be corrupt, or even in league with the carjackers, so that more police could worsen the problem.
3 There might be other reasons for tax withholding, beyond promoting compliance. As people seem to find it harder to give up something they already count as theirs as opposed to something that has yet to gain that mental status ("the endowment effect"), withholding can reduce the pain that taxes impose on taxpayers. See Stake (1995).
4 Thoreau (1992, p. 233). This quote and the following one are from "Resistance to Civil Government," which was first published in 1849.
5 Thoreau (1992, p. 233).
6 Some forms of civil disobedience involve breaking certain rules, such as trespassing, with the hope of bringing attention to a campaign to change other rules. See Rawls (1977).
7 From an 1862 poem by Arthur Hugh Clough, "The Latest Decalogue."
8 On the role of failure in civil engineering, see Petroski (1992); in policy analysis, see chapter 2 in Wildavsky (1996).
9 Compare this claim with Wildavsky (1996, p. 32), where he notes that error recognition and error correction are not always compatible: small errors are correctable but they are not detectable, whereas large policy mistakes might be detectable but not correctable. Small-scale (as opposed to widespread) evasion and avoidance might hide the information that a policy is failing, while reducing the incentive to implement a reform.
10 Hirschman (1995). The Berlin Wall case is discussed in more detail in Chapter 2.

1 Rules and their circumvention

1 On compliance, see Tyler (1990).
2 The lack of detail in the inventory or accounting procedures governing pens or photocopiers isn't accidental, of course; rather, it reflects the cost and efficacy of such procedures relative to the (generally small) costs imposed by higher levels of misappropriation.
3 The division of rules and regulations into three components – standards, enforcement, and sanctions – is developed by Bardach (1989).
4 Oliver Wendell Holmes, Jr., suggested that the ability to predict how judicial

authorities will handle a situation is equivalent to knowing the law: "The prophesies of what the courts will do in fact, and nothing more pretentious, are what I mean by the law." From "The Path of the Law," reprinted in Posner (1992, p. 163).

5 *Politics*, Book II, Chapter 8.
6 Actually, states and actions need only be differentiated to the extent that anyone could possibly care about the differences; in economics language, only "payoff relevant" distinctions need be made. Marschak and Miyasawa (1968). The technical name for a contract that covers all payoff-relevant contingencies is a "complete contingent contract." See, e.g., Shavell (1984), and Leitzel (1989).
7 Another problem with this contract is that it might be undermined by the potential for later renegotiation. For example, the contract might specify that if person A robs person B, then person A will have to go to prison, providing an incentive for person A to refrain from theft. But it is costly to society to maintain prisons, so person A and society might have an incentive, after a theft has been committed, to forgo the punishment. Anticipation of such a renegotiation, then, can undermine the intended deterrence in the original contract.
8 Hobbes (1970 [1651], p. 93).
9 See, e.g., Ellickson (1991).
10 Williamson (1985) provides a discussion of general rules in the context of transactions mediated across markets or within firms. On the Greeks and the incompleteness of rules, see, for instance, Book VI of Plato's *Laws*, or Book II, Chapter 8, of Aristotle's *Politics*. There is an extensive legal literature concerning "rules" as opposed to "standards," with the difference being that rules specify compliance behavior before the action has been taken (the car cannot travel faster than 55 miles per hour) whereas the determination of whether standards have been met (was the speed "reasonable" given road conditions?) can only take place with an adjudication after the fact. See Kaplow (1992). While I discuss *ex ante* versus *ex post* controls on behavior (see Chapter 5), I do not make a distinction between rules and standards. In my framework, both "rules" and "standards" are examples of rules, though presumably the actor is more confident of his or her knowledge of the relevant compliance actions under a "rule" than under a "standard."
11 The constitutional guarantee of due process in the US, as well as the constitutional prohibition of cruel and unusual punishment, helps to insulate individuals from arbitrary determinations of guilt based on *ex post* or vague rules.
12 The "invisible hand" quote is, of course, from *The Wealth of Nations*; Smith (1991 [1776], p. 400).
13 The "bad man" discussion is in "The Path of the Law," *Harvard Law Review*, 1897; excerpts reprinted in Posner (1992). Rules or legal institutions might help to promote the development of virtuous preferences. See Huck (1998).
14 Compare Buchanan and Tullock (1992 [1962], p. 27): "Insofar as possible, institutions and legal constraints should be developed which will order the pursuit of private gain in such a way as to make it consistent with, rather than contrary to, the attainment of the objectives of the group as a whole."
15 Both the fire in the theater example and the clear and present danger test were enunciated by Holmes for the Supreme Court in *Schenck v. United States*, 249 U.S. 47 (1919), excerpted in Posner (1992, pp. 314–16).
16 Schelling (1971 [1960], p. 112). "Slippery slope" arguments in policy debates are premised on the notion that an initial change will more-or-less automatically lead to further, perhaps undesired changes. See Hirschman's (1991, pp. 81–132) discussion of the "jeopardy thesis;" Hirschman also notes (p. 50) that with respect to the nineteenth-century spread of voting rights, "There was no obvious stopping point on the way to universal suffrage, which soon appeared to contemporary observers to be the inevitable outcome of the process." See also Lode (1999) and Schauer (1985) on slippery-slope reasoning.

17 This passage appears in the infamous decision in *Buck* v. *Bell*, 274 U.S. 200 (1927), upholding the Commonwealth of Virginia's right to sterilize a "feeble-minded" woman who had been committed. Posner (1992, p. 105).

18 From Lewis Carroll's untitled poem that opens *Through the Looking Glass.*

19 See the discussion of philosopher Henry Sidgwick in Bakalar and Grinspoon (1984, p. 152). Such deception, however, has costs of its own; thus, John Stuart Mill in *On Liberty*, 1859: "A state of things in which a large portion of the most active and inquiring intellects find it advisable to keep the general principles and grounds of their convictions within their own breasts, and attempt, in what they address to the public, to fit as much as they can of their own conclusions to premises which they have internally renounced, cannot send forth the open, fearless characters, and logical, consistent intellects who once adorned the thinking world." Ryan (1997, p. 66). See also Kuran (1995) on preference falsification.

20 The exclusionary rule has been diluted since the 1961 ruling. Rothwax (1996, pp. 35–65) presents a broad critique of the rule from the point of view of a trial judge. A central component of his discussion is how the complexity of the rule renders it almost impossible to know in advance if a search will be judged to meet the standards (p. 48): "in more than 90% of the cases, the police don't know what the law is. A chief judge riding in the backseat of a police car wouldn't know what the law is!" Evidence of substantial misconceptions on the part of police, lawyers, and the lay public as to what constitutes a legal search is provided in Heffernan and Lovely (1991).

21 See Bakalar and Grinspoon (1984, p. 119), and Dershowitz (1994, pp. 233–6).

22 In a survey reported in Heffernan and Lovely (1991, p. 349), almost half of the responding officers indicated that in some circumstances they would willingly engage in search practices they thought to be illegal. Former police chief Anthony Bouza (2001, p. 25) suggests that police do not find it shameful to provide perjured testimony.

23 Kleiman (1992, pp. 102–3), and MacCoun, Reuter, and Schelling (1996). One extraordinary example of reluctant denial took place in July, 2002, when Greece banned all electronic games, such as those on home computers. The rationale for this expansive measure was that it was necessary to effectively enforce prohibitions against illegal gambling. Thanks to Will Baude for bringing this case to my attention.

24 Justice Potter's comment appears in his concurring opinion in *Jacobellis* v. *Ohio*, 378 U.S. 184 (1964). An alternative anti-child pornography policy might be to maintain the ban on all such images, but, in effect, to switch the burden of proof to defendants to demonstrate that the images in question did not involve the use of actual children. This might be accomplished by acknowledging such a demonstration as an affirmative defense against child pornography charges. The US Supreme Court struck down a ban on the possession of computer-generated child pornography in April 2002.

25 Basu (1999).

26 Cheung (1977) examines a situation where, with price differentiation, the high-priced tickets are priced somewhat lower than they otherwise would be, in order to ensure enough people legitimately sitting in the high-priced seats that they can perform some of the policing themselves.

27 *Greater New Orleans Broadcasting Association, Inc, etc., et al., Petitioners* v. *United States et al.*, 98 U.S. 387 (1999).

28 Dworkin (1977, p. 208).

29 On vagueness and discretion in US criminal law, see Maclin (2001).

30 Consider, for example, Berns (1987, p. 165): ". . . the great English statute of 1689. The Toleration Act, as it is known, abounds in contradictions and inconsistencies, but, as Macauley correctly points out, it managed to remove 'a vast mass of evil without shocking a vast mass of prejudice,' achievements that can be credited precisely to its employment of those contradictions and inconsistencies. No law based on a clear statement of principle could have succeeded, but, however dimly, the principle is there

for those who seek it [endnotes omitted]." On the potential benefits of discretion in enforcement, see Chapters 2 and 4 below.

31 Schauer (1985, p. 372).
32 See Scotchmer and Slemrod (1990), and the discussion in Andreoni, Erard, and Feinstein (1998, pp. 852–3).
33 Knight (1996, p. 172). Alternatively, the appearance of foolishness in delineating the exclusionary rule might suggest that the rule itself is misguided. Standen (2000) argues that the exclusionary rule might be dominated by a regime where civil damages are assessed against police who conduct unconstitutional searches.
34 Smith (1976 [1759], p. 155).
35 See "Off On A Terror" (February 19, 2002), by Scott Shuger, archived at http://slate.msn.com/?id=2062267 (accessed March 23, 2002).
36 Epstein (1995) provides one approach to developing a system of desirable rules, with a focus on the advantages of relatively simple rules.
37 Harrington (1999) presents a formal model that shows how rigid rules can be favored in bureaucracies, in part because of their high fidelity.
38 The actual puzzle was stated: "Think of a feasible change in the U.S. economy that does not involve payment of compensation and that would be a Pareto improvement." Farrell (1988, p. 178).
39 The suggestion was from Curt Anderson, and was reported in Nalebuff (1989, pp. 172–3.)
40 See the untitled report assessing right-turn-on-red laws prepared for the US National Highway Traffic Safety Administration, at www.nhtsa.dot.gov/people/injury/research/pub.rtor.pdf (accessed January 29, 2002). I would like to thank David Hemenway for alerting me to the literature evaluating the consequences of right-turn-on-red laws.
41 If these adaptations sufficiently blur the bright line of "red means stop, green means go," then they may pave the way for the full "right through red" reform. Though the adaptions allow many of the benefits (in terms of reduced waiting time) of the full reform to be captured in the unreformed setting, the pre-reform blurring of the bright line means that the costs of the full policy change are also reduced.
42 Higher wage rates (or more generally, higher opportunity costs of time) tend to increase the cost of delays at traffic signals, however.
43 Olson (1971).
44 See the model of policy reform in Kane (1996).
45 See, e.g., Winston and Crandall (1994) on theories of regulatory policies.
46 Irwin and Kroszner (1998).
47 This notion is formalized in the "political cost-benefit ratio" of Rodrik (1994).
48 Kane (1996, p. 158). On the pressure towards efficiency in the common law, see Rubin (1977) and chapter 19 of Friedman (2000).
49 Risk aversion alone makes people wary of trading a rule with known outcomes for a reformed rule with unknown outcomes. A sophisticated analysis of how uncertainty over individual outcomes can lead to a bias towards the *status quo*, even among risk-neutral individuals, is provided by Fernandez and Rodrik (1991).
50 This reasoning is consonant with the approach to deregulation in Peltzman (1989) and Kane (1996).
51 Gutmann (1977).
52 Biological evolution also is limited by the need for intermediate forms to be viable.
53 See, e.g., Barzel (1974) and Deacon and Sonstelie (1989).
54 See Lott and Roberts (1989). The enforcement of vice laws, including bans on drugs, prostitution, and gambling, tend to involve more severe sanctions on sellers than on buyers.
55 On wartime price controls, see, e.g. Mills and Rockoff (1987).
56 The estimate on compliance with the US minimum wage, for 1973, is from Ashenfelter

and Smith (1979). Squire and Suthiwart-Narueput (1997) present minimum-wage compliance information from many developing countries.
57 OMRI Daily Digest, No. 61, Part I, March 26, 1996.
58 Barzel (1989, pp. 22–5).
59 Cheung (1975).
60 This point is highlighted in Squire and Suthiwart-Narueput (1997).
61 *Washington Post*, May 24, 1995, p. A1, and May 27, 1994, p. A23.

2 Evasion

1 Cowell (1993, p. 19). Jeff Stake has pointed out to me that were there perfect enforcement, the rules would change to reflect that state of affairs. While this chapter focuses on evasion, much of the discussion does not require that the rule circumvention be illegal, and hence applies to avoidance activities as well.
2 Crime data from the Crime in the United States Press Release, Federal Bureau of Investigation, available at www.fbi.gov/pressrel/pressrel01/cius2000.htm (accessed on February 1, 2002.) The violent crime figure represents a fall of 25.5 percent from the level of 1991.
3 On 55 miles-per-hour US interstate highways in 1992, 70.1 percent of the vehicles exceeded the speed limit; 41.5 percent were at least 5 miles per hour in excess of the speed limit, and 17.5 percent were 10 miles per hour or more in excess. Highway Statistics 1992, p. 222.
4 Andreoni, Erard, and Feinstein (1998, p. 819).
5 Frey (1993) presents a model where increased monitoring can reduce total work effort.
6 Becker (1968). For a thorough review of the economic approach to optimal enforcement, see Polinsky and Shavell (2000a). The level of expected punishment need not precisely determine the extent of deterrence. Some people may be more deterred by a high probability–low severity punishment regime than by a low probability–high severity regime that generates the same expected punishment. Also, it may not be possible to adjust the magnitude of punishment without simultaneously affecting the probability of punishment. Juries might refuse to convict violators, for instance, following the adoption of punishments that jury members view as too severe.
7 Polinsky and Shavell (1979) discuss the possibility of combining a low probability of detection with a high punishment for apprehended malefactors.
8 On how considerations of fairness might influence optimal enforcement, see Polinsky and Shavell (2000b).
9 Courts (as opposed to school officials) generally separate the determination of guilt or innocence from the severity of punishment. Once a defendant is convicted, the strength of the evidence should have no influence on sentencing.
10 Behr (1997, p. 169).
11 The law's indifference between compliance and breach with damages was asserted, controversially, by Oliver Wendell Holmes, Jr. (1991 [1881], p. 301): "The only universal consequence of a legally binding promise is, that the law makes the promisor pay damages if the promised event does not come to pass." See also Posner (1992, p. 164).
12 See the discussion of "the Victorian compromise" in Friedman (1985, pp. 585–6).
13 From *On Liberty*; Ryan (1997, p. 119).
14 Heyes and Rickman (1999) interpret the tolerance by the US Environmental Protection Agency of evasion of regulations as part of a strategy to induce compliance in other dimensions.
15 The quotation is from Wilde's 1891 essay "The Soul of Man Under Socialism," available on the web at http://flag.blackened.net/revolt/hist_texts/wilde_soul.html (accessed February 2, 2002).

16 Chapter 19 in Friedman (2000) examines the extent to which the common law evolves towards efficiency.

17 That is, with appropriately calculated damages, decisions to breach should be "efficient." See, for instance, pp. 162–5 in Friedman (2000).

18 See, e.g., Baker and Holmstrom (1995).

19 On selective intervention, see Williamson (1985); Prendergast and Topel (1996) examine favoritism within firms, while Tirole (1986) looks at intra-firm collusion.

20 Lott (1990) notes that post-conviction income losses are greater for those earning higher incomes.

21 As an example, consider these words of Karl Marx, who in part echoes Wilde, but who also seems to discount the costs that protecting against evasion entails: "Would locks ever have reached their present degree of excellence had there been no thieves? Would the making of banknotes have reached its present perfection had there been no forgers? . . . And has not the Tree of Sin been at the same time the Tree of Knowledge ever since the time of Adam?" The passage is from *Theories of Surplus Value*, and is quoted from Wheen (1999, p. 309).

22 Alford and Feige (1989) note this problem in connection with underground economic activity.

23 Sah (1991). See also the fascinating story in the autobiography of journalist Lincoln Steffens (1931, pp. 285–91), in a chapter entitled "I Make a Crime Wave," where a perceived (but not actual) crime wave was engendered by a temporarily increased rivalry among journalists assigned to the crime beat.

24 The phrase is from *The Imitation of Christ* (1415), and is quoted from the CD-ROM, *Library of the Future*, third edition, 1991.

25 See Kleiman (1992, p. 48).

26 This example is drawn from Smith and Wright (1992).

27 The "broken-window" parable is from Wilson and Kelling (1982); see also Kelling and Coles (1996).

28 Banfield (1974, pp. 211–33).

29 See, for instance, David Ross, "Lasting Symbol of Scots Rebellion," *The Herald* (Glasgow), October 16, 1997, p. 15.

30 See Anthony Browne, "Cannabis Cafes Set to Open All Around Britain as Law Changes," *The Observer*, March 17, 2002, p. 5.

31 In terms of the approach to rules developed in Chapter 1, delineating exceptions implies that the set of states of the world is partitioned more finely (fewer states in a typical set A), with some states receiving an enhanced set (B) of compliance actions. Closing loopholes, alternatively, consists of either bringing more states into the "equivalence class" (A) for which a more restrictive set of compliance actions is applied, or redesignating some compliance actions as breaching actions, or both.

32 See the discussion in Twining and Miers (1991, pp. 46–51).

33 Wildavsky (1996 [1979], p. 64).

34 Quoted in Hawkins and Zimring (1988, pp. 140–1).

35 Kennedy (1997, p. 163), footnote omitted. I endorse this contention in the race and policing section in Chapter 5. A formal model of how legal rules can shape preferences in the long run appears in Huck (1998).

36 Leitzel and Weisman (1999); for a discussion of preserving policy options and "hysteresis," see Dixit (1996, pp. 67–71).

37 Kleiman (1992, p. 276). The hundreds of thousands of Americans arrested each year for marijuana possession might not view the current policy as involving "salutary neglect."

38 See Kuran (1995, p. 294), where he suggests that the US Congress might consider changing presidential terms from four to six years, but wouldn't bother to make a change to four and a half years. Reluctance to reform is perhaps characteristic of bureaucracies generally. Crozier (1964, p. 196) suggests that "a bureaucratic system will

resist change as long as it can; it will move only when serious dysfunctions develop and no other alternatives remain."

39 See Kane (1996, p. 142), where this notion is presented with respect to the financial services industry. Budget constraints always require some prioritizing of enforcement; therefore, the changing of *de facto* rules through altered enforcement generally cannot be viewed as a subterfuge aimed at foisting an unpopular reform upon an unsuspecting populace. Nevertheless, such changes are less immediately visible than legislated changes in the rules.

40 See Perkins (1994, p. 35) and Krugman (1994, p. 75).

41 See Barnaby J. Feder, "A Study Finds That Teen-Agers are Buying Cigarettes With Ease," *New York Times*, February 16, 1996, p. A24.

42 See the discussion of 'reluctant denial' in MacCoun, Reuter, and Schelling (1996, p. 336).

43 See Hirschman (1995, Chapter 1), which provides an elegant analysis of the fall of East Germany in terms of the author's exit–voice framework. The statistics on emigration are taken from this source. The population of East Germany at the time was around 17 million.

44 The extent to which the collapse of the Berlin Wall was unintentional is chronicled in Roger Cohen, "Haphazardly, Berlin Wall Fell a Decade Ago," *New York Times*, November 9, 1999, and in Ray Moseley, "Witness Finds Real Story of the Berlin Wall's End," *Chicago Tribune*, November 7, 1999.

45 Information on the Church of England case is drawn from "Church of England May Allow Divorced People to Remarry," *Chicago Tribune*, January 26, 2000, p. 3. In July 2002, the Church's General Synod voted to permit remarriage in "exceptional" cases.

46 Information on the proposed reforms to state laws on child abandonment is drawn from Dara Akiko Williams, "California Debates Measure to Set Rules for Abandoning Babies," *Chicago Tribune*, February 2, 2000, p. 9. Mary Anne Case has brought to my attention the long history of social contrivances to protect unwanted infants from unsafe abandonment.

47 Alexeev (1991).

48 Leitzel (1998a).

49 See, for example, the discussion in Hirschman (1963, p. 257).

50 Rosenberg (1991, pp. 178–80).

51 Kane (1996, p. 142).

52 ". . . they used the debris of the old order for building up the new." de Tocqueville (1983 [1856], p. vii). Also, see the discussion of de Tocqueville in Hirschman (1991, pp. 45–50). Rosenberg (1991) argues that the conditions under which the US Supreme Court can effect significant social change are quite limited.

53 Zimring (1993, p. 100).

54 In risk-adjusted terms, smugglers might not earn extraordinary profits, though those attracted into smuggling are likely to be those who are least sensitive to the risk. Even risk-adjusted profits might persist, however, if through collusion with corrupt officials or threats of violence, would-be competitors are dissuaded from entering into smuggling. Note also that consumers of the smuggled goods might prefer legalization and hence lower prices, but as the stakes will typically be small for any one consumer, the interests of consumers in public policy tend to carry less weight than the significant, concentrated interests of the relatively small number of "producers."

55 This discussion echoes Rubin's (1977) analysis of the pressure towards efficiency in common law.

56 See the discussion and citations in Zimring and Hawkins (1992, pp. 66–67).

57 Knight (1996, p. 61).

58 Schanze (1995, p. 165).

59 Cao, Fan, and Woo (1997, p. 31).

60 Ellickson (1991, pp. 254–6).

61 On adverse possession, see Stake (2001). The principle that tolerance of breach leads to an erosion of a legal right is quite general; see Ben-Shahar (1999).

62 Merton (1936) identifies such an atmosphere, more generally, as a cause of unintended consequences from policies.

63 The benefit of dissent from received opinion or established ways of doing things runs through Mill's *On Liberty*. See, e.g., Ryan (1997, p. 75). See also Kuran (1995, p. 19) and Dworkin (1977, p. 212).

64 The Smith (1991 [1776]) quotes are from *The Wealth of Nations*, Volume II, Book V, Chapter I, Part I, p. 229.

65 Hirschman (1970, p. 121).

66 Collecting the tax might itself be costly, but often these administrative costs are minor compared to the revenues. For instance, the expenses of collecting tobacco and alcohol taxes in the US comprise approximately 0.5 percent of the revenue. See Kleiman (1992, p. 70n).

67 Some of the expenses involved in evading prohibitions might be revenues to other private individuals; sellers of fake identification papers, for instance, gain from teenagers' desire to evade drinking laws. But real resources – the forger's time, the papers themselves, the peace of mind of the illegal transactors – are also consumed by evading the prohibition.

68 Society as a whole (and not just the illicit market participants) might find such organization beneficial. For example, the official salaries of the police might fall, reflecting the informal payments, and thereby reduce the tax payments of other citizens. Official wages in the Soviet Union, it appears, did adjust in precisely this fashion, in recognizing the opportunities that various jobs presented for illicit earnings. See Gaddy (1991).

69 See Kenkel (1993) for an analysis of replacing underage drinking bans with a "teen tax" on alcohol consumption.

70 Collecting a small tax is relatively easy for market-style exchanges such as alcohol or drug sales. Other legal prohibitions, such as those against violent crime, concern activities in which all of the main interested parties do not voluntarily engage. So replacing a prohibition on robbery with a tax would not be a good idea, perhaps for many reasons, not the least of which being that the tax would almost certainly be evaded.

71 The distributional impact might be consequential even if the overall social benefit of replacing a prohibition with a tax is minuscule. Certainly many of those who evade the ban will be happy that they no longer face arrest when the tax regime comes into effect.

72 MacCoun and Reuter (2001, pp. 362–3).

73 The claim that the majority of gun crime in Britain involves illegally owned guns applies to those offenses that are not committed with low-powered air guns. Such air guns actually account for the majority of recorded gun crime in England and Wales.

74 Another dramatic tightening of firearm controls occurred in Australia following a gun massacre in Port Arthur in April, 1996, that left thirty-five dead.

75 Any disturbances from the high gun "equilibrium" will also tend to be more costly than similar departures from equilibrium in the low gun setting. (Incidentally, there is a famous joke in transition economics along these lines, about a country that decides to switch from driving on the left side of the road to driving on the right. The country elects to adopt a gradual strategy, with trucks being the first to switch.)

76 See the discussion in Drazen (1996), and in Kuran (1995, pp. 105–17).

77 Fernandez and Rodrik (1991).

78 As in Olson (1982).

79 Alesina and Drazen (1991).

80 See, e.g., Drazen and Grilli (1993), and Bruno and Easterly (1996).

81 Hirschman (1970, pp. 44–54).

82 Kuran (1995, pp. 105–17).

83 See Labán and Sturzenegger (1994).

84 Individuals could still be harmed by output falls during a stabilization program, but hyperinflations are themselves so detrimental to output that stabilizations tend to be associated with output growth; see Easterly (1996).

85 The closer the substitute the informal reform provides for the formal reform, the smaller the efficiency gain from going ahead with the official reform. So while widespread evasion reduces the distributional consequences of an official reform, and thus helps to promote policy change, it is possible that evasion simultaneously reduces the benefit of official reform to the point that there is little interest in the formal change. But frequently the informal reform is a poor substitute for a formal policy change.

86 See, e.g., the discussion in Wilson (1989, chapter 18).

87 An important determinant of the nature of the bargaining at the time of rule formation is whether the interested parties are well-informed about how their interests will be affected by different rules. Two settlers coming into a new area might quickly agree to split a parcel of land down the middle, 50–50. If it were known, however, that some part of the land had better soil, or contained valuable subterranean minerals, it could become more difficult to devise a rule governing the distribution of ownership. See the discussion of the North Sea in Barzel (1989, pp. 72–2), and more generally, Buchanan and Tullock (1992 [1962], pp. 77–80).

88 See the discussion of this issue in Dixit and Nalebuff (1991, p. 146).

89 See, e.g., Cogan, Muris, and Schick (1994).

90 See "Rules and Discretion in Monetary Policy," a special issue (June 1997) of the *Journal of Monetary Economics* devoted to this topic. Another important contribution to the economics literature within the rules v. discretion framework is Heiner (1983), which examines individual choice behavior.

91 On the shift in the relationship between a standard measure of the money supply and economic activity, see Duca (1995).

92 Stigler (1970, p. 536).

3 Zero tolerance

1 A senior at a Newport News, Virginia high school was suspended for eleven days for bringing a heavy duty pair of scissors to class in her purse; she had been using the scissors earlier for a school project and forgot they were in her purse. See Yasmin Anwar, "Threat of Violence Throughout School Year. 'Sweet' Student Suspended for Scissors," *USA Today*, April 14, 2000, p. 13A.

2 Kleiman (1998, p. 2) refers to "the usual meaning of zero tolerance" as "a policy of making arrests for every observed violation of the law." Jacobs (1999, p. 74) similarly notes that zero tolerance "indicates increased attention to minor offenses that previously might have escaped much, if any, attention." The terminology "zero tolerance" with respect to rule enforcement dates at least to the early 1980s, when the US Navy strengthened its policy against illegal drug use by sailors.

3 Enforcement can be distinguished from adjudication. A zero tolerance enforcement policy might involve arresting any person involved in a minor crime, while considerable discretion could later be afforded to judges. Many zero tolerance policies, however, are associated with institutions such as schools where the enforcement and judicial functions are largely combined. Also, in other zero tolerance situations, such as those concerned with soccer-related violence, it is the arrest (i.e. the enforcement) that is the real threat, largely irrespective of later adjudication.

4 Again, this is a version of the rule trichotomy developed by Bardach (1989).

5 In late March, 2000, the city of Baltimore appointed an acting police commissioner who is committed (as is Baltimore's mayor) to a policy of zero tolerance against crime. The *Baltimore Sun* asked various Baltimoreans how they defined zero tolerance policing. The president of the city's Fraternal Order of Police said "Zero tolerance is less a crime-

fighting strategy and more an attitude. It's about a community taking a stand against pervasive lawlessness that has negatively affected its quality of life." See "Zeroing in on Policing Styles," *Baltimore Sun*, April 20, 2000, p. 25A.

6 See Kelling and Coles (1996, p. 164). Part of the benefit claimed for strict policing of minor crimes is that such practices simultaneously provide a means to identify and arrest serious criminals.

7 Threats to punish can be expensive even if no one engages in the proscribed activity, if the number of enforcers needed to keep the threat credible is exorbitant, or if the compliance costs imposed on those wishing to avoid technical violations of the policy are substantial.

8 See Sah (1991) and Kleiman (1993).

9 Thucydides (1952 [c. 400 BC], p. 505).

10 See, e.g., Sah (1991).

11 See Gladwell (2000).

12 Rosen (2001, p. 49).

13 See Milgrom and Roberts (1988) on lobbying, or "influence activities."

14 See Polinsky and Shavell (2000b, pp. 235–6).

15 See, for instance, the discussion and citations in Heymann (2000, p. 419).

16 See, e.g., Skolnick (1999, pp. 184–5). Also see the discussion of "fortress" and "stepladder" approaches to the severity of punishment in Zimring and Hawkins (1973, pp. 203–4).

17 See, e.g., Scheck, Neufeld, and Dwyer (2000).

18 Nor is lobbying undesirable in and of itself. Lobbying is one method whereby the preferences of individuals are communicated to policy makers. Reducing the incentives to lobby could result in policies that are less reflective of societal preferences.

Mandatory sentencing laws represent a related attempt to limit discretion within law enforcement. Discretion is not eliminated by these laws, however. First, police may not arrest all malefactors whom they come across. Second, prosecutors might not bring maximal charges against defendants. Third, some parole possibilities often remain, as a carrot in helping prison officials maintain order. Fourth, executive branch officials such as governors or presidents have the power to commute sentences or to pardon prisoners. In November, 2001 and again in February, 2002, some aspects of California's well-known "three strikes" mandatory sentencing law were ruled to be unconstitutional by a federal appeals court on the grounds that they constituted cruel and unusual punishments.

19 Information about the Decatur incident is taken from Johnson (2001).

20 Hymowitz (2000).

21 Even a zero tolerance policy fairly enforced might be perceived as being unfair, if the targeted activity is one that is associated with homelessness or poverty.

22 See Kenneth Cooper, "Group Finds Racial Disparity in Schools' 'Zero Tolerance,'" *Washington Post*, June 15, 2000, p. A08.

23 Nor is it the case that a zero tolerance regime necessarily minimizes the amount of evasive behavior. See Caulkins (1993).

24 The "broken windows" metaphor derives from Wilson and Kelling (1982).

25 Order maintenance policing frequently is conflated with zero tolerance in policy discussions, despite the distinctions that can be made between them. Rosen (2000) offers an interesting analysis of how a "broken windows" approach metamorphosed into a zero tolerance campaign in New York City. Kelling, one of the founders of "broken windows," also tries to distinguish that approach from zero tolerance: "the equation made in some quarters between police order maintenance activities ('broken windows') and 'zero tolerance' for disorderly behavior raises issues that go beyond semantics. Without further comment, it is an equation that I have never made, find worrisome, and have argued against, considering the phrase 'zero tolerance' not credible and smacking of zealotry" (1999, p. 3, note 3).

26 Rosen (2000, p. 25).
27 See Kleiman (1998) and Rosen (2000). Ellickson (1996) provides a good description of a formal system of policing that incorporates near-zero tolerance in restricted urban areas.
28 Kelling and Coles (1996, chapter 4); these authors do not describe the anti-graffiti and other order maintenance activities in the New York City subway system as a zero tolerance policy.
29 The Euro 2000 soccer tournament, held in Belgium and the Netherlands in June 2000, implemented a zero tolerance policy against fan violence.
30 These considerations underlying a harm reduction policy are adapted from Drucker (1995).
31 See Zimring and Hawkins (1999).

4 Avoidance, futility, and reform

1 The term "balloon effect" is taken from Andreas (1994), where it is used in the context of attempts to control illegal immigration.
2 Viscusi (1984, p. 327).
3 Sargent and Wallace (1975). Many futility results are more familiarly known in terms of "neutrality," where some variable of interest is unaffected when conditions change.
4 Coase (1960). The "theorem" also requires the condition that income effects are zero.
5 See Bernheim and Bagwell (1988), which presents a general neutrality result; see also Bergstrom and Varian (1985).
6 For some perversity-type arguments, see Schelling (1960); for examples within the political science discipline, see Jervis (1991).
7 Peltzman (1975, p. 677). An interesting sidelight is that Peltzman's empirical work employs 1966 as the first year of the safety regulation, even though the regulations did not become law until 1968. His reasoning is that pressure from regulators created a situation of *de facto* regulation prior to the *de jure* acknowledgment.
8 Tsebelis (1989, p. 82).
9 Andreoni (1995) finds that the marginal deterrence effect of more severe penalties is approximately zero for each of twelve categories of crime.
10 Philipson and Posner (1996, p. 408).
11 Nadelmann (1998, p. 111).
12 Larkey and Caulkins (1992). See also Baker (1992). The longevity of institutions that do not seem to serve their stated purpose suggests that there is another purpose that they do serve. See Wildavsky (1996, pp. 28–9).
13 See the discussion of this issue in the National Gambling Impact Study Commission's report on lotteries, available at http://govinfo.library.unt.edu/ngisc/research/lotteries.html.
14 Hirschman (1991, pp. 41–2), and Jervis (1991, pp. 109–10). In the safety caps on aspirin bottle case, Viscusi (1984, p. 325) notes the rather stringent conditions needed to generate a perverse result from safety regulation in a simple model of precautionary behavior.
15 See Chirinko and Harper (1993). Peterson, Hoffer, and Millner (1995), however, find (in the Peltzman tradition) that driver response to the presence of air bags offsets the safety benefits of the bag for the driver, while increasing the risk of death for others. Incidentally, the increased risks facing individuals other than drivers from more intense driving (spurred by safety regulations) should in turn induce efforts by passengers and pedestrians to offset, to some extent, their increased danger. The per-mile rate of motor vehicle fatalities in the US fell by 60 percent between 1972 and 1996; see Bonnie, Fulco, and Liverman (1999, pp. 115–16).
16 Downs (1992, p. 37). Beyond this futility-style result, perverse outcomes in traffic congestion (increased travel times after road expansion) are also possible. See Arnott

and Small (1994). For some general futility-style reasoning in economics, see chapter 4 of Landsburg (1993).

17 Or, alternatively, prior to the policy change, the "inframarginal" individuals who begin to switch had a strict preference for their original route. Though induced to shift by the policy reform, then, they do not view their new route as equivalent to their old one.

18 Better ways to adapt to the rules of baseball, for example, are discovered and propagate over time. As a result, the variance in baseball performance measures such as batting averages has declined throughout the twentieth century; while batting has improved in absolute terms, improved pitching and defense with lower variance has led to the lessened variance in batting average. See Gould (1996).

19 Graham and Lee (1986).

20 Miron and Zweibel (1991); but see Miron (1999) for a different view of the effect of Prohibition on alcohol consumption.

21 On the stimulus to marijuana consumption provided by the Volstead Act, see the discussion in Zimring and Hawkins (1992, pp. 70–1).

22 Friedman, Hakim, and Spiegel (1989).

23 Lindbeck (1995a, b) employs this reasoning in analyzing the dynamics of social welfare policies. For a discussion of informal constraints on behavior, see North (1991), chapter 5.

24 See the discussion and references in Kane (1996, pp. 146–7), and the section on "The Logic of Regulatory Expansion" in Bardach and Kagan (1982, pp. 19–22).

25 See Hirschman (1995, pp. 62–4).

26 Lindbeck (1995a, b) notes that those who determine eligibility for social benefits tend to become more liberal over time.

27 Translated and quoted by Stille (1996, pp. 142–3). Note a similar sentiment in a public policy context in Wildavsky (1996, p. 4): "The more the nation attempted to control public policy, the less control there seemed to be. A troublesome parallel aspect of this expanding public sector was the feeling that unintended consequences were overwhelming the ability to cope. Vast changes were taking place amid suspicion that here was change for change's sake alone. Immobility and change appeared to be different sides of the same coin."

28 Kovacic (1990).

29 Crozier (1964, p. 193).

30 Suetonius (1931, pp. 74–5).

31 This echoes Lindblom's (1959) notion of "muddling through." For a mathematical treatment and critique, see Bendor (1995).

32 The legal doctrine of *stare decisis*, in which precedents are used to decide cases, reflects the value of rule stability. Dixit (1996, pp. 26–8) discusses some of the benefits of policy durability, and Rodrik (1991) indicates some of the costs of uncertainty over the sustainability of a reform.

33 See, e.g., Howard (1994) and Epstein (1995), both of whom, incidentally, compare complex US regulations with Soviet central planning. Austin and Larkey (1992) show how "micromanagement" has had perverse effects for Department of Defense computer procurements. Stiglitz (1995, pp. 133–4) suggests that simple *per se* rules could provide no worse incentives, at reduced cost, than the current US antitrust regime.

34 This argument appears in Kaufmann (1994), based on an analysis of transitional Ukraine. Cowell and Gordon (1995) provide a model in which better enforcement of the tax law among formal firms can lead to more tax evasion, as increased numbers of firms elect to operate exclusively in the informal sector.

35 Kaplow (1995) presents a model in which the optimal regime might involve widespread ignorance of the laws, and potentially high non-compliance, while large players would invest in learning the relevant laws to avoid large fines.

36 The discussion of the "at will" and "just cause" doctrines relies heavily upon Epstein (1995); the example of just cause dismissal indicates that some complex rules can nevertheless be stated very easily.

37 Leitzel and Conrad (1997). Methods of measuring complexity can themselves be complicated. For a biological example, see the discussion in Gould (1996, pp. 202–3), and in economics, see Rosser (1999).

38 *Politics*, Book II, Chapter 8.

39 de Tocqueville (1983 [1856], p. 194). Thomas Jefferson voiced a similar sentiment in 1816 [Hunt (1996, p. 313)]: "I am certainly not an advocate for frequent and untried changes in laws and constitutions. I think moderate imperfections had better be borne with; because, when once known, we accommodate ourselves to them, and find practical means of correcting their ill effects."

40 Hirschman (1970).

41 White (1991, p. 55).

42 White (1991, p. 59). In an endnote omitted here, White identifies the 3–6–3 observation as "attributed to Maurice Mann by Kane (1983, p. 56)."

43 This paragraph draws heavily on White (1991, pp. 63–4).

44 The insolvency problem would have been lessened had thrifts been allowed at an earlier stage to employ adjustable-rate mortgages (ARMs), so that their revenues on existing loans would increase when market interest rates (and hence their costs of attracting funds) climbed. But it was not until 1979 that limited ARMs were permitted, with a further liberalization in 1982. Barth (1991, pp. 127–8).

45 The combination of (implicit) government insurance and little oversight over asset portfolios of financial institutions was a central feature of the Asian financial crisis that rocked Indonesia, Thailand, Korea, and other countries in 1997–8.

46 Akerlof and Romer (1993).

5 Preventive and punitive controls

1 Hobbes (1970 [1651], p. 85).

2 See the discussion in Epstein (1995, pp. 281–2), for instance.

3 This example is drawn from Heyes (2001).

4 For an analysis of the divergence between outputs and the actual end in view, in the context of environmental taxes, see Fullerton, Hong, and Metcalf (1999).

5 Miller (1984).

6 Akerlof and Romer (1993).

7 Goodhart (1981), as quoted in Issing (1997, p. 74). The Issing article challenges Goodhart's Law, by suggesting that adherence to a rule aimed at steadiness reinforces the stability of the monetary relationship and hence reinforces the foundation of the policy itself.

8 From *On Liberty*; Ryan (1997, p. 116).

9 From *On Liberty*; Ryan (1997, p. 117).

10 Borooah (2001, p. 18).

11 The "Traffic Stops Statistics Act of 1999," which would require the attorney general to collect such information from a nationwide sample of jurisdictions, was introduced in April, 1999, in both the House (HR 1443) and Senate (S.821).

12 Cole (1999, p. 36), endnote omitted. This disparity is particularly remarkable given that the state police understood their actions were being monitored, and had been given written notice of a policy prohibiting stops based on race.

13 Merida (1999, p. 26). On disproportionate stops and searches of racial minorities in New York City, see Fagan and Davies (2000).

14 See, e.g., the discussion in Gray (1998, pp. 24–30).

15 Harris (1999, p. 7).

16 Quoted in Cole (1999, p. 41); see also Kennedy (1997, p. 15). This entire section is

indebted to these two sources, and to some degree offers an economist's reinterpretation of many of their ideas.

17 Kennedy (1997, p. 166), footnote omitted.
18 Kelling and Coles (1996, p. 93).
19 See, e.g., Kennedy (1998, p. 35), and Cole (1999, pp. 11–12).
20 Further, the practice of profiling can lead to overlooking rather obvious signs of criminality in those who do not meet the profile. See Williams (2000, pp. 154–6).
21 Kennedy (1998, p. 35). The San Diego case is *Kolendar v. Lawson* 461 U.S. 352 (1983). Mr Lawson was detained under a California statute that required wanderers or loiterers to give account for their presence and to provide reliable identification to police. The Supreme Court struck down the statute as unconstitutionally vague, as it encouraged arbitrary enforcement.
22 Crouch (2000, p. 164).
23 Alexeev and Leitzel (2002) note that a focus on arrests as opposed to the amount of illegal activity itself also tends to lead to socially excessive amounts of racial profiling.
24 Alexeev and Leitzel (2002) demonstrate that in settings such as airports where police have the resources to track a considerble portion of potential offenders, some profiling is often sensible.
25 See the incident in a Santa Monica hotel parking garage described in Harris (1999, p. 9), for an abusive use of a description of suspects.
26 Kennedy (1997, p. 163).
27 These alternatives are discussed in Kennedy (1998, pp. 35–6).
28 Cole (1999) argues that the current system of criminal justice in the US depends on equality in theory but wide race- and class-based disparities in practice. An elimination of the disparities, by his reckoning, might also lead to weaker constitutional protections than are now enjoyed by the favored citizens.
29 See, e.g., Davis (1999), Cole (1999, pp. 34–41), and Harris (1999).

6 Corruption

1 Klitgaard (1991, p. 221).
2 Huberts (2000, p. 214).
3 Noonan (1984, pp. xi–xii) notes different standards underlying the notion of bribery.
4 Huntington (1968, pp. 59–60).
5 See the recollections of work in the USSR in the late 1930s in Andreev-Khomiakov (1997 [1954]), particularly chapters 4, 5, and 7, as well as Ledeneva (1998).
6 Ross (1992, p. 10).
7 Segrave (1994) provides an excellent history and analysis of payola. Payments to play songs on the air are legal if the payments are disclosed.
8 Anechiarico and Jacobs (1996, p. 25).
9 The list is from Klitgaard (1991).
10 The principal–agent–client framework for analyzing corruption is developed in Klitgaard (1988).
11 Tanzi (1995, p. 167).
12 Gerth and Mills (1946, p. 215); italics in the original. Also, see the discussion of the Weberian ideal bureaucracy in Tanzi (1995).
13 Klitgaard (1991, p. 225).
14 O'Brian (1993, p. 82).
15 Stone (1989, pp. 28–9) suggests that a better English equivalent of this charge against Socrates might be "subverting" or "alienating."
16 Acemoglu and Verdier (2000) present a model of corruption when rules are good, in that they counteract market failures.
17 In a first-best world, legitimate businesses would probably not be forced out of the marketplace by general taxes (as opposed to user fees). The necessity to collect taxes

from marginal businesses, and potentially then to drive them out of business, is motivated by the desire to provide incentives for non-marginal businesses to pay their taxes, given that marginal and non-marginal businesses cannot be easily delineated by the taxation authorities. Also, recall from an earlier endnote the possibility that tax evasion can have little or no impact on overall tax collections, if the activity made profitable by evasion has multiplier effects on the taxed portion of the economy. See Peacock and Shaw (1982) and Mercouiller and Young (1995).

18   Becker and Stigler (1974). The official salary of the bribed officials can also be reduced to reflect the opportunities for bribe collection.
19   Walzer (1983, p. 147).
20   Rodger (1988, p. 302).
21   Anechiarico and Jacobs (1996, p. 37).
22   Tanzi (1995, pp. 164–7). The strength of reciprocity in human relations is generally very significant. See, e.g. Fehr and Gächter (2000).
23   Gerth and Mills (1946, pp. 220–21, 231).
24   Lippmann (1989 [1930], p. 569).
25   Fischer (1992, p. 191).
26   Gupta, Davoodi, and Alonso-Terme (1998).
27   Mauro (1998) presents empirical evidence suggesting that, holding other factors constant, the extent of corruption tends to reduce government spending on education.
28   Huntington (1968, p. 64): "Corruption itself may be a substitute for reform and both corruption and reform may be substitutes for revolution."
29   Wei (1997b) provides empirical evidence of the extent to which the uncertainty generated in a corrupt environment reduces foreign direct investment.
30   "At times they [established music promoters] become annoyed when they feel they are all paying out payola just to avoid having their records fall into the no-play pile, as opposed to receiving extra plays." Segrave (1994, p. 221).
31   A 1983 investigation of electrical inspectors in New York city indicated that inspectors were expected to turn over half of their bribe income to supervisors. Anechiarico and Jacobs (1996, p. 84).
32   For a sophisticated discussion of Say's Law, see Sowell (1974, pp. 35–52).
33   On the applicability of Say's Law to corruption, see Andvig and Moene (1990).
34   As with other forms of evasion, one source of positive feedback in corruption is that with a fixed level of anti-corruption enforcement resources, a perception of increased corruption reduces the subjective probability of being caught, and therefore may result in more individuals choosing to behave corruptly. Sah (1991).
35   Mauro (1995). The interpretation of statistical analyzes suggesting a negative relationship between corruption and growth is not always straightforward. As noted earlier, for instance, expert evaluations of corruption might already be tainted by knowledge of the extent of economic growth, so that poorly performing economies are spuriously claimed to have relatively high corruption.
36   Huntington (1968, p. 69).
37   Huntington (1968, p. 69).
38   Excessive efforts at corruption control might also undermine governmental responsiveness. Further, even if the corrupt behavior is legalized – perhaps campaign contributions from PACs is a case in point – the diminished responsiveness to broad societal interests might remain.
39   Shleifer and Vishny (1993) analyze some of the differences between organized and disorganized corruption.
40   Sherman (1978, pp. 256–7).
41   Crozier (1964, p. 196). This passage may look familiar, as it appeared in an endnote in Chapter 2.
42   The differential response to big and little scandals in police departments is discussed in Sherman (1978, pp. 206–7).

43 Jacobs (1999, p. 78).
44 See the discussion in Smart (1999, pp. 108, 117).
45 Banfield (1975).
46 Dalton (1959).
47 Dalton (1959). Behr (1997, p. 159) relates how two Prohibition agents who were too successful at arresting violators found themselves fired during a reorganization.
48 Retailers expect some theft as a normal cost of business. Anechiarico and Jacobs (1996, p. 194).
49 Simis (1982, pp. 218–21).
50 See, e.g., Anechiarico and Jacobs (1996, pp. 11–14).
51 Wildavsky (1996, pp. 43–53). See also Crozier (1964, p. 193).
52 Anechiarico and Jacobs (1996, p. 28).
53 Anechiarico and Jacobs (pp. 17, 37–9). Huntington (1968): "in a society where corruption is widespread the passage of strict laws against corruption serves only to multiply the opportunities for corruption."
54 Anechiarico and Jacobs (1996, p. 44).
55 Transparency International (TI) is a well-known Germany-based non-profit organization aimed at advancing good government through increased openness in government decision making. TI produces an important country corruption rating by aggregating multiple rankings of the previously mentioned expert-opinion type. See www.transparency.org (accessed March 26, 2002).
56 Segrave (1994, p. 221). Earlier on the same page is the futility claim that "Attempts to eradicate payola by attacking the recipients, or gate-keepers, are doomed to total failure." Note the totality of the proclaimed failure.
57 See the discussion of steps that potential or actual victims of corruption might take to shield themselves from costs imposed by corruption in Alam (1995).
58 This distinction between the corruption of the poor and the corruption of the rich is due to Huntington (1968, p. 61).
59 Bliss and Di Tella (1997) note that corruption itself can influence the extent of competition.
60 As Huntington (1968, p. 59) notes, however, the emergence of "new sources of wealth and power" may be a stimulus to corruption.
61 See Sherman (1978, p. 250).
62 For one argument against transparency, see Dixit (1996, p. 106).
63 Walzer (1983, p. 127).
64 Leff (1989, p. 402).
65 This section draws heavily on Potter (1997) and Mann (1999). Sabato and Simpson (1996) also provide some useful description and analysis. The description of the rules regarding campaign finance (which may undergo substantial reform) applies to the situation in early 2002.
66 Surprisingly, a donation after the fact that is given explicitly in gratitude for a particular vote is not illegal. Further, the US Senate has adopted a stricter though seemingly unenforced (and probably unenforceable) rule that permits senators to engage in constituent service, as long as the service is not undertaken on the basis of campaign contributions. See Matt Alsdorf, "Is it Illegal to Do Favors for Campaign Donors?," in Explainer, *Slate. com*, posted January 12, 2000, available at http://slate.msn.com/?id=1004365 (accessed March 26, 2002). Both this and a second *Slate* article, Timothy Noah, "Congressional Ethics for Dummies," posted January 14, 2000, available at http://slate.msn.com/?id=73029 (accessed March 26, 2002) are drawn upon in my discussion of campaign finance.
67 Again, this summary of US campaign finance regulations applies to the system as of the beginning of 2002. Reform is likely soon, including, perhaps, the banning of "soft money" and increased control over "issue advocacy" advertizements.
68 *Buckley* v. *Valeo*, 424 US 1 (1976), excerpted in Corrado et al. (1997).
69 Rosenkranz (1999, p. 3).

70 See, e.g., Drew (1999, p. 48).
71 The loophole that led to the creation of unregulated "stealth PACs" (which engaged in issue advocacy while avoiding disclosure requirements) was closed by legislation in mid-2000. Following the legislation, sufficiently large groups that previously operated in the loophole (called "Section 527" groups after the relevant part of the income tax code) had to disclose donations of $200 or more.
72 Potter (1997, p. 15) notes that the soft money loophole was created by some amendments to campaign finance laws in 1979 that introduced a more precise definition of "contribution," probably without the intention of creating pools of unregulated soft money. Corrado (2001) offers a different account of the source of the soft money loophole, though in this account soft money continues to be an unanticipated consequence of attempts to avoid campaign finance restrictions.
73 Sorauf (1999, pp. 21–2).
74 Mann (1999), and http://commoncause.org/publications/feb01/020701st.htm (accessed February 17, 2002). The 2000 figure includes soft money collected not just by the national committees (the large majority of the soft money), but also by their senatorial, congressional, and dinner committees.
75 Drew (1999, p. 8).
76 Issue advertizements are followed closely by the Annenberg Public Policy Center of the University of Pennsylvania, which produced the spending estimate. See www.appcpenn.org/issueads/estimate.htm (accessed February 18, 2002).
77 Mann (1999).
78 Drew (1999, p. ix).
79 Rosenkranz (1999, p. 5).
80 Mann (1999).
81 One intriguing proposal is to mandate that donors remain anonymous. A politician, then, could not be sure of the identity of major contributors, and hence could not easily reciprocate for donations. The incentive to make large donations would be greatly diminished if a workable version of this scheme – one that could overcome the seemingly significant opportunities for evasion and avoidance – could be implemented. See Ayres and Bulow (1998).
82 Calavita, Pontell, and Tillman (1997, p. 87), citing Joseph A. Grundfest, "Son of S&L – The Sequel: The Conditions that Caused the Crisis Are Still With Us," *Washington Post*, June 3, 1990, D1.
83 Calavita, Pontell, and Tillman (1997, p. 107), citing Waldman (1990).
84 Thompson (1995).
85 Corrado (2001, p. 2).

7 Evasion and the demise of the Soviet Union

1 See, e.g., Hayek (1945), and Friedman (1988).
2 See Leitzel (1995) for a argument that the what-to-produce question was at the heart of the inferiority of Soviet central planning.
3 Treml (1993).
4 de Tocqueville (1983 [1856], p. 188).
5 A similar sentiment for an earlier historical epoch was voiced by Friedrich Engels: "In default of a Napoleon, another would have filled his place." Quoted in Kuran (1995, p. 284).
6 de Tocqueville (1983 [1856], pp. 66–7).
7 The term "second economy" also incorporates legal activity undertaken for private gain, most notably sales of food on collective farm markets. See Grossman (1977). Widespread rule evasion has been characteristic of other (i.e. non-Soviet) controlled economies, as Wallich (1955, p. 119), for instance, noted in the case of immediate postwar Germany: "Controls were universal and so was evasion."
8 "I suspect that in the Soviet Union and even in China, if you could only find some

way to quantify it, you would discover that most resources are organized through the principle of the market, of voluntary cooperation by people pursuing their own interests, rather than through the elaborate structure of direct command." Friedman (1988, pp. 28–9).

9 Grossman (1977, p. 29).

10 Gaddy (1991).

11 Grossman (1977, p. 40).

12 Andrei Grachev, cited in Grossman (1998).

13 See, e.g., Treml and Alexeev (1993), Grossman (1987), and Millar (1988).

14 de Tocqueville (1983 [1856], p. 188).

15 de Tocqueville (1983 [1856], pp. 176–7).

16 On the decline in alcohol sales, see White (1996, p. 141). The more than 50 percent decline is in terms of liters of pure alcohol per capita; higher prices to some extent offset the quantity decline. The anti-alcohol campaign was itself undone in large measure by evasion, most particularly of laws forbidding the home production and sale of alcohol.

17 Johnson and Kroll (1991) offer a good description and analysis of this process.

18 This argument is spelled out in Leitzel (1998a).

19 de Tocqueville (1983 [1856], p. 1).

20 See Schroeder (1979) on the "treadmill" of Soviet reforms. Even if certain features of the economy, such as poor work discipline, did reassert themselves in the face of reforms, other dimensions of Soviet life were impacted by policy changes. The anti-alcohol campaign, for example, seemed to be a success in terms of public health. See White (1996).

21 Grossman (1963) contains an important analysis of the potential for a market sector to persist within a centrally planned economy. I briefly discuss the implications of this analysis for Russian and Chinese reforms in Leitzel (1995, pp. 146–148).

22 The Soviet government became substantially more attuned to citizen preferences under Gorbachev. "In 1962 the response of the authorities to a strike in the north Caucasian town of Novocherkassk was to call in the army to break the strike by force. In 1989, the official response to the coal-miners' strike was to recognize their grievances and talk to their representatives." Ellman and Kontorovich (1992, p. 5).

23 From Hicks (1963), as quoted in Dallago (1990, p. ix).

24 The 1986 Soviet campaign against unearned incomes, for instance, quickly led to worsening economic conditions and higher prices in kolkhoz markets, resulting in a hasty relaxation of enforcement. Grossman (1989, pp. 89–90).

25 Official price indices did not record near-hyperinflationary rates in late 1991, because fixed prices within the state sector implied that the inflation was largely of the "repressed" variety, and therefore not recorded in standard indices. Price indices based on the free price collective farm markets, however, did display high inflation rates in late 1991. See Leitzel (1995).

26 The distinction between liberalization and deregulation is a theme of Vogel (1996).

27 The non-state sector includes township-village enterprises, which tend to operate in a market-oriented manner.

28 See, e.g., Naughton (1996, chapter 1).

29 On the dual-track system, see Cao, Fan and Woo (1997).

30 On the extent and impact of corruption in China, see, e.g., Johnston (1997).

31 Cao, Fan and Woo (1997, pp. 20–1).

32 Cao, Fan, and Woo (1997, p. 20).

33 Qian (1999).

34 There is evidence that there was substantial diversion of goods out of the planned sector in China even as early as 1980. See the discussion in Roland (2000, p. 149), which is drawn in part from Li (1999).

35 Cao, Fan, and Woo (1997, p. 25).

36 Gambetta (1994).
37 See Suvorov (1986, p. 1).
38 Falcone (1993, p. 102). For the mid-1990s structure of mafia elements in the Russian city of Perm', see Varese (1997).
39 See, e.g., Handelman (1995).
40 Industries that involve a significant monopoly element, such as having a workforce drawn from a powerful labor union, also appear to be more likely to have organized crime connections.
41 Grossman (1989, p. 81).
42 Simis (1982) details the systemic nature of Soviet corruption.
43 An early sociological study showed how perceptions of crime were related to crime news, but not to the actual amount of crime. See the discussion of Davis (1952) in Becker (1973, p. 12). Also, recall from an endnote in Chapter 2 how journalist Lincoln Steffens (1931, pp. 285–91) generated a perceived crime wave.
44 The centralization of news in Moscow, which was relatively strongly policed during the Soviet era, also contributed to misleading perceptions of increased crime. See Alexeev, Gaddy and Leitzel (1995, p. 687), for a discussion of this Moscow bias.
45 This point is commonly made; see, e.g. Goldman (1996, p. 43). In many instances, laws are contradictory, so it is not even possible to be in business and be law-abiding – a situation reminiscent of the era of central planning.
46 In one survey of Moscow shop managers, the average number of inspections reported was more than eighteen per year, double the amount reported in Warsaw. See Shleifer (1997).
47 OMRI Daily Digest, March 12, 1997. Perhaps not coincidentally, the number of "organized criminal groups" that had come to the attention of the authorities in mid-1997 also exceeded 9,000. RFE/RL, June 13, 1997. It is easy to overlook the large role that private security plays in Western market economies. In 1996, there were more than 155,000 licensed private security guards in the state of California alone, excluding off-duty public police officers who often moonlight as security guards. Sklansky (1999, p. 1174, n. 28).
48 On protection rents, see Lane (1958); this concept has been applied to Russian organized crime in Lotspeich (1996).
49 Shleifer and Vishny (1993) analyze some of the differences between stable and more competitive forms of corruption.
50 The 1990 figure is from Rossiyskaya Federatsiya v Tsifrakh v 1992 Godu [1993], and the 1996 figure (actually a decline of some 2,000 from 1995) was announced by the Interior Minister, as reported in OMRI Daily Digest, January 20, 1997. Note also that these figures include attempted murders, and therefore are not directly comparable with homicide statistics from many Western countries.
51 Johnson and Loveman (1995) document the importance of new firms in the Polish transition.
52 See Halligan and Teplukhin (1995, pp. 119–21), and OMRI Daily Digest, March 21, 1997. The surveys reported in these sources involved foreign firms that had already invested. Fears of crime or the mafia might be more important in preventing initial investments.
53 Putnam (1993, p. 183). The statement would look considerably less foreboding if placed at a higher level of aggregation: Italy may represent the future of Russia.
54 Tirole (1996). On the legacy of corruption of Russia, see Stephan (1999).
55 An environment with lower corruption can then feed back on transition, by being a spur to foreign investment, for instance. See Wei (1997a).
56 Similar suggestions for combatting the mafia can be found in such otherwise dissimilar analyzes as Goldman (1996) and Layard and Parker (1996, pp. 167–72).
57 See, for instance, Matt Bivens, "Back to the USSR," *Brill's Content*, at www.brillscontent.com/August2000/russia_0700.html (accessed July 1, 2000). Measures

taken in 2000 and 2001 against oligarch Vladimir Gusinsky and his Media-Most company, as well as other Kremlin maneuvers, seem to threaten media freedoms in Russia.
58 In this, I am in agreement with "oligarch" Boris Berezovsky. See "Tycoon Resigns from Duma as Relations with Kremlin Cool," by Amelia Gentleman, *The Guardian*, July 18, 2000, p. 12.

8 Gun control

1 The futility syllogism is addressed in Cook and Leitzel (1996), and Leitzel (1998b). Polsby (1994, p. 60) presents a "futility theorem," based on the notion that criminals have a relatively high willingness to pay for firearms.
2 A gun control might be a sound policy even if it has no impact on criminal violence, if it reduces suicides or accidents.
3 The analogy between drunk driving and gun control is noted in Jacobs (1989, p. 60). For a fuller discussion of the principles underlying preemptive gun control, see Cook and Leitzel (1996, pp. 94–101).
4 See the discussion of futility arguments in Cook and Leitzel (1996).
5 Wolfgang (1958).
6 See the discussion of the instrumentality effect in Cook and Moore (1995). The probability of an injury during a robbery attempt, as opposed to a fatality, is higher if the attacker does not have a gun, reflecting the different approaches used by robbers and their victims in these two circumstances.
7 See, e.g., Kleck (1984).
8 Sawed-off shotguns are themselves illegal in the US and Britain, but because shotguns are legal – and in the US, almost uncontrolled – and the alteration required to turn a shotgun into a sawed-off shotgun only involves a hacksaw, the ban of sawed-off shotguns can be evaded at very low cost, and hence generally is enforceable only after the fact, when someone has been caught employing such an altered gun in a misdeed.
9 Ash *et al.* (1996).
10 For 1994, the US firearm percentage of homicides (and legal interventions) was 71.7 percent, calculated from Centers for Disease Controls and Prevention (1996) data. In England and Wales, for 1999/2000, 8.1 percent of homicides were committed with firearms; *Criminal Statistics, England and Wales, 1999*.
11 Canada (1995). This quote and the two following ones are from pp. 96 and 97.
12 Some burglaries are motivated by the possibility of stealing firearms, however, and this component of burglaries would presumably decline as home ownership of guns decreases.
13 On gun prevalence in the US, see Cook and Moore (1995).
14 Lord Cullen, who headed the British government's inquiry into the Dunblane massacre, characterized this argument as one suggesting a "net benefit" to increased gun availability; he concluded that he did "not see anything in the net benefit argument which is relevant to this country [Britain]." *The Cullen Report* (1996, p. 112).
15 See, e.g., Greenhut (2001, p. 29).
16 Recall Klitgaard's (1988) heuristic equation Corruption = Monopoly + Discretion – Accountability; the discretion afforded by the lack of a complainant, and the reluctance of law breakers to push for an internal police investigation (low accountability), indicate that the potential for police corruption in the presence of victimless crime is quite high. See also Barnett (1994, p. 2623).
17 Wright (1995, p. 68).
18 "When, in the interests of fighting crime, we advocate restrictions on their rights to own guns, we are casting aspersions on their decency, as though we somehow hold them responsible for the crime and violence that plague this nation." Wright (1995, p. 68).

19 Hirschman (1991, p. 83).

20 Perhaps those who argue against a control on slippery-slope grounds aren't so much claiming that the way will be paved for socially undesirable future reforms, but rather believe that the future reforms will damage their own interests. Then the issue would seem to be whether one "good" reform today will make it more likely that a measure one segment of society opposes will be adopted in the near future. It is unclear whether this is the case in general. See the brief discussion of this question in Stiglitz (1998, pp. 9–10). Lode (1999) provides an excellent analysis of slippery-slope arguments, and notes that they may have more weight (due, for instance, to *stare decisis*) in adjudication than in legislation. Constitutional protections, of course, are provided in part to ensure that temporarily popular measures do not easily override individual rights.

21 I owe this point to Michael Alexeev.

22 See, e.g., LaPierre (1994, pp. 17–18).

23 Polsby (1994, p. 59). Snyder (1993, p. 55) goes further, arguing that even if the Second Amendment were repealed, the right to private ownership of firearms could not be rescinded by a legitimate government: "The repeal of the Second Amendment would no more render the outlawing of firearms legitimate than the repeal of the due process clause of the Fifth Amendment would authorize the government to imprison and kill people at will."

24 Hirschman (1991, pp. 149–54) notes that a standard "progressive" counterpoint to jeopardy arguments is that the failure to reform will bring on undesired consequences.

25 The discussion here concerning gun prevalence and policy draws on Cook and Leitzel (1996).

26 See, e.g., Killias (1993), and the discussion of this issue in *The Cullen Report* (1996, pp. 106–13).

27 Donohue and Levitt (1998) note that unpredictability can lead to high violence. To the extent that transitional environments involve more uncertainty, we would therefore expect high social costs from violence in such settings.

28 Following Dunblane, high-calibre handguns were banned under the Conservative government, with full implementation of the ban becoming effective on October 1, 1997. The Labour government which came to power in May 1997 then extended the ban to handguns of all calibres, with full implementation of that ban becoming effective on March 1, 1998.

29 On the British stock, see *Possession of Handguns*, Volume 2 (1996, p. 38). Two million is an estimate of the legal gun stock in England, Scotland, and Wales for the mid-1990s. This figure is imprecise for various reasons, including the fact that the shotgun certification system permitted multiple guns per certificate, so the legally owned number of shotguns was unknown, and further, there was no notification requirement for when guns were disposed of. To the two million figure should be added the illegal gun stock, for which there is a wide range of estimates; see *The Cullen Report* (1996, pp. 106–7). On the US stock, see Cook and Moore (1995) and Cook and Ludwig (1996).

30 This description of firearm regulation in the US is general, ignoring the substantial variation across states and municipalities.

31 The US firearm homicide figure is from the FBI's Crime in the United States, while the England and Wales figure, for the statistical year 1999/2000, is from Criminal Statistics England and Wales, 1999.

32 For example, the conviction and one-year prison term of a prominent former MI6 agent for the sale of one 0.32 calibre gun and eighteen rounds of ammunition is the sort of evidence that can help to assure people that the illegal market for guns is being effectively policed. See "Prison for Ex-MI6 Agent Trapped into Supplying Gun," by Richard Norton-Taylor, *The Guardian*, May 3, 1997, p. 4.

33 See, e.g., Guns and Violence Symposium (1995), and Lott and Mustard (1997).

34 One might expect, then, that the long-run impact of liberalized concealed carry laws will depend partly on complementary regulations, such as safe storage rules, and on

details of the laws themselves – requisite training and prohibited carrying areas, for instance.
35 Blumstein and Cork (1996).
36 See *Following the Gun: Enforcing Federal Laws Against Firearm Traffickers* (2000).
37 Occasional newspaper accounts as well as the economics of illicit markets suggest a connection between drug and gun selling. In recommending federal prosecution in trafficking investigations, the Bureau of Alcohol, Tobacco, and Firearms suggested narcotics violation charges against 12.1 percent of defendants, and firearm use in a drug crime charges against 6.3 percent of defendants. *Following the Gun: Enforcing Federal Laws Against Firearm Traffickers* (2000, p. 33).
38 Decker, Pennell, and Caldwell (1997).
39 Approximately one-third of the handguns in the US are kept loaded and unlocked; see Cook and Ludwig (1996, pp. 20–1). The annual average number of fatal firearm accidents in the US was 1,181 for the period 1993–8; see Table 5 in Gotsch et al. (2001).
40 See Cook and Leitzel (2002).
41 On the rationale for preventive measures with weapons of mass destruction, see Heymann (1998, p. 80).
42 On the significant costs of a deployable nuclear arsenal, see Schwartz (1998).
43 The very strong mutual interest in ensuring stability allowed distrust to be overcome in the case of the Anti-Ballistic Missile Treaty, which limited defensive capabilities. Because stability was dependent on the credibility of retaliation by either side should an attack be launched, an effective defense would have been extremely destabilizing, and perhaps have led the undefended side to launch its missiles prior to the defensive capability becoming fully operational. Recall that, presumably in an effort to overcome this destabilizing feature of defensive measures, President Reagan suggested that should the US Strategic Defense Initiative result in an effective nuclear shield, he would give the technology to the Soviet Union.
44 Schelling (1971 [1960], p. 107n).
45 See, e.g., Singh (1998).
46 A more optimistic scenario appears in Perkovich (1998).
47 An initial draft of this chapter was completed before the nuclear tests by India and Pakistan in May, 1998. Part of the Indian justification for their 1998 tests – they had exploded one nuclear device underground in 1974 – was evasion of the Non-Proliferation Treaty: "India was left with no option but to go in for overt nuclear weaponization. The Sino-Pakistani nuclear weapons collaboration – a flagrant violation of the NPT – made it obvious that the NPT regime had collapsed in India's neighborhood." Singh (1998, p. 44).
48 Betts (1998, p. 32).
49 Many experts believe that effective measures to prevent terrorist attacks with weapons of mass destruction can be undertaken in the US without threatening the existing civil liberties. See, e.g., Heymann (1998) and Falkenrath, Newman, and Thayer (1998).

Conclusions

1 It is likely that the original owner values the stolen goods more highly than the thief does; otherwise, the owner and thief might previously have agreed to a voluntary sale – though if the thief can steal the goods with impunity, he'll have little incentive to pay for them. And the indirect costs of theft, including the resources that go into theft prevention and into apprehension and punishment of thieves, are very significant, of course. The notion that benefits tend to be obvious while costs are hidden is a theme pursued by the French economist-journalist Frederic Bastiat, who in 1850 wrote an essay entitled "That Which Is Seen, and That Which Is Not Seen."

Bibliography

Acemoglu, D., and T. Verdier, "The Choice Between Market Failures and Corruption." *American Economic Review* 90(1): 194–211, 2000.

Akerlof, G. A., and P. M. Romer, "Looting: The Economic Underworld of Bankruptcy for Profit." *Brookings Papers on Economic Activity*, 1–73, 1993.

Alam, M. S., "A Theory of Limits on Corruption and Some Applications." *Kyklos* 48(3): 419–35, 1995.

Alesina, A., and A. Drazen, "Why Are Stabilizations Delayed?" *American Economic Review* 81: 1170–88, 1991.

Alexeev, M., "If Market Clearing Prices Are So Good, Then Why Doesn't (Almost) Anyone Want Them?" *Journal of Comparative Economics* 15: 380–90, 1991.

—— and J. Leitzel, "Racial Profiling." Mimeo, Indiana University, September 2002.

——, C. Gaddy, and J. Leitzel, "Economic Crime and Russian Reform." *Journal of Institutional and Theoretical Economics* 151(4): 677–92, 1995.

Alford, R. R., and E. L. Feige, "Information Distortions in Social Systems: The Underground Economy and Other Observer-Subject-Policymaker Feedbacks." In E. L. Feige (ed.) *The Underground Economies*, Cambridge: Cambridge University Press, 1989.

Andreas, P., "The Making of Amerexico. (Mis)Handling Illegal Immigration." *World Policy Journal* 11(2): 45–56, Summer 1994.

Andreev-Khomiakov, G., *Bitter Waters: Life and Work in Stalin's Russia*. Boulder: Westview Press, 1997.

Andreoni, J., "Criminal Deterrence in the Reduced Form: A New Perspective on Ehrlich's Seminal Study." *Economic Inquiry* 33: 476–83, July 1995.

——, B. Erard, and J. Feinstein, "Tax Compliance." *Journal of Economic Literature* 36: 818–60, June 1998.

Andvig, J. C., and K. O. Moene, "How Corruption May Corrupt." *Journal of Economic Behavior and Organization* 13: 63–76, 1990.

Anechiarico, F., and J. B. Jacobs, *The Pursuit of Absolute Integrity*. Chicago: University of Chicago Press, 1996.

Aristotle, *The Works of Aristotle*. Great Books of the Western World, Chicago: Encyclopedia Britannica, Inc., 1952.

Arnott, R., and K. Small, "The Economics of Traffic Congestion." *American Scientist* 82: 446–55, September–October 1994.

Ash, P., A. L. Kellermann, D. Fuqua-Whitley, and A. Johnson, "Gun Acquisition and Use by Juvenile Offenders." *Journal of the American Medical Association* 275: 1754–58, 1996.

Ashenfelter, O., and R. Smith, "Compliance with the Minimum Wage Law." *Journal of Political Economy* 87: 333–50, April 1979.

Austin, R., and P. D. Larkey, "The Unintended Consequences of Micro-Management." *Policy Sciences* 25(1): 3–28, February 1992.

Ayres, I., and J. Bulow, "The Donation Booth: Mandating Donor Anonymity to Disrupt the Market for Political Influence." *Stanford Law Review* 50: 837–91, February 1998.

Bakalar, J. B., and L. Grinspoon, *Drug Control in a Free Society*. Cambridge: Cambridge University Press, 1993 [1984].

Baker, G. P., "Incentive Contracts and Performance Measurement." *Journal of Political Economy* 100(3): 598–614, 1992.

Baker, G., and B. Holmstrom, "Internal Labor Markets: Too Many Theories, Too Few Facts." *American Economic Review* 85(2): 255–9, May 1995.

Banfield, E. C., "Corruption as a Feature of Governmental Organization." *Journal of Law and Economics* 18: 587–605, 1975.

——, *The Unheavenly City Revisited*. Boston: Little, Brown and Company, 1974.

Bardach, E., "Social Regulation as a Generic Policy Instrument." In L. M. Salamon and M. S. Lund (eds), *Beyond Privatization: The Tools of Government Action*, Washington, DC: Urban Institute Press, 1989.

—— and R. A. Kagan, *Going By The Book: The Problem of Regulatory Unreasonableness*. Philadelphia: Temple University Press, 1982.

Barnett, R., "Bad Trip: Drug Prohibition and the Weakness of Public Policy." *Yale Law Journal* 103: 2593–630, 1994.

Barth, J. R., *The Great Savings and Loan Debacle*. Washington, DC: AEI Press, 1991.

Barzel, Y., *Economic Analysis of Property Rights*. Cambridge: Cambridge University Press, 1989.

——, "A Theory of Rationing By Waiting." *Journal of Law and Economics* 17(1): 73–95, April 1974.

Basu, K., "Child Labor: Cause, Consequence, and Cure, with Remarks on International Labor Standards." *Journal of Economic Literature* 37(3): 1083–119, September 1999.

Becker, G. S., "Crime and Punishment: An Economic Approach." *Journal of Political Economy* 76: 169–217, 1968.

—— and G. J. Stigler, "Law Enforcement, Malfeasance, and Compensation of Enforcers." *Journal of Legal Studies* 3: 1–18, January 1974.

Becker, H. S., *Outsiders: Studies in the Sociology of Deviance*. New York: The Free Press, 1973 [1963].

Behr, E., *Prohibition: The 13 Years that Changed America*. London: BBC Books, 1997.

Bendor, J., "A Model of Muddling Through." *American Political Science Review* 89(4): 819–40, December 1995.

Ben-Shahar, O., "The Erosion of Rights by Past Breach." *American Law and Economics Review* 1: 190–238, Fall 1999.

Bergstrom, T. C., and H. R. Varian, "When Are Nash Equilibria Independent of the Distribution of Agents' Characteristics?" *Review of Economic Studies* 52: 715–18, 1985.

Bernheim, B. D., and K. Bagwell, "Is Everything Neutral?" *Journal of Political Economy* 96: 308–38, April 1988.

Berns, W., *Taking the Constitution Seriously*. Lanham, MD: Madison Books, 1987.

Betts, R. K., "The New Threat of Mass Destruction." *Foreign Affairs* 77: 26–41, January/February 1998.

Bliss, C., and R. Di Tella, "Does Competition Kill Corruption?" *Journal of Political Economy* 105: 1001–23, 1997.

Blumstein, A., and D. Cork, "Linking Gun Availability to Youth Gun Violence." *Law and Contemporary Problems* 59: 5–24, Winter 1996.

Bonnie, R. J., C. E. Fulco, and C. T. Liverman (eds), *Reducing the Burden of Injury: Advancing Prevention and Treatment.* Committee on Injury Prevention and Control, Division of Health Promotion and Disease Prevention, Institute of Medicine, Washington, DC: National Academy Press, 1999.

Borooah, V. K., "Racial Bias in Police Stops and Searches: An Economic Analysis." *European Journal of Political Economy* 17: 17–37, 2001.

Bouza, A. V., *Police Unbound: Corruption, Abuse, and Heroism by the Boys in Blue.* Amherst, NY: Prometheus Books, 2001.

Bruno, M., and W. Easterly, "Inflation's Children: Tales of Crises that Begat Reforms." *American Economic Association Papers and Proceedings* 86: 213–17, 1996.

Buchanan, J. M., and G. Tullock, *The Calculus of Consent.* Ann Arbor: University of Michigan Press, 1992 [1962].

Calavita, K., H. N. Pontell, and R. H. Tillman, *Big Money Crime: Fraud and Politics in the Savings and Loan Crisis.* Berkeley: University of California Press, 1997.

Canada, G., *Fist Stick Knife Gun: A Personal History of Violence in America.* Boston: Beacon Press, 1995.

Cao, Y. Z., G. Fan, and W. T. Woo, "Chinese Economic Reforms: Past Successes and Future Challenges." In W. T. Woo, S. Parker, and J. D. Sachs (eds), *Economies in Transition: Comparing Asia and Europe.* Cambridge, MA: MIT Press, 1997.

Caulkins, J.P., "Zero-Tolerance Policies: Do They Inhibit or Stimulate Illicit Drug Consumption?" *Management Science* 39: 458–76, 1993.

Caulkins, J.P., and P. Reuter, "Setting Goals for Drug Policy: Harm Reduction or Use Reduction?" *Addiction* 92(9): 1143–50, 1997.

Centers for Disease Controls and Prevention, *National Summary of Injury Mortality Data, 1988– 1994.* Atlanta: Centers for Disease Control and Prevention, National Center for Injury Prevention and Control, November 1996.

Cheung, S. N. S., "Why are Better Seats 'Underpriced'?" *Economic Inquiry* 15(3): 513–22, 1977.

——, "Roofs or Stars: The Stated Intents and Actual Effects of a Rents Ordinance." *Economic Inquiry* 13: 1–21, March 1975.

——, "A Theory of Price Control." *Journal of Law and Economics* 17(1): 53–71, April 1974.

Chirinko, R. S., and E. P. Harper, Jr., "Buckle Up or Slow Down? New Estimates of Offsetting Behavior and Their Implications for Automobile Safety Regulation." *Journal of Policy Analysis and Management* 12(2): 270–96, 1993.

Clark, J., and A. Wildavsky, *The Moral Collapse of Communism: Poland as a Cautionary Tale.* San Francisco: ICS Press, 1990.

Coase, R., "The Problem of Social Cost." *Journal of Law and Economics* 3(1): 1–44, 1960.

Cogan, J. F., T. J. Muris, and A. Schick, *The Budget Puzzle: Understanding Federal Spending.* Stanford: Stanford University Press, 1994.

Cole, D., *No Equal Justice: Race and Class in the American Criminal Justice System.* New York: The New Press, 1999.

Cook, P., "The 'Saturday Night Special': An Assessment of Alternative Definitions From a Policy Perspective." *Journal of Criminal Law and Criminology* 72(4): 1735–45, 1981.

—— and J. Leitzel, "'Smart Guns': A Technological Fix for Regulating the Secondary Market." *Contemporary Economic Policy* 20(1): 38–49, January 2002.

—— and ——, "Perversity, Futility, Jeopardy: An Economic Analysis of the Attack on Gun Control." *Law and Contemporary Problems* 59: 91–118, Winter 1996.

—— and J. Ludwig, *Guns in America. Results of a Comprehensive National Survey on Firearm Ownership and Use. Summary Report.* Washington, DC: Police Foundation, 1996.

—— and M. H. Moore, "Gun Control." In J. Q. Wilson and J. Petersilia (eds), *Crime*, San Francisco: ICS Press, 1995.

Corrado, A., "A History of Federal Campaign Finance Law." Available at www.brookings.org/dybdocroot/gs/cf/cf_hp.htm2001 (accessed March 26, 2002), 2001.

——, T. E. Mann, D. R. Ortiz, T. Potter, and F. Sorauf (eds), *Campaign Finance Reform: A Sourcebook*. Washington, DC: Brookings Institution Press, 1997.

Cowell, F. A., "What's Wrong With Going Underground?" *International Economic Insights*, 18–20, November/December 1993.

—— and J. P. F. Gordon, "Auditing with 'Ghosts'." In G. Fiorentini and S. Peltzman (eds), *The Economics of Organized Crime*, Cambridge: Cambridge University Press, 1995.

Criminal Statistics, England and Wales, 1999. London: HMSO Available at www.archive.official-documents.co.uk/document/cm50/5001/5001.htm (accessed March 26, 2002).

Crouch, S., "What's New? The Truth, As Usual." In J. Nelson (ed.), *Police Brutality*, New York: W. W. Norton and Company, 2000.

Crozier, M., *The Bureaucratic Phenomenon*. Chicago: University of Chicago Press, 1964.

The Cullen Report. The Hon Lord Cullen, "The Public Inquiry into the Shootings at Dunblane Primary School on 13 March 1996." London: HMSO, October 1996.

Dallago, B., *The Irregular Economy*. Aldershot, UK: Dartmouth Publishing Company, 1990.

Dalton, M., *Men Who Manage*. New York: John Wiley and Sons, Inc., 1959.

Davis, F. J., "Crime News in Colorado Newspapers." *Amercian Journal of Sociology* 57: 325–30, January 1952.

Davis, M., "Traffic Violation: Racial Profiling is a Reality for Black Drivers." *Emerge* 10(8): 42–8, June 1999.

Deacon, R. T., and J. Sonstelie, "The Welfare Costs of Rationing By Waiting." *Economic Inquiry* 27: 179–96, April 1989.

Decker, S. H., S. Pennell, and A. Caldwell, "Illegal Firearms: Access and Use by Arrestees." US Department of Justice, Office of Justice Programs, National Institute of Justice, Research in Brief, January 1997.

Dershowitz, A. M., *The Abuse Excuse*. Boston: Little, Brown and Company, 1994.

DiIulio, J. J., Jr., "Help Wanted: Economists, Crime, and Public Policy." *Journal of Economic Perspectives* 10(1): 3–24, Winter 1996.

Dixit, A. K., *The Making of Economic Policy: A Transaction-Cost Politics Perspective*. Cambridge, MA: MIT Press, 1996.

—— and B. J. Nalebuff, *Thinking Strategically*. New York: W. W. Norton, 1991.

Donohue, J. J., III, and S. D. Levitt, "Guns, Violence, and the Efficiency of Illegal Markets." *American Economic Review* 88(2): 463–7, May 1998.

Downs, A., *Stuck in Traffic*. Washington, DC: Brookings Institution, 1992.

Drazen, A., "The Political Economy of Delayed Reform." *Journal of Policy Reform* 1: 25–46, 1996.

—— and V. Grilli, "The Benefit of Crises for Economic Reforms." *American Economic Review* 83: 598–607, 1993.

Drew, E., *The Corruption of American Politics: What Went Wrong, and Why*. Secaucus, NJ: Birch Lane Press, 1999.

Drucker, E., "Harm Reduction: A Public Health Strategy." *Current Issues in Public Health* 1: 64–70, 1995.

Duca, J. V., "The Changing Meaning of Money." *The Southwest Economy*, Federal Reserve Bank of Dallas, 6: 6–9, 1995.

Dworkin, R., *Taking Rights Seriously*. Cambridge, MA: Harvard University Press, 1977.

Easterly, W., "When is Stabilization Expansionary?" *Economic Policy* 22: 67–107, April 1996.

Ellickson, R. C., "Controlling Chronic Misconduct in City Spaces: Of Panhandlers, Skid Rows, and Public-Space Zoning." *Yale Law Journal* 105: 1165–248, March 1996.

——, *Order Without Law: How Neighbors Settle Disputes*. Cambridge, MA: Harvard University Press, 1991.

Ellman, M., and V. Kontorovich, "Overview." In M. Ellman and V. Kontorovich (eds), *The Disintegration of the Soviet Economic System*, London: Routledge, 1992.

Epstein, Richard, *Simple Rules for a Complex World*. Cambridge, MA: Harvard University Press, 1995.

Fagan, J., and G. Davies, "Street Stops and Broken Windows: *Terry*, Race, and Disorder in New York City." *Fordham Urban Law Journal* 28: 457–504, December 2000.

Falcone, G., with M. Padovani, *Men of Honour*. London: Warner Books, 1993.

Falkenrath, R. A., R. D. Newman, and B. A. Thayer, *America's Achilles' Heel: Nuclear, Biological, and Chemical Terrorism and Covert Attack*. Cambridge, MA: MIT Press, 1998.

Farrell, J., "Puzzles." *Journal of Economic Perspectives* 2: 175–82, Summer 1988.

Fehr, E., and S. Gächter, "Fairness and Retaliation: The Economics of Reciprocity," *Journal of Economic Perspectives* 14(3): 159–81, Summer 2000.

Fernandez, R., and D. Rodrik, "Resistance to Reform: Status quo Bias in the Presence of Individual-Specific Uncertainty." *American Economic Review* 81(5): 1146–55, 1991.

Fiorentini, G., and S. Peltzman (eds), *The Economics of Organized Crime*. Cambridge: Cambridge University Press, 1995.

Fischer, T., *Under the Frog*. New York: The New Press, 1992.

Following the Gun: Enforcing Federal Laws Against Firearm Traffickers. US Department of the Treasury, Bureau of Alcohol, Tobacco and Firearms, June 2000.

Franzoni, L. A., "Tax Evasion and Tax Compliance." Mimeo, University of Bologna, 1998.

Frey, B. S., "Does Monitoring Increase Work Effort? The Rivalry with Trust and Loyalty." *Economic Inquiry* 31: 663–70, October 1993.

Friedman, D., *Law's Order: What Economics Has to Do with Law and Why It Matters*. Princeton: Princeton University Press, 2000.

Friedman, J., S. Hakim, and U. Spiegel, "The Difference Between Short and Long Run Effects of Police Outlays on Crime: Policing Deters Criminals Initially, But Later They May 'Learn By Doing'." *American Journal of Economics and Sociology* 48(2): 177–91, April 1989.

Friedman, L. M., *A History of American Law*, second edition. New York: Simon and Schuster, 1985.

Friedman, M., "Market Mechanisms and Central Economic Planning." In *Ideas, Their Origins, and Their Consequences: Lectures to Commemorate the Life and Work of G. Warren Nutter*, Washington, DC: American Enterprise Institute for Public Policy Research, 1988.

Frisby, T., "The Rise of Organised Crime in Russia: Its Roots and Significance." *Europe-Asia Studies* 50: 27–49, 1998.

Fullerton, D., I. Hong, and G. E. Metcalf, "A Tax on Output of the Polluting Industry is Not a Tax on Pollution: The Importance of Hitting the Target." NBER Working Paper 7259, July 1999.

Gaddy, C. G., "The Labor Market and the Second Economy in the Soviet Union." *Berkeley-Duke Occasional Papers on the Second Economy in the USSR* January 24, 1991.

Gambetta, D., *The Sicilian Mafia*. Cambridge, MA: Harvard University Press, 1994.

Gerth, H. H., and C. W. Mills, *From Max Weber: Essays in Sociology*. New York: Oxford University Press, 1946.

Gladwell, M., *The Tipping Point*. Boston: Little, Brown and Company, 2000.

Goldman, M. I., "Why is the Mafia so Dominant in Russia?" *Challenge* 39(1): 39–47, January–February 1996.

Goodhart, C., "Problems of Monetary Management: the U.K. Experience." In A. S. Courakis (ed.), *Inflation, Depression, and Economic Policy in the West*, Totowa, NJ: Barnes and Noble Books, 1981.

Gotsch, K. E., J. L. Annest, J. A. Mercy, and G. W. Ryan, "Surveillance for Fatal and Nonfatal Firearm-Related Injuries – United States, 1993–1998." *MMWR Surveillance Summaries* 50(SS02): 1–32, April 13, 2001.

Gould, S. J., *Full House: The Spread of Excellence from Plato to Darwin*. New York: Three Rivers Press, 1996.

Graham, J. D., and Y. Lee, "Behavioral Response to Safety Regulation. The Case of Motorcycle Helmet-wearing Legislation." *Policy Sciences* 19: 253–73, 1986.

Gray, M., *Drug Crazy: How We Got Into This Mess and How We Can Get Out*. New York: Random House, 1998.

Greenhut, S., "What's Wrong with Registration?" *America's 1st Freedom* 2(5): 28, May 2001.

Grossman, G., "Subverted Sovereignty: Historic Role of the Soviet Underground." Working Paper 2.63, Political Relations and Institutions Research Group (PRI), University of California, Berkeley, July 1998.

——, "The Second Economy: Boon or Bane for the Reform of the First Economy." In S. Gomulka, Y. Ha, and C. Kim (eds), *Economic Reforms in the Socialist World*, Armonk, NY: M. E. Sharpe, 1989.

——, "Roots of Gorbachev's Problems: Private Income and Outlay in the Late 1970s." In *Gorbachev's Economic Plans*, Joint Economic Committee, US Congress, Washington, DC: US Government Printing Office, vol. 1, 1987.

——, "The 'Second Economy' of the USSR," *Problems of Communism* 26(5): 25–40, September–October 1977.

——, "Notes for a Theory of the Command Economy." *Soviet Studies* 15: 101–23, 1963.

——, and V. G. Treml, "Measuring Hidden Personal Incomes in the USSR." In S. Alessandrini and B. Dallago (eds), *The Unofficial Economy*, Aldershot, UK: Gower Publishing Company Limited, 1987.

Guns and Violence Symposium. A Special Issue of the *Journal of Criminal Law and Criminology* 86(1), 1995.

Gupta, S., H. Davoodi, and R. Alonso-Terme, "Does Corruption Affect Income Inequality and Poverty?" International Monetary Fund Working Paper WP98/76, 1998.

Gutmann, P. M., "The Subterranean Economy." *Financial Analysts Journal* 33: 26–8, 1977.

Halligan, L., and P. Teplukhin, " Investment Disincentives in Russia." In *Russian Economic Trends*, Centre for Economic Reform, Whurr Publishers, Vol. 4, No. 1, 1995.

Handelman, S., *Comrade Criminal*. New Haven: Yale University Press, 1995.

Harrington, J. E., Jr., "Rigidity of Social Systems." *Journal of Political Economy* 107: 40–64, 1999.

Harris, D. A., "Driving While Black: Racial Profiling on our Nation's Highways." American Civil Liberties Union Special Report, June 1999, available at www.aclu.org/profiling/report/index.html (accessed April 5, 2002).

Hawkins, G., and F. Zimring, *Pornography in a Free Society*, New York: Cambridge University Press, 1988.

Hayek, F. A., "The Use of Knowledge in Society." *American Economic Review* 35: 519–30, 1945.

Heffernan, W. C., and R. W. Lovely, "Evaluating the Fourth Amendment Exclusionary Rule: The Problem of Police Compliance with the Law." *University of Michigan Journal of Law Reform* 24: 311–69, Winter 1991.

Heiner, R. A., "The Origin of Predictable Behavior." *American Economic Review* 73: 560–95, September 1983.

Heyes, A., "Honesty in a Regulatory Context – Good Thing or Bad?" *European Economic Review* 45(2): 215–32, 2001.

Heyes, A., and N. Rickman, "Regulatory Dealing: Revisiting the Harrington Paradox." *Journal of Public Economics* 72: 361–78, 1999.

Heymann, P. B., "The New Policing." *Fordham Urban Law Journal* 28: 407–56, December 2000.

——, *Terrorism and America: A Commonsense Strategy for a Democratic Society*. Cambridge, MA: MIT Press, 1998.

Hicks, J. R., *The Theory of Wages*, second edition. London: Macmillan, 1963.

Highway Statistics 1992. Federal Highway Administration, US Department of Transportation. Washington, DC: US Government Printing Office, 1992.

Hirschel, J. D., and W. Wakefield, *Criminal Justice in England and the United States*. Westport, CT and London: Praeger, 1995.

Hirschman, A. O., *A Propensity to Self-Subversion*. Cambridge, MA: Harvard University Press, 1995.

——, *The Rhetoric of Reaction: Perversity, Futility, Jeopardy*. Cambridge, MA: Harvard University Press, 1991.

——, *Exit, Voice, and Loyalty*. Cambridge, MA: Harvard University Press, 1970.

——, *Journeys Toward Progress: Studies of Economic Policy-Making in Latin America*. New York: The Twentieth Century Fund, 1963.

Hobbes, T., *Leviathan*, ed. F. B. Randall. New York: Washington Square Press, 1970 [1651].

Holmes, O. W., Jr., *The Common Law*. New York: Dover Publications, Inc., 1991 [1881].

Howard, P. K., *The Death of Common Sense*. New York: Random House, 1994.

Huberts, L. W. C. J., "Anticorruption Strategies: The Hong Kong Model in International Context." *Public Integrity* 211–28, Summer 2000.

Huck, S., "Trust, Treason, and Trials: An Example of How the Evolution of Preferences Can Be Driven by Legal Institutions." *Journal of Law, Economics, and Organization* 14: 44–60, 1998.

Hunt, J. G. (ed.), *The Essential Thomas Jefferson*. Avenel, NJ: Portland House, 1996.

Huntington, S., *Political Order in Changing Societies*. New Haven: Yale University Press, 1968.

Hymowitz, K. S., "Who Killed School Discipline?" *City Journal* 10(2): 34–43, Spring 2000.

Irwin, D., and R. Kroszner, "The Roles of Interests, Institutions, and Ideology in Durable Policy Change: Evidence from the Republican Conversion to Trade Liberalization." National Bureau Of Economic Research Working Paper 6112, 1998.

Issing, O., "Monetary Targeting in Germany: The Stability of Monetary Policy and of the Monetary System." *Journal of Monetary Economics* 39: 67–79, 1997.

Jacobs, J., "Dilemmas of Corruption Control." Presentation to the National Institute of Justice, May 18, 1999. Perspectives on Crime and Justice: 1998–1999 Lecture Series, available at www.ojp.usdoj.gov/nij/pubs-sum/178244.htm (accessed April 5, 2002.)

——, *Drunk Driving: An American Dilemma*. Chicago: University of Chicago Press, 1989.

Jervis, R., "Systems Effects." In R. J. Zeckhauser (ed.), *Strategy and Choice*, Cambridge, MA: MIT Press, 1991.

Johnson, S., and H. Kroll, "Managerial Strategies for Spontaneous Privatization." *Soviet Economy* 7: 281–316, 1991.

Johnson, S., and G. W. Loveman, *Starting Over in Eastern Europe: Entrepreneurship and Economic Renewal*. Boston: Harvard Business School Press, 1995.

Johnson, V., "Decatur: A Story of Intolerance." In W. Ayers, B. Dohrn, and R. Ayers (eds), *Zero Tolerance: Resisting the Drive for Punishment in Our Schools*, New York: The New Press, 2001.

Johnston, M., "The Vices – and Virtues – of Corruption." *Current History* 96: 270–3, September 1997.

Kane, E. J., "De Jure Interstate Banking: Why Only Now?" *Journal of Money, Credit, and Banking* 28: 141–61, 1996.

——, "The Role of Government in the Thrift Industry's Net Worth Crisis." In G. J. Benston (ed.), *Financial Services: The Changing Institutions and Government Policy*, Englewood Cliffs, NJ: Prentice Hall, 1983.

Kaplow, L., "A Model of the Optimal Complexity of Legal Rules." *Journal of Law, Economics, and Organization* 11(1): 150–63, 1995.

——, "Rules Versus Standards: An Economic Analysis." *Duke Law Journal* 42: 557–629, December 1992.

Kaufmann, D., "Diminishing Returns to Administrative Controls and the Emergence of the Unofficial Economy: A Framework of Analysis and Applications to Ukraine." *Economic Policy* 19 (Supplement): 52–69, December 1994.

Kelling, G. L., "'Broken Windows' and Police Discretion." National Institute of Justice Research Report (NCJ 178259), US Department of Justice, October 1999.

——, and C. M. Coles, *Fixing Broken Windows: Restoring Order and Reducing Crime in Our Communities*. New York: Simon and Schuster, 1996.

Kenkel, D. S., "Prohibition Versus Taxation: Reconsidering the Legal Drinking Age." *Contemporary Policy Issues* 11: 48–57, 1993.

Kennedy, R., "Race, the Police, and 'Reasonable Suspicion.'" Presentation to the National Institute of Justice, February 3, 1998. Perspectives on Crime and Justice: 1997–1998 Lecture Series, available at www.ojp.usdoj.gov/nij/pubs-sum/172851.htm (accessed March 26, 2002).

——, *Race, Crime, and the Law*. New York: Random House, 1997.

Killias, M., "Gun Ownership, Suicide, and Homicide: An International Perspective." In A. del Frate, U. Zvekic, and J. J. M. van Dijk (eds), *Understanding Crime and Experiences of Crime and Crime Control*, UNICRI Publication No. 49, Rome: UNICRI, 1993.

Kleck, G., "Handgun-Only Gun Control: A Policy Disaster in the Making." In D. B. Kates (ed.), *Firearms and Violence: Issues of Public Policy*. San Francisco: Ballinger Publishing Company, 1984.

Kleiman, M. A. R., "Getting Deterrence Right: Applying Tipping Models and Behavioral Economics to the Problems of Crime Control." Presentation to the National Institute of Justice, December 3, 1998. Perspectives on Crime and Justice: 1998–1999 Lecture Series, available at www.ojp.usdoj.gov/nij/pubs-sum/178244.htm (accessed March 26, 2002).

——, "Enforcement Swamping: A Positive-Feedback Mechanism in Rates of Illicit Activity." *Mathematical and Computer Modeling* 17(2): 65–75, January 1993.

——, *Against Excess: Drug Policy for Results*. New York: Basic Books, 1992.

Klitgaard, R., "Gifts and Bribes." In R. J. Zeckhauser (ed.), *Strategy and Choice*, Cambridge, MA: MIT Press, 1991.

——, *Controlling Corruption*. Berkeley: University of California Press, 1988.

Knight, A. H., *The Life of the Law*. Oxford: Oxford University Press, 1996.

Kovacic, W. E., "Blue Ribbon Defense Commissions: The Acquisition of Major Weapons Systems." In R. Higgs (ed.), *Arms, Politics, and the Law: Historical and Contemporary Perspectives*, New York: Holmes and Meier, 1990.

Krugman, P., "The Myth of Asia's Miracle," *Foreign Affairs* 62–78, November/December 1994.

Kuran, T., *Private Truths, Public Lies: The Social Consequences of Preference Falsification*. Cambridge, MA: Harvard University Press, 1995.

Labán, R., and F. Sturzenegger, "Fiscal Conservatism as a Response to the Debt Crisis." *Journal of Development Economics* 45: 305–24, 1994.

Landsburg, S. E., *The Armchair Economist: Economics and Everyday Life*. New York: The Free Press, 1993.

Lane, F. C., "Economic Consequences of Organized Violence." *Journal of Economic History*, 18: 401–10, 1958.

LaPierre, W. R., *Guns, Crime, and Freedom*. Washington, DC: Regency Publishing, Inc.,1994.

Larkey, P. D., and J. P. Caulkins, "All Above Average and Other Unintended Consequences of Performance Appraisal Systems." Heinz School of Public Policy and Management, Carnegie Mellon University, Working Paper 92–41, 1992.

Layard, R., and J. Parker, *The Coming Russian Boom*. New York: The Free Press, 1996.

Ledeneva, A. V., *Russia's Economy of Favours: Blat, Networking, and Informal Exchange*. Cambridge: Cambridge University Press, 1998.

Leff, N. H., "Economic Development through Bureaucratic Corruption." *American Behavioral Scientist* 8: 8–14, 1964. Reprinted in A. J. Heidenheimer, M. Johnston, and V. T. LeVine (eds), *Political Corruption: A Handbook*, New Brunswick: Transaction Publishers, 1989.

Leitzel, J., "Goods Diversion and Repressed Inflation: Notes on the Political Economy of Price Liberalization." *Public Choice* 94: 255–66, March 1998a.

——, "Evasion and Public Policy: US and British Firearm Regulation." *Policy Studies* 19: 141–57, 1998b.

——, *Russian Economic Reform*, London: Routledge, 1995.

——, "Damage Measures and Breach of Contract." *Rand Journal of Economics* 20: 92–101, Spring 1989.

—— and R. Conrad, "Evasion and Russian Tax Reform," *Eurasia Economic Outlook*, The WEFA Group, November 1997.

—— and E. Weisman, "Investing in Policy Reform." *Journal of Institutional and Theoretical Economics* 155(4): 696–709, December 1999.

Li, W., "A Tale of Two Reforms." *Rand Journal of Economics* 30: 120–36, 1999.

Lindbeck, A., "Hazardous Welfare-State Dynamics." *American Economic Association Papers and Proceedings* 85(2): 9–15, May 1995a.

——, "Welfare State Disincentives with Endogenous Habits and Norms." *Scandinavian Journal of Economics* 97(4): 477–94, 1995b.

Lindblom, C., "The Science of 'Muddling Through.'" *Public Administration Review* 19: 79–88, 1959.

Lippmann, W., "A Theory About Corruption." Reprinted in *Political Corruption: A*

Handbook, A. J. Heidenheimer, M. Johnston, and V. T. LeVine (eds), New Brunswick: Transaction Publishers, 1989.

Lode, E., "Slippery Slope Arguments and Legal Reasoning." *California Law Review* 87: 1469– 543, December 1999.

Lotspeich, R., "An Economic Analysis of Extortion in Russia." Working paper, Indiana State University, Department of Economics, November 1996.

Lott, J. R., Jr., "The Effect of Conviction on the Legitimate Income of Criminals." *Economic Letters* 34(4): 381–5, 1990.

—— and D. B. Mustard, "Crime, Deterrence, and Right-to-Carry Concealed Handguns." *Journal of Legal Studies* 26: 1–68, January 1997.

—— and R. D. Roberts, "Why Comply?: One-Sided Enforcement of Price Controls and Victimless Crime Laws." *Journal of Legal Studies* 18: 403–14, June 1989.

Lui, F., "A Dynamic Model of Corruption Deterrence." *Journal of Public Economics* 31: 215–36, 1986.

MacCoun, R. J., and P. Reuter, *Drug War Heresies: Learning from Other Vices, Times, and Places*. Cambridge: Cambridge University Press, 2001.

——, ——, and T. Schelling, "Assessing Alternative Drug Control Regimes." *Journal of Policy Analysis and Management* 15(3): 330–52, 1996.

Maclin, T., "What Can Fourth Amendment Doctrine Learn From Vagueness Doctrine?" *University of Pennsylvania Journal of Constitutional Law* 3: 398–454, February 2001.

Mann, T. E., "The U.S. Campaign Finance System Under Strain." In H. J. Aaron and R. D. Reischauer (eds), *Setting National Priorities: The 2000 Election and Beyond*, Washington, DC: Brookings Press, 1999.

Marcouiller, D., and L. Young, "The Black Hole of Graft: The Predatory State and the Informal Economy." *American Economic Review* 85(3): 630–46, June 1995.

Marschak, J., and K. Miyasawa, "Economic Comparability of Information Systems." *International Economic Review* 9: 137–74, 1968.

Mauro, P., "Corruption and the Composition of Government Expenditure." *Journal of Public Economics* 69: 263–79, 1998.

——, "Corruption and Growth." *Quarterly Journal of Economics* 111: 681–712, August 1995.

Merida, K., "Capital Scene: Decriminalizing 'Driving While Black.'" *Emerge* 26, December/January 1999.

Merton, R. K., "The Unanticipated Consequences of Purposive Social Action." *American Sociological Review* 1(5): 894–904, October 1936.

Milgrom, P., and J. Roberts, "An Economic Approach to Influence Activities in Organizations." *American Journal of Sociology* 94 (Supplement): S154–S179, 1988.

Millar, J. R., "The Little Deal: Brezhnev's Contribution to Acquisitive Socialism." In T. L. Thompson and R. Sheldon (eds), *Soviet Society and Culture*, Boulder: Westview Press, 1988.

Miller, J. B., "The Big Nail and Other Stories: Product Quality Control in the Soviet Union." *ACES Bulletin* 26(1): 43–57, 1984.

Mills, G., and H. Rockoff, "Compliance with Price Controls in the United States and the United Kingdom During World War II." *Journal of Economic History* 47(1): 197–213, March 1987.

Miron, J. A., "The Effect of Alcohol Prohibition on Alcohol Consumption." National Bureau of Economic Research Working Paper 7130, May 1999.

——, and J. Zweibel, "Alcohol Consumption During Prohibition." *American Economic Review Papers and Proceedings* 81(2): 242–7, 1991.

Nadelmann, E. A., "Commonsense Drug Policy." *Foreign Affairs* 77(1): 111–26, January/February 1998.

Nalebuff, B., "Puzzles." *Journal of Economic Perspectives* 3: 165–74, Summer 1989.

National Gambling Impact Study Commission, "Lotteries." At http://govinfo.library.unt.edu/ngisc/research/lotteries.html (accessed April 5, 2002).

National Summary of Injury Mortality Data, 1988–1994. Atlanta: Centers for Disease Control and Prevention, National Center for Injury Prevention and Control, November 1996.

Naughton, B., *Growing Out of the Plan*. Cambridge: Cambridge University Press, 1996.

Noonan, J. T., Jr., *Bribes*. New York: Macmillan, 1984.

North, D. C., *Institutions, Institutional Change, and Economic Performance*. Cambridge: Cambridge University Press, 1991.

O'Brian, P., *The Nutmeg of Consolation*. New York: Norton, 1993.

Olson, M., *The Rise and Decline of Nations: Economic Growth, Stagflation, and Social Rigidities*. New Haven: Yale University Press, 1982.

——, *The Logic of Collective Action*. Cambridge, MA: Harvard University Press, 1971.

Peacock, A. T., and G. K. Shaw, "Tax Evasion and Tax Revenue Loss." *Public Finance* 37(2): 269–78, 1982.

Peltzman, S., "The Economic Theory of Regulation after a Decade of Deregulation." *Brookings Papers on Economic Activity, Microeconomics* 1989: 1–59, 1989.

——, "The Effects of Automobile Safety Regulation." *Journal of Political Economy* 83(4): 677–725, 1975.

Perkins, D., "Completing China's Move to the Market." *Journal of Economic Perspectives* 8: 23–46, Spring 1994.

Perkovich, G., "Nuclear Proliferation." *Foreign Policy* 112: 12–23, Fall 1998.

Peterson, S., G. Hoffer, and E. Millner, "Are Drivers of Air-Bag-Equipped Cars More Aggressive? A Test of the Offsetting Behavior Hypothesis." *Journal of Law and Economics* 38(2): 251–64, 1995.

Petroski, H., *To Engineer is Human: The Role of Failure in Successful Design*. New York: Random House, 1992.

Philipson, T. J., and R. A. Posner, "The Economic Epidemiology of Crime." *Journal of Law and Economics* 39: 405–33, October 1996.

Polinsky, A. M., and S. Shavell, "The Economic Theory of Public Enforcement of Law." *Journal of Economic Literature* 38: 45–79, March 2000a.

—— and ——, "The Fairness of Sanctions: Some Implications for Optimal Enforcement Policy." *American Law and Economics Review* 2: 223–37, Fall 2000b.

—— and ——, "The Optimal Tradeoff Between the Probability and Magnitude of Fines." *American Economic Review* 69(5): 880–91, 1979.

Polsby, D. P., "The False Promise of Gun Control." *Atlantic Monthly* x: 57–70, March 1994.

Posner, R. A. (ed.), *The Essential Holmes*. Chicago: University of Chicago Press, 1992.

Possession of Handguns, Volumes I and II. Home Affairs Committee, House of Commons, London: HMSO, 1996.

Potter, T., "The Current State of Campaign Finance Law." In A. Corrado, T. E. Mann, D. R. Ortiz, T. Potter, and F. Sorauf (eds), *Campaign Finance Reform: A Sourcebook*, Washington, DC: Brookings Institution Press, 1997.

Prendergast, C., and R. H. Topel, "Favoritism in Organizations." *Journal of Political Economy* 104 (5): 958–78, 1996.

Pressman, J. L., and A. Wildavsky, *Implementation*, third edition. Berkeley: University of California Press, 1984.

Putnam, R., *Making Democracy Work*. Princeton: Princeton University Press, 1993.

Qian, Y., "The Process of China's Market Transition (1978–98): The Evolutionary, Historical, and Comparative Perspectives." Mimeo, University of California, Berkeley, April 1999.

Rawls, J., "A Theory of Civil Disobedience." In R. M. Dworkin (ed.), *The Philosophy of Law*, Oxford: Oxford University Press, 1977.

Rodger, N. A. M., *The Wooden World: An Anatomy of the Georgian Navy*. London: Fontana Press, 1988.

Rodrik, D., "The Rush to Free Trade in the Developing World: Why So Late? Why Now? Will it Last?" In S. Haggard and S. B. Webb (eds), *Voting for Reform: Democracy, Political Liberalization, and Economic Adjustment*, New York: Oxford University Press, 1994.

——, "Policy Uncertainty and Private Investment in Developing Countries." *Journal of Development Economics* 36: 229–42, October 1991.

Roland, G., *Transition and Economics*. Cambridge, MA: MIT Press, 2000.

Rosen, J., "In Lieu of Manners." *New York Times Magazine*, pp. 46–51, February 4, 2001.

——, "Excessive Force." *The New Republic*, pp. 24–7, April 10, 2000.

Rosenberg, G. N., *The Hollow Hope: Can Courts Bring About Social Change?* Chicago: University of Chicago Press, 1991.

Rosenkranz, E. J., "Introduction." In E. J. Rosenkranz (ed.), *If Buckley Fell: A First Amendment Blueprint for Regulating Money in Politics*, New York: The Century Foundation Press, 1999.

Ross, I., *Shady Business: Confronting Corporate Corruption*. New York: Twentieth Century Fund Press, 1992.

Rosser, J. B., Jr., "On the Complexities of Complex Economic Dynamics." *Journal of Economic Perspectives* 13(4): 169–92, Fall 1999.

Rothwax, H. J., *Guilty: The Collapse of Criminal Justice*. New York: Warner Books, 1996.

Rubin, P., "Why is the Common Law Efficient?" *Journal of Legal Studies* 6(1): 51–64, 1977.

"Rules and Discretion in Monetary Policy." Special issue of the *Journal of Monetary Economics* 39(1), 1997.

Ryan, A., *Mill*. New York: W. W. Norton and Company, Inc., 1997.

Sabato, L. J., and G. R. Simpson, *Dirty Little Secrets: The Persistence of Corruption in American Politics*. New York: Times Books, 1996.

Sah, R. K., "Social Osmosis and Patterns of Crime." *Journal of Political Economy* 99(6): 1272–95, 1991.

Sargent, T., and N. Wallace, "Rational Expectations, the Optimal Monetary Instrument, and the Optimal Money Supply Rule." *Journal of Political Economy* 83: 241–54, 1975.

Schanze, E., "Hare and Hedgehog Revisited: The Regulation of Markets That Have Escaped Regulated Markets." *Journal of Institutional and Theoretical Economics* 151(1): 162–76, 1995.

Schauer, F., "Slippery Slopes." *Harvard Law Review* 99: 361–383, December 1985.

Scheck, B., P. Neufeld, and J. Dwyer, *Actual Innocence*. New York: Doubleday, 2000.

Schelling, T. C., *The Strategy of Conflict*. London: Oxford University Press, 1971 [1960].

Schroeder, G. E., "The Soviet Economy on a Treadmill of 'Reforms.'" In *Soviet Economy in a Time of Change*, Washington, DC: Joint Economic Committee, US Congress, 1979.

Schwartz, S. (ed.), *Atomic Audit*. Washington, DC: Brookings Institution, 1998.

Scotchmer, S., and J. Slemrod, "Randomness in Tax Enforcement." *Journal of Public Economics* 38: 17–32, 1989.

Segrave, K., *Payola in the Music Industry: A History, 1880–1991*. Jefferson, NC: McFarland & Company, Inc., 1994.

Shavell, S., "The Design of Contracts and Remedies for Breach." *Quarterly Journal of Economics* 99: 121–48, 1984.

Sherman, L. W., *Scandal and Reform: Controlling Police Corruption*. Berkeley: University of California Press, 1978.

Shleifer, A., "Government in Transition." *European Economic Review* 41: 385–410, 1997.

Shleifer, A., and R. W. Vishny, "Corruption," *Quarterly Journal of Economics* 108(3): 599–617, 1993.

Simis, K., *USSR: The Corrupt Society*. New York: Simon and Schuster, 1982.

Singh, J., "Against Nuclear Apartheid." *Foreign Affairs* 77(5): 41–52, September/October 1998.

Sklansky, D. A., "The Private Police." *UCLA Law Review* 46: 1165–287, April 1999.

Skolnick, J., "Drug Enforcement, Violent Crime, and the Minimization of Harm." In E. L. Rubin (ed.), *Minimizing Harm: A New Crime Policy For America*, Boulder: Westview Press, 1999.

Slemrod, J., and S. Yitzhaki, "Tax Avoidance, Evasion, and Administration." National Bureau of Economic Research Working Paper 7473, January 2000.

Smart, A., "Predatory Rule and Illegal Economic Practices." In J. McC. Heyman (ed.), *States and Illegal Practices*, Oxford: Berg, 1999.

Smith, A., *The Wealth of Nations*. New York: Knopf, 1991 [1776].

——, *The Theory of Moral Sentiments*. Oxford: Clarendon Press, 1976 [1759].

Smith, E., and R. Wright, "Why is Automobile Insurance in Philadelphia So Damn Expensive?" *American Economic Review* 82: 756–72, 1992.

Snyder, J. R., "A Nation of Cowards." *Public Interest* 40–55, Fall 1993.

Sorauf, F. J., "What *Buckley* Wrought." In E. J. Rosenkranz (ed.), *If Buckley Fell: A First Amendment Blueprint for Regulating Money in Politics*, New York: The Century Foundation Press, 1999.

Sowell, T., *Classical Economics Reconsidered*. Princeton: Princeton University Press, 1974.

Squire, L., and S. Suthiwart-Narueput, "The Impact of Labor Market Regulations." *World Bank Economic Review* 11: 119–43, 1997.

Stake, J. E., "The Uneasy Case for Adverse Possession." *Georgetown Law Journal* 89: 2419–74, August 2001.

——, "Loss Aversion and Involuntary Transfers of Title." In R. P. Malloy and C. K. Braun (eds), *Law and Economics: New and Critical Perspectives*, New York: Lang, 1995.

Standen, J., "The Exclusionary Rule and Damages: An Economic Comparison of Private Remedies for Unconstitutional Police Conduct." *Brigham Young University Law Review* 2000: 1443–88, 2000.

Steffens, L., *The Autobiography of Lincoln Steffens*. New York: Harcourt, Brace and Company, 1931.

Stephan, P. B., "Rationality and Corruption in the Post-Socialist World." *Connecticut Journal of International Law* 14: 533–49, 1999.

Stigler, G. J., "The Optimum Enforcement of Laws." *Journal of Political Economy* 78: 526–36, May/June 1970.

Stiglitz, J., "The Private Uses of Public Interests: Incentives and Institutions." *Journal of Economic Perspectives* 12: 3–22, Spring 1998.

——, *Whither Socialism?* Cambridge, MA: MIT Press, 1995.

Stille, A., *Excellent Cadavers: The Mafia and the Death of the First Italian Republic*. London: Vintage (Random House), 1996.

Stone, I. F., *The Trial of Socrates*. New York: Doubleday, 1989.

Suetonius, *The Lives of the Twelve Caesars*. New York: Modern Library, 1931.

Suvorov, V., *Inside the Aquarium. The Making of a Top Soviet Spy*. New York: Macmillan, 1986.

Tanzi, V., "Corruption: Arm's Length Relationships and Markets." In G. Fiorentini and S. Peltzman (eds), *The Economics of Organized Crime*, Cambridge: Cambridge University Press, 1995.

Thompson, D. F., *Ethics in Congress: From Individual to Institutional Corruption*. Washington, DC: The Brookings Institution, 1995.

Thoreau, H. D., *Walden and Resistance to Civil Government*, ed. W. Rossi. Norton Critical Edition, New York: W. W. Norton and Company, 1992.

Thucydides, *The History of the Peloponnesian War*. In R. M. Hutchins (ed.), *Great Books of the Western World*, Chicago: Encyclopedia Britannica, 1952 [c. 400 BC].

Tirole, J., "A Theory of Collective Reputations." *Review of Economic Studies* 63: 1–22, 1996.

——, "Collusion and the Theory of Organizations." In J. Laffont (ed.), *Advances in Economic Theory: Sixth World Congress*, vol. 2, Cambridge: Cambridge University Press, 1992.

——, "Hierarchies and Bureaucracies: On the Role of Collusion in Organizations." *Journal of Law, Economics, and Organization* 2(2): 181–214, Fall 1986.

Tocqueville, A. de, *The Old Régime and the French Revolution*, translated by S. Gilbert. New York: Doubleday, 1983 [1856].

Treml, V. G., "Two Schools of Thought." *RFE/RL Research Report* 2(23), 4 June 1993.

—— and M. Alexeev, "The Second Economy and the Destabilizing Effect of its Growth on the State Economy in the Soviet Union: 1965–1989." *Berkeley-Duke Occasional Papers on the Second Economy in the USSR* 36, December 1993.

Tsebelis, G., "The Abuse of Probability in Political Analysis: The Robinson Crusoe Fallacy." *American Political Science Review* 83(1): 76–91, March 1989.

Twining, W., and D. Miers, *How to Do Things With Rules*, third edition. London: Weidenfeld and Nicolson, 1991.

Tyler, T. R., *Why People Obey the Law*. New Haven: Yale University Press, 1990.

Varese, F., "The Structure of Criminal Groups Compared: Perm', Sicily and the USA." Paper prepared for BASEES Annual Conference, Cambridge, UK, 12–14 April 1997.

Viscusi, W. K., "The Lulling Effect: The Impact of Child-Resistant Packaging on Aspirin and Analgesic Ingestions." *American Economic Association Papers and Proceedings* 74(2): 324–7, 1984.

Vogel, S. K, *Freer Markets, More Rules: Regulatory Reform in Advanced Industrial Countries*. Ithaca: Cornell University Press, 1996.

Waldman, M., *Who Robbed America? A Citizen's Guide to the Savings & Loan Scandal*. New York: Random House, 1990.

Wallich, H. C., *Mainsprings of the German Revival*. New Haven: Yale University Press, 1955.

Walzer, M., *Spheres of Justice*. Oxford: Blackwell, 1983.

Wei, S., "How Taxing is Corruption on International Investors?" National Bureau of Economic Research Working Paper 6030, May 1997a.

——, "Why is Corruption So Much More Taxing than Tax? Arbitrariness Kills." National Bureau of Economic Research Working Paper 6255, November 1997b.

Wheen, F., *Karl Marx: A Life*. New York: Norton, 1999.

White, L. J., *The S&L Debacle: Public Policy Lessons for Bank and Thrift Regulation*. New York: Oxford University Press, 1991.

White, S., *Russia Goes Dry*. Cambridge: Cambridge University Press, 1996.

Wildavsky, A., *Speaking Truth to Power: The Art and Craft of Policy Analysis*, second edition. New Brunswick: Transaction Publishers, 1996 [1979].

Williams, P. J., "Obstacle Illusions: The Cult of Racial Appearance." In J. Nelson (ed.), *Police Brutality*, New York: W. W. Norton and Company, 2000.

Williamson, O., *The Economic Institutions of Capitalism*. New York: The Free Press, 1985.

Wilson, J. Q., *Bureaucracy: What Government Agencies Do and Why They Do It*. New York: Basic Books, 1989.

——, *Thinking About Crime*, revised edition. New York: Basic Books, 1983.

—— and G. L. Kelling, "The Police and Neighborhood Safety." *The Atlantic Monthly* 29–38, March 1982.

Winston, C., and R. Crandall, "Explaining Regulatory Policy." *Brookings Papers on Economic Activity, Microeconomics* 1994: 1–49, 1994.

Wolfgang, M. E., *Patterns in Criminal Homicide*. Philadelphia: University of Pennsylvania Press, 1958.

Wright, J. D., "Ten Essential Observations on Guns in America." *Society* 63–8, March/April 1995.

Zawitz, M. W., "Guns Used in Crime: Firearms, Crime, and Criminal Justice. Selected Findings." US Department of Justice, Office of Justice Programs, Bureau of Justice Statistics, NCJ-148201, July 1995.

Zimring, F. E., "Comparing Cigarette Policy and Illicit Drug and Alcohol Control." In R. L. Rabin and S. D. Sugarman (eds), *Smoking Policy: Law, Politics, and Culture*, New York: Oxford University Press, 1993.

—— and G. Hawkins, "Public Attitudes Towards Crime. Is American Violence a Crime Problem?" In E. L. Rubin (ed.), *Minimizing Harm: A New Crime Policy For America*. Boulder: Westview Press, 1999.

—— and ——, *The Search for Rational Drug Control*. Cambridge: Cambridge University Press, 1992.

—— and ——, *Deterrence: The Legal Threat in Crime Control*. Chicago: University of Chicago Press, 1973.

Index

absolute prohibition: creation of bright lines 14
accountability, lack of: role in corruption 94
agents: role in corruption 93–4
anti-bribery laws: impotency 110
anti-corruption measures: leading to increase in rules 107
anti-futility argument 67–70; *see also* futility argument
anti-gun control arguments 137; guns as defense against governmental tyranny 145–6; Second Amendment 145–6
arbitrage: effect on outcomes 69
Aristotle 74
authoritarian regimes: evasion and avoidance under 71, 72
avoidance 13–14; authoritarian regimes, 71, 72; balloon effects 65; defined 3, 13; determinant of input/output regulations 83; futility argument 65–70; gun control and 138–41; leading to policy reform 13; loopholes 36

bad rules 17–18; avoided by corruption 95; breaking 32
balloon effects: avoidance and 65
Berlin Wall 5, 39, 103; link between exit and voice 5
Bogota traffic signal case 1–2, 4, 5, 26, 62, 103
breaching action 9, 10
bribery 98–9, 100; *see also* corruption
bright lines 14–16; dimming of 19; ease of enforcement 74; nuclear weapons 153–4; poor quality rules 73, 74; use v. misuse of office 91, *see also* corruption; useful in children's rules 15
"broken windows" strategy 62; zero-tolerance policy 62, *see also* zero tolerance policy

bureaucracy: at odds with socially best actions 13
bureaucrats: role in corruption 93–4
business: corruption in 104–6

cascade of corruption 99–100
cascade of disobedience 33–5, 70
central authorities: role in corruption 93–4
central planning 115; failures of 117, 118–19, 121–2; illegal economic activity, and 117–18; limitations 123; rule evasion within 117–19
China: dual track reform of economy 125–6; law of motion of socialism 124–7; stability v. political pluralism 126–7
civil disobedience 34–5; incentive for political reform 5; racial segregation in USA 43; unintentional 2–3
civil liberties: gun control and 145–6, 149, 155; racial discrimination 84–5
clarity in rules 17–18
client: involved in corruption 93–4
Coase Theorem 66
Cold War: weapons control 152
competition: role in limiting corruption 108–9
compliance: achieved by "legal bribes" 30–1; compliance actions 9, 10
computer-generated child pornography: rule complexity 16
consensual crimes: zero tolerance v. harm reduction 63–4
controls: complementarity of *ex ante* and *ex post* controls 80, 83; conflict with liberty 83–4; mix of approaches 80; preventive *see ex ante* controls; punitive *see ex post* controls; *see also* rules